The Rice-Paper Ceiling

Breaking through

Japanese Corporate Culture

Stone Bridge Press • *Berkeley, California*

The

Rice-Paper

Ceiling

ROCHELLE KOPP

Published by STONE BRIDGE PRESS
P.O. Box 8208
Berkeley, California 94707
TEL 510-524-8732
FAX 510-524-8711

10 9 8 7 6 5 4 3 2 1

Printed in the United States of America.

Library of Congress Cataloging-in-Publication Data

Kopp, Rochelle.
    The rice-paper ceiling: breaking through Japanese corporate
culture / Rochelle Kopp.
        p.   cm.
    Includes bibliographical references and index.
    ISBN 1-880656-14-0.
    1. Corporate culture—Japan.   2. Corporations, Japanese—Social aspects.
  3. Americans—Employment—Japan.   I. Title.
    HD58.7.K656   1994
    650.1'089'13052—dc20   94-27608
                                                                    CIP

Contents

THREE: LONG-TERM PROSPECTS FOR NON-JAPANESE EMPLOYEES

Acknowledgments

I would like to thank the following individuals who helped bring this book to fruition: my parents David and Jacquelyn Kopp, who provided me with continual encouragement as well as tireless proofreading and editing; Robin Nakamura and Adam Rice, who were invaluable sounding boards for my ideas and helped me to clarify my prose; Robert Harper, Kristin Hoganson, Carollina Song, and Elizabeth Floyd Wood, who read and commented on various drafts of the manuscript; Assistant Professor Canice Prendergast of the University of Chicago Graduate School of Business, who provided valuable guidance on my research methodology; Tom Fiffer, who helped me begin this project; and Reiko Kimura and Yoshimi Tominaga, who provided assistance during my research in Japan.

Many other friends, too numerous to list here, also provided important ideas and insights. However, any weaknesses of this book are solely my responsibility.

I am also grateful to the human resource managers at Fuji Bank, Nippon Credit Bank, Nissan Motor, Sony, and other major Japanese firms who shared their insights and experiences with me. In addition, I owe a great debt to my former colleagues at the financial institution where I worked in Tokyo, who provided me with a wonderful learning experience and helped me understand the inner workings of a large Japanese company. Last but not least I also want to thank the over one hundred Japanese and American employees of Japanese companies whom I interviewed for this book. They have asked to remain anonymous, but their experiences and opinions were the most important basis for this volume.

Introduction

The Japanese have many wonderful qualities. It's difficult to keep that fact in perspective when you're working with them on a day-to-day basis. There's total quality management, consensus decision-making, and a concern for employees that's greater than at any American company I've worked for. However, all of these positive factors are overshadowed by communication difficulties. So that they can benefit more from these positives, Japanese companies should learn to modify what we Americans see as negatives. For Americans, the better we can learn how to adapt and function with other nationalities, the better it is for our economy. There's a lot we can teach each other. As long as cultural barriers prevent that, we miss this opportunity.

AN AMERICAN MANAGER AT A JAPANESE MANUFACTURING FIRM

An American who joins a Japanese company enters a working environment unlike any he or she has encountered before. Few American businesspeople have had the opportunity to visit Japan or to meet and work with Japanese. In fact, relatively few have had in-depth interactions with anyone from another country. Combine this with a similar lack of experience on the part of Japanese managers and the fact that many Japanese business customs are vastly different from those in America, and you get a recipe for frustration and cultural clashes when Japanese companies hire Americans. And even when Americans and Japanese are familiar with each others' languages and cultures, conflicts can emerge from differences in deeply held beliefs and assumptions.

The tremendous difference between Japanese and American workstyles creates problems at both the organizational and individual levels. For an individual employee trying to acclimate himself to a Japanese firm, the environment can be stressful and confusing, while failure to adapt can hinder job performance and may even result in a career disaster. Not understanding how to skillfully work with, and for, Japanese can render even the most qualified and capable employee completely ineffective. As one manager at a Japanese manufacturer describes it, "When I applied for this job, I tried to match my qualifications to the job description. At no time did I ever consider that the biggest part of my job would be dealing with the fact that this is a Japanese company. That factor totally overwhelms my qualifications. The stress of my actual job content has paled by comparison with the difficulty of adjusting to the fact that it's a company from such a different culture."

Many Japanese companies have encountered a variety of problems as a result of their failure to effectively integrate American employees into their management culture and processes. These include high turnover, low morale, internal strife, and poor productivity. In the words of a senior executive at the New York branch of a Japanese securities firm, "One of my fellow managers here is totally insensitive to the cultural issues involved in working with the Japanese, and as a result can't function productively. He will probably quit soon in frustration. This has great costs for the company: his salary, the low productivity of the people below him, and the fact that the company will have to pay a headhunter to get someone else. It hurts business, and costs money."

American employees of Japanese companies need useful information that can help them to address differences in work style and culture. They are looking for techniques that they can use to improve their working relationships and career prospects, as well as their company's effectiveness and profitability. Unfortunately, most of the books currently available about Japanese business have few practical insights for someone who is working daily alongside Japanese colleagues. This book is specifically designed to address the issues faced by Americans who work at or are considering joining Japanese firms. The information it contains will also be useful to others, such as suppliers, joint venture partners, consultants, and attorneys, who need to understand the organizational dynamics of Japanese companies.

This book describes the cultural and organizational issues at Japanese companies in the United States, focusing primarily on the white-collar and managerial levels. Against the background of the recent controversy over alleged discrimination against Americans, I will explore the factors that often inhibit the success of Americans in Japanese companies, as well as those that contribute to Japanese companies' success in America. My goal is to provide the insights and information that employees of Japanese companies have often been forced to learn the hard way.

Although I will talk at length about "cultural" issues, this book is not intended to provide an overview of Japanese culture. Nor will this book provide instructions on how to exchange business cards, how to use chopsticks, or other mechanical aspects of Japanese business etiquette. In fact, more than culture per se is behind many of the frictions that develop when Americans work for Japanese firms. The typical organizational structure and human resource policies of Japanese companies, as well as the conflicting expectations of American and Japanese employees, are often the root causes of difficulties. Also, while I will touch on the special issues for female employees of Japanese firms, my primary focus is on issues that affect both American men and women who work with Japanese.

I begin by examining the current debate about the "rice-paper ceiling"—the artificial barrier to advancement for non-Japanese employees of Japanese companies. This debate has been fueled by a spate of lawsuits by employees who allege discrimination by Japanese firms, an acrimonious trio of Congressional hearings led by Congressman Tom Lantos (D-California), and a steady stream of newspaper and magazine articles. I present statistics I have gathered documenting the existence of a rice-paper ceiling and a discussion of why Japanese firms are more prone to have such barriers to advancement by non-native employees. A checklist to help potential employees of Japanese firms measure the rice-paper ceiling is provided.

The next section of the book deals with short-term issues—aspects of the Japanese company environment that become important from one's first day on the job. The section begins with some general considerations for potential and new employees of Japanese firms. The following chapters explore some common issues that are frequently faced by Americans who work at Japanese companies. These include a shortage of clear-cut instructions and feedback, the cryptic behavior of Japanese managers, and the mysterious decision-making process. I examine the cultural and structural reasons behind these recurring difficulties, with the aim of enabling the reader to understand and defuse problems before they occur.

The third section of the book focuses on long-term issues—more subtle organizational and cultural issues that will be of significant concern to anyone desiring a long-term career at a Japanese company. The section begins by discussing to what extent American employees are allowed to participate in internal management processes and then goes on to describe the organizational barriers to Americans' full integration into the managerial hierarchy. I discuss the traditional Japanese human resources paradigm—the so-called lifetime employment system—and the reasons why it tends to relegate non-Japanese employees to the periphery. One factor examined in depth is the different employee classifications given Americans and Japanese. Non-Japanese tend to be placed in a second-tier "contract worker" category (*shokutaku*) while Japanese employees are regarded as "real employees" (*seishain*). The formal effects of this distinction in terms of opportunities for training and advancement, as well as the informal effects in terms of Japanese managers' attitudes, is described in detail. This discussion will help the employee of a Japanese company to make an informed decision about his or her future prospects.

The final chapter discusses the extent to which current economic and social pressures in Japan may be altering the Japanese approach to human resource management. The recent recession in particular is causing Japanese firms to rethink their commitment to lifetime employment, seniority promotion, and consensus management. This shift will have important repercussions for Japanese firms' overseas employees, both now and in the future.

In this book I aim to take an objective rather than a "Japan-bashing" approach. Many positive aspects of working for a Japanese company will be examined. However, the common complaints about Japanese managers and the inequities built into many Japanese companies' organizational structures will not be glossed over. If I seem to dwell on the negative aspects of Japanese management style, it is because I wish to analyze common problems so that potential and current employees of Japanese firms can have a greater understanding of the situations they are likely to face.

Working for a Japanese company in the short run can be a tremendous opportunity for personal growth and career development, especially when steps are taken to avoid common misunderstandings and pitfalls. Depending on the organization, the long-term career prospects for a non-Japanese in a Japanese company may be less bright, although there are opportunities for committed individuals to go far if they understand how to interact skillfully with Japanese colleagues and make the most of their position in the company. The situation of non-Japanese employees may also begin to improve as various pressures are brought to bear on the way Japanese companies manage themselves both in Japan and overseas. And of course, although this book makes many generalizations, every Japanese company and each Japanese expatriate do not necessarily fit the patterns I describe. Overall, it is my hope that this book will provide meaningful information for Americans working in Japanese firms and contribute to a decrease in frictions between Japanese and Americans in the workplace.

On a broader note, the clashes between cultures and workplace customs described here will become a more prominent feature of business life as Americans have more opportunities to work with, or for, companies from many different countries and as immigrants to the United States continue to take on important roles in the American workforce. In the future, the ability to interact smoothly with people who have different assumptions and values will be a requirement for business success. Americans working with Japanese can thus be considered a case study of an increasingly important theme in American business life.

I became interested in the topic of human resource management at Japanese companies during the time I worked at the Tokyo head office of a large Japanese bank. As a non-Japanese working at corporate headquarters, I experienced firsthand the contrasts between Japanese and western business styles. The differences went far beyond language and culture. The company's structure, its policies, and the motivations of my Japanese colleagues were completely unlike those in analogous large American firms. Meanwhile, since one of my responsibilities was to improve communication between personnel in Japan and the firm's non-Japanese employees at its various offices around the world, I observed the challenges my company faced in integrating overseas employees into the overall organization.

I wondered whether my experiences and observations were unique, so when I returned to the United States to study at the University of Chicago Graduate School of Business, I interviewed over one hundred Americans working at Japanese companies and conducted comparative survey research in order to better understand the situations at other Japanese firms and to discern patterns and trends. This book is the result of that exploration. My goal is to draw from and analyze the experiences of many to provide the information and insights I wish had been available when I joined a Japanese firm. I had to learn many things by trial and much error—I hope that this book will give others a bit of a head start.

The Rice-Paper Ceiling is the sister of my Japanese-language book, *Koyo Masatsu*, which was published in December 1993 by the Sanno Institute of Management Press, Tokyo. That book is in a sense a mirror image of this one, conveying the same information from a different perspective. While my basic conclusions are the same, *Koyo Masatsu's* thrust is to explain to Japanese readers the concerns and motivations of American employees of Japanese firms. That book also discusses the economic and political danger to Japanese companies of employment-related friction in their U.S. operations.

Direct quotes and anecdotes from American employees of Japanese firms appear throughout this book. Fictional names have been used and other details have been changed to preserve their anonymity.

ONE

Measuring the
Rice-Paper Ceiling

1

What Happens When Japanese Companies Hire Americans?

Are American citizens becoming second-class citizens in their own country if they work for Japanese companies?

U.S. REPRESENTATIVE TOM LANTOS[1]

The young woman standing in front of the House of Representatives subcommittee had all-American, blond-haired blue-eyed good looks. In a simple dark-colored dress adorned only with a small gold pin in the shape of a rose, her image was conservative and businesslike. Yet this girl-next-door type was holding up a scanty pair of pink G-string panties that she had recently discovered on her Japanese boss's desk. The woman portrayed the atmosphere at her employer, the trading company Sumitomo Corporation, as rife with sexual harassment and discrimination against Americans. As the Congressmen listened, she described how Japanese managers openly traded pornographic magazines and videos in the office, distributed girlie calendars embossed with the company logo, and asked female employees for photographs of themselves in swimsuits. She said she was told that women could never hold upper-level positions because they "become too emotional once every month" and that Americans at the company received promotions only so that lawsuits could be avoided.[2] Seeing that advancement prospects in the

QUOTES FROM THE LANTOS HEARINGS

"Japanese employees from the Tokyo headquarters were treated by management in subtle but significant ways that enhanced their status relative to the non-Japanese employees."[a]

"There were two standards at the agency. One was for Japanese and the other for Americans. It was actually the stated policy of Japanese management that they could not treat the two groups alike."[b]

"Frequent reorganizations are a type of Japanese management training . . . Americans are not allowed or even encouraged to participate in this managerial pattern. Therefore, no matter what their gender, race or nationality, their promotional opportunities within a Japanese company are greatly diminished."[c]

"Non-Japanese middle management has in all instances been required to report to Japanese nationals. The effect of these practices has been the creation of the so-called 'glass ceiling' which keeps non-Japanese employees from rising to the higher executive levels."[d]

"They have refused to rotate me or other non-Japanese nationals to Japan and have prevented me from working with Japanese officials overseas, both of which activities are considered crucial to an employee's ability to advance within the corporation."[e]

company were limited for American men as well as women, she concluded that "Japanese corporations operating in the United States have determined that there are two sets of rules: Those that apply to other companies, and those that apply to themselves."[3]

At the hearings of the Employment and Housing Subcommittee of the House Committee on Government Operations held in July, August, and September 1991 and chaired by Representative Tom Lantos of California, a parade of witnesses told similar horror stories about their experiences at Japanese-owned firms. A former human resource manager at a Japanese bank claimed that he was told not to consider women and African Americans for loan officer positions. A man who worked for ten years at an auto manufacturer, despite good performance and Japanese language ability, described how he watched as openings above him were consistently filled with Japanese expatriates. A female advertising executive related how she had been barred from a promotion due to her sex, and how she and other Americans were ultimately laid off while Japanese colleagues kept their jobs. An employee of a Japanese employment agency described a system of codes used to screen candidates by age, sex, and race. A man in the technology field told how he had laid the groundwork for a new product launch by his Japanese employer, and then been dismissed once he had completed this task and his usefulness had ended. A woman who was let go by a Japanese electronics firm called her six years there "a daily rollercoaster ride of humiliation, despair, demoralization, and fear, which culminated in an overwhelming sense of sadness about the professional time I had wasted with the company."[4]

The hearings were convened soon after a resident of Lantos' Congressional district was featured in a *New York Times* article describing his lawsuit against his former employer, a Japanese electronics firm. The very fact that the hearings were titled "Employment Discrimination by Japanese-Owned Companies in the United States" suggested that Lantos' opening statement, ". . . employment discrimination by Japanese-owned companies against American citizens in the United States is a problem,"[5] was a predetermined conclusion. Many of the American witnesses were people who had sued their former or current Japanese employers—hardly a representative sample. Their statements were accepted for the most part at face value, while the representatives of Japanese firms who testified were questioned harshly and impatiently. Lantos was also unable to produce reliable statistics to support his contention that Japanese firms are somehow more likely to discriminate than either American or other foreign firms.

These aspects of the hearings prompted a great deal of criticism. Many Americans were appalled by the tone of the proceedings, and expressions of dismay from the Japanese American community in particular caused Lantos to drop his plans to pursue the topic further. For their part, the Japanese media reported on the hearings as just another example of the U.S. government engaging in Japan-bashing. One prominent Japanese scholar, Professor Yoshihiro Tsurumi of Baruch College, City University of New York, called the hearings "a witch-hunt inquisition" reminiscent of McCarthyism that showcased "one-sided and isolated tales of woe" from "disgruntled individuals."[6]

However, despite their plentiful hot air, the Lantos hearings weren't just Japan-bashing histrionics—there was a kernel of truth behind them.

The witnesses told stories with uncannily similar themes, despite their different industries, ages, and types of positions. Although they often tended toward the emotional, the testimonies addressed real and important issues faced by Japanese firms: Who makes decisions? Whose values should prevail? How can barriers of language and culture be overcome? Should American employees be treated differently from Japanese employees? How can American employees build meaningful careers in organizations that are dominated by the Japanese parent company and the expatriates it has sent from Japan?

The hearings crystallized what has been a significant undercurrent in much of the debate over Japanese investment, U.S.-Japan trade friction, and the future of the United States economy: the issue of how American employees are faring at Japanese firms. With the number of Americans employed by Japanese companies rising rapidly in the past decade and now exceeding 700,000,[7] the way in which these Americans are treated is an issue at the core of American anxiety about Japanese investment.

QUESTIONING JAPANESE CORPORATE VALUES

As the pace of Japanese investment in the United States has slowed, the outcry about "selling the country to the Japanese" has died down. Yet, as economic friction between Japan and the United States continues, the concerns voiced by Lantos still remain in the American consciousness. Somehow, the investments of Japanese companies have inspired a greater degree of public anxiety than those of investors from other countries.

What is it about Japanese investors in particular that has generated uneasiness among Americans? Some ascribe it to American racism, fears of declining competitiveness, ignorance about Japan, and emotions left over from World War II. While these factors undoubtedly play a part, it also seems that Americans are questioning the fundamental values of Japanese firms.

American media coverage of Japanese companies has often emphasized the negative aspects of corporate life in Japan. Japanese workers who pledge lifetime loyalty to the company, wear uniforms, and sing company songs are portrayed as conformists, and their employers hopelessly paternalistic. Their long working hours, refusal to take vacation time, and marathon commutes to cramped housing have prompted derogatory metaphors such as "robots," "ants," and "worker bees." The American media have devoted significant attention to issues such as the less-than-equal status of Japanese working women and the emergence of "death from overwork" (*karoshi*) as a Japanese social problem. Articles describing the plight of Japan's native minority groups—the Ainu people of the north, the descendants of feudal period lower castes, and ethnic Koreans—appear frequently in the United States press. The underlying theme of these reports is often one of a human cost behind the Japanese economic miracle. At some deep level, Americans seem to want to say to themselves, "It's okay if the Japanese are beating us economically, because they have to pay the price for it." Americans have been further sensitized by a stream of disparaging comments by Japanese politicians about American minority groups, the quality of American workers and managers, and the country's overall work ethic. The American public's reaction to this stream of negative images of Japanese management and society is a concern that racism, sexism, and harsh treatment of workers will somehow be imposed by Japanese companies when they invest in the United States and hire Americans.

In the context of such worries, any evidence that Japanese firms are discriminating against Americans in the United States is quickly seized upon by the media. Lawsuits and other problems are given a great deal of attention—sometimes more than they would deserve on an objective basis—simply because they involve Japanese firms. As Ronald Morse of the Economic Strategy Institute described it in his statement submitted at the Lantos hearings, ". . . the American perception of Japan as an economic threat continues to be one-sided and exaggerated. This creates a concern with their business practices that is sometimes taken out of context and can be interpreted as [a] reverse form of discrimination."[8] In this environment of extreme scrutiny of Japanese firms' conduct in the United States, every report of an American's negative experience at a Japanese firm fuels American fears and adds to U.S.-Japan friction.

KEEPING THINGS IN PERSPECTIVE

The Equal Employment Opportunity Commission representatives who spoke at the Lantos hearings made an important point: "For every example you can give regarding the Japanese, we can give you one regarding an American company."[f] Certainly, American firms are hardly perfect when it comes to issues of employee welfare and discrimination. While lapses by American companies should, of course, be no excuse for foreign investors to flout U.S. laws, there is a danger of a double standard. As Congresswoman Ileana Ros-Lehtinen (R-Florida) pointed out at the hearings, "Let's not fool ourselves into thinking that all is right in our own back yard and that American-owned and American-administered companies are paragons of virtue when we discuss patterns of discrimination. I would be glad to have Lee Iacocca come and testify about the number of Hispanic women vice presidents he might have in Chrysler."[g] Also, the fact that Japanese companies are facing many lawsuits may not in itself be that unusual, given the litigiousness of American society and the fact that deep-pocketed, publicity-shy Japanese companies may be tempting targets for nuisance suits.

Japanese companies often seem to underestimate Americans' sensitivity to these issues. Nothing in their prior experience prepares them for American society's standards concerning fair treatment toward all employees. Japan lacks the legal framework and social consciousness of discrimination issues that characterize the United States. Also, in its domestic context Japanese business has seldom confronted issues of a diverse workforce. Yet Japanese companies operating in the United States face a veritable minefield in terms of attitudes about discrimination, expectations for corporate behavior, and views concerning the proper role of the legal system. Racial and gender issues are hot topics in the United States, and Americans are sensitized to them. The concepts of individual rights, equality, and fairness are highly developed, and Americans are willing to use the courts to assert them.

This clash between American sensitivities and Japanese unfamiliarity with American standards has led to a well-publicized rash of discrimination and other employment-related lawsuits against Japanese companies in the United States. Nearly a third of the U.S. affiliates of Japanese firms responding to a recent Japan Society poll reported having received complaints of discrimination in their hiring and promotion practices,[9] and 57 percent of the Japanese companies responding to a Japanese Ministry of Labor survey reported that they face possible equal employment-related lawsuits in the United States.[10] More than one expert has claimed that any major Japanese company operating in the United States is likely to have at least one employment lawsuit pending against it.[11] The list of Japanese firms that have been involved in employment-related litigation in the United States reads like a Who's Who of Japanese industry: Canon, C. Itoh, Dentsu, Fujitsu, Hakuhodo, Hitachi, Honda, Kyocera, Mitsubishi Bank, NEC, Nikko Securities, Nissan, Ricoh, Sumitomo Corporation, Suzuki Motor, Toshiba, and Toyota, among others. Covering this trend, prominent newspapers have also run stories with troubling headlines, such as: "U.S. Managers Claim Job Bias by the Japanese" (*New York Times*), "Differences Between U.S. Workers and Japanese Managers Wind Up in Court" (*New York Times*), "A Collision of Corporate Cultures: Bias Charges Grow at Japanese Firms in the U.S." (*Chicago Tribune*), and "Are Japanese Firms Importing Prejudice?" (*Los Angeles Times*). Magazines such as *Business Week, Business Month, Business Tokyo,* and *Fortune* have weighed in with coverage of their own, and popular television shows such as "20-20" and "The MacNeil/Lehrer NewsHour" have also investigated this topic. The Lantos hearings simply added momentum to what had already become a familiar media theme.

This media coverage, combined with individual stories that quickly travel the business grapevine, has given many Americans the impression that Japanese companies are not good employers. Many businesspeople think twice before applying for work at a Japanese firm, and headhunters report that some candidates refuse to consider positions at Japanese companies. Is the poor reputation of Japanese companies just a myth, fed by American racism and media-fueled fears about the Japanese "taking over"? Are Japanese firms really such bad places to work? The emotional overtones of the subject have largely prevented dispassionate analysis of how Japanese companies manage their American employees.

CORPORATE CULTURE SHOCK

Eileen is a one of a handful of American managers at a Japanese manufacturing plant on the East Coast. She spends most of her time working directly with Japanese expatriate colleagues—and trying to figure out better ways to communicate with them:

"Part of it's language. One of my colleagues speaks so little English that I need a translator to have anything more than a simple conversation with him. But even beyond that, it's like there's a secret code that I haven't cracked yet. Some days I go home and I wonder: 'What happened? What was that? What went on here? Why did I get that reaction?' Finally I've come to realize that the management style I've developed over the years is completely at odds with the way this company does business. Acting independently, taking risks, making fast decisions, moving quickly—those are all qualities considered valuable in U.S. companies, but not here.

"People like me waste a lot of time trying to deal with the environment here. We get dissatisfied and eventually we leave. Then it will start all over. The next person who comes into my position will be just as overwhelmed as I was trying to adapt to this place."

COMMON PROBLEMS AT JAPANESE FIRMS

Given the tremendous differences in language, culture, work style, and management techniques between Japan and the United States, it would be surprising if Japanese firms didn't encounter difficult issues when they hire Americans. The gap between the expectations, assumptions, and incentives of Japanese expatriates and American staff results in a recurring pattern of frictions and problems:

- Decision-making is dominated by Japanese expatriates.

- Non-Japanese employees are frequently excluded from information flow, which occurs primarily in the Japanese language among Japanese expatriates and head office employees.

- The language barrier prevents effective communication between locally hired and Japanese staff.

- Locally hired employees seldom reach upper-level positions, which are reserved for Japanese.

- When staff reductions occur, local employees may lose their jobs, but Japanese parent-company employees do not.

- There are few management development programs, training opportunities, or clear career paths for locally hired employees.

- There is an atmosphere of mutual distrust between locally hired and Japanese expatriate employees.

- Japanese and non-Japanese employees seldom socialize together or develop friendly relationships.

- Locally hired employees feel that they receive little praise for their efforts or constructive feedback on how to improve their work.

- Women and minorities may be discriminated against in hiring, promotion, or general treatment.

- The organization has difficulty attracting and retaining high-caliber local employees.

- Small matters frequently escalate into major misunderstandings that pit Japanese and locally hired employees against each other.

- Japanese managers feel that locally hired employees do not meet their expectations—they perceive them as sloppy, uncommitted, and unwilling to take initiative.

- Japanese managers experience great stress in managing locally hired employees, and it is difficult for the parent company to identify potential expatriates who are up to the task.

- Frictions are more pronounced at the white-collar and managerial staff levels.

Probably no Japanese company has experienced all of these problems in its U.S. operations, but none is likely to have escaped them altogether. In some cases, the problems spin out of control, straining the workplace atmosphere, making employees frustrated and resentful, and perhaps even culminating in a discrimination suit or a sudden spurt of resignations. In other firms, these issues become a steady low-level "background noise" that the company either has chosen to ignore or accepts as inevitable. Meanwhile, some Japanese companies have been able to minimize or eliminate frictions and problems through effort and wise personnel policies. However, Japanese firms that have been able to break this pattern have first had to openly recognize it and then decide to address it directly.

These problems have surfaced in the media coverage of employment issues at Japanese firms as well as in many of the recent discrimination cases against Japanese employers. Also, a sizable academic literature has emerged in recent years that documents these issues, not only in the United States but also in other countries where Japanese companies have invested.[12] The interviews with American employees of Japanese firms conducted for this book also turned up the same pattern of frictions and problems. Significantly, both those who were happy with their positions at Japanese firms and those who were not reported the same pattern of conflicts and issues at their companies, although in different degrees.

ROOT CAUSES OF FRICTION

The frictions and problems at Japanese firms in the United States result from a combination of structural differences and mutual misunderstandings. In addition to the different levels of sensitivity to discrimination issues discussed above, typical problem areas include the following:

Language.   Few Americans speak and read Japanese well enough to use it for conducting business. Although Japanese businesspeople usually have some command of English, it is often tenuous at best, especially in conversation. Few Japanese businesspeople are comfortable with conducting detailed discussions or reading long documents in English. Like anyone else, they naturally prefer to do business in their native language.

Cross-cultural communications skills.   Both American and Japanese businesspeople tend to have little experience in dealing with people from

IT'S THEIR BANK

Andy, an American marketing officer at a Japanese bank, tells new hires that "at the beginning the job's great. For the first three to five years it's a good place to learn. But if you want to make a future here, you're joining the wrong firm." He himself has been at the company for seven years, has performed well, and has been promoted to a managerial position. Yet the increased status has not led to any significant change in Andy's job responsibilities. Nor has it increased his participation in the company's decision-making process, which is the exclusive province of the Japanese expatriates. Important meetings are commonly held with only the Japanese staff, excluding American employees like himself who hold management titles.

Andy comments: "It's not the language barrier—they all speak English. If they want to have a meeting and get our input they can talk to us, but they don't think it's necessary, so they don't. Their mentality is 'It's our bank.' As Americans, we're not employees of the bank in Tokyo, we're just employees of the branch here." Further career progression seems unlikely, since all the posts above him are filled with Japanese expatriates.

---

other countries, and generally lack the skills needed to overcome cross-cultural challenges.

Communication patterns.   Japanese and American communication patterns are quite different. The American style is direct, and values discussion. The Japanese style is more vague and roundabout, placing greater emphasis on nonverbal cues and subtle nuances of tone and wording. Informal debate and the act of openly challenging another's opinions are often viewed negatively.

Leadership styles.   Americans expect their managers to attack problems head-on, set the agenda, make detailed plans, and then delegate the implementation to subordinates. Charisma and motivational ability are considered crucial. Yet Japanese often feel that American-style "strong leadership" is insensitive and dictatorial. Rather than giving detailed direction, Japanese managers strive to create an environment in which self-motivated subordinates can take initiative.

Internal management and decision-making patterns.   American companies tend to be financially oriented, and value individual leadership and autonomy. Each employee's role is clearly defined, and he or she is

I'M EXPENDABLE

Jack is proud of the work he has done over the past three years setting up and running a Japanese construction firm's branch office on the West Coast. However, he has come to feel that in his company "there is definitely a class situation. If you're not Japanese you're not considered part of the team. You're expendable." Two months ago, Jack was told that the company had decided to roll up the rugs on the operation he was hired for. He is now the only American left in the office. He has dismissed the staff that he had so care- fully assembled, and once he ties up loose ends he will be gone too. All the Japanese staff have been transferred back to Japan, or to the company's other locations in the United States. However, the option of transfer was not offered to Jack or any of the office's other American employees despite their years of good performance. The bottom line, Jack has decided, is "there is no reward for hard work. You know that you're the outsider. You're going to be gone and they're going to be there."

responsible for those activities. Individuals make decisions in their realm of authority or expertise, and the company clearly defines who can make which decisions about what. In contrast, Japanese companies tend to take a more intuitive approach to management. Employees have undefined roles and are expected to work as teams to meet group goals. Decision-making is a group process, with large numbers of people involved in each decision.

Centralized management processes. At many Japanese firms, the head office has significant input into decision-making at the U.S. affiliate. This necessitates constant, detailed communication across the Pacific. Due to language and cultural barriers, such communication is often dominated by Japanese employees. The result can be an exclusion of American employees from managerial processes. The large role of the head office also diminishes the U.S. operation's ability to act independently.

Ethnocentricity. Many Japanese are uncomfortable interacting with foreigners and frequently hold negative stereotypes about Americans in particular. Many Japanese also lack the flexibility to consider doing things differently from the way they are done in Japan. By the same token, Americans often hold negative views about the Japanese, and often seem convinced that the American way is best.

Employment system differences. In comparison with the American free market for labor, the Japanese tradition of lifetime employment leads to vastly different career patterns. As a result, Americans and Japanese tend to have radically different assumptions about basic features of the employment relationship such as compensation, performance evaluation, the pace of advancement, and when it is appropriate to change jobs.

Japanese personnel management. Many authors, both western and Japanese, have praised the Japanese system of "lifetime employment" for its ability to foster individual loyalty and encourage the development of firm-specific skills. However, the domestic personnel management system is a weakness when the Japanese company expands overseas. The typical Japanese company's personnel management style is quite rigid and makes demands on employees that few non-Japanese would tolerate. This is because the Japanese system is predicated on the lack of an external labor market—Japanese employees have few other employment options, so once they join a firm they have little choice but to go along with the demands of the company. Unable to absorb non-Japanese into this system, companies tend to relegate them to separate employment categories that may not provide equivalent advancement opportunities or job security.

Corporate cultures. Since most Japanese employees work for the same firm for their entire careers, Japanese companies tend to develop their own distinct, inbred corporate cultures. These corporate cultures are so strong that they tend to exclude even native Japanese who might join a company at midcareer. It is extremely difficult for non-Japanese employees to break into the circle, especially given the other barriers listed above.

As this list suggests, the possibilities for misunderstandings are endless when Americans work at Japanese firms. Frictions and frustrations arise from complicated combinations of these various factors. Thus, the pattern of problems at Japanese firms is, in effect, a set of typical cultural and systemic clashes that play themselves out over and over again. These issues add up to a significant set of challenges that Americans who work for Japanese firms, as well as the companies themselves, will have to face.

On an everyday basis, linguistic and cross-cultural issues cause frustrations and prevent Japanese and Americans from developing effective working relationships. Communication is hampered, and Americans are often left out of important information-sharing and decision-making processes. Over the longer run, the fact that American employees are in a separate employment category can have a negative impact on their opportunities for advancement and even their job security. Collectively, this phenomenon can be thought of as a "rice-paper ceiling" that frequently prevents non-Japanese employees from enjoying successful careers and rising to key managerial positions in Japanese firms. However, just as there are rice papers of varying strengths and thicknesses, the nature of the rice-paper ceiling may be quite different from one Japanese company to another. It might be translucent and easily punctured, or it might be virtually unbreakable.

Citing rising employment by Japanese-owned companies in the United States, the *National Law Journal* has observed, "Until the Japanese fully understand the reach of American labor laws—and until American workers grasp the traditions of the Japanese workplace—each of those newly created jobs represents a potential lawsuit."[13] This statement could be expanded to say that:

- until Japanese companies are willing to recognize and deal with the difficult cultural and structural issues that often lead to problems at their overseas operations, they will face, if not lawsuits, then certainly misunderstandings, frictions, decreased productivity, and difficulties in recruiting and retaining high-caliber local employees, and that

- until Americans develop a better understanding of Japanese corporate culture and the typical issues that are likely to develop at Japanese companies' U.S. operations, they will find it difficult to have satisfying employment experiences at Japanese firms.

2

Personnel Management Problems in Japanese Multinationals

In the competition for global talent, corporations that are reluctant to consider foreign nationals for top managerial positions will lose out: the most talented people simply will not join an organization that holds out no promise of promotion. Japanese-owned companies that have been notoriously slow to open their top executive ranks to non-Japanese will operate at a competitive disadvantage.

ROBERT B. REICH, U.S. SECRETARY OF LABOR,
FORMER HARVARD UNIVERSITY PROFESSOR[1]

Many of the management challenges described in the previous chapter are common to all multinationals, not only Japanese. Any firm that operates internationally will have to contend with cultural, linguistic, legal, and social differences from country to country, in addition to the logistical difficulties of managing an organization over long distances. However, not all multinationals respond to these challenges in the same way.

JAPANESE VS. WESTERN MULTINATIONALS

In order to test whether Japanese multinationals conduct their international personnel management differently from American and European multinationals, I conducted a survey of international human resource

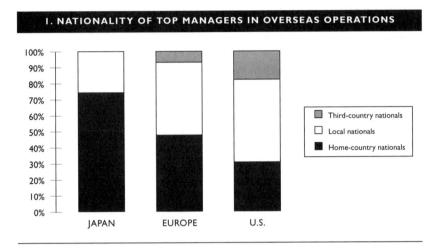

I. NATIONALITY OF TOP MANAGERS IN OVERSEAS OPERATIONS

managers at the headquarters of major multinationals in these three regions in the spring of 1992.[2] Each respondent was asked to provide data about international staffing, policies, and problems at their firms. The results suggest that there are indeed differences between Japanese and western multinationals in the international human resource area. Three main differences emerged from the survey results: a lower glass ceiling for local managers, less use of progressive international personnel policies, and greater susceptibility to international human resource management problems.

Lower Glass Ceiling for Local Managers

Japanese multinationals are less likely than western ones to use local nationals in managerial positions at their overseas operations. In other words, they are more likely to send home-country expatriates to fill management positions abroad than are western multinationals. This is true both for top management positions (e.g., country manager or president of the overseas operation) and for managerial positions in general (defined as supervisory, white-collar; see Charts 1 and 2). The survey results indicate that there is a glass ceiling at every type of multinational, in that home-country expatriates occupy a certain percentage of managerial positions. However, the height of this ceiling is significantly lower

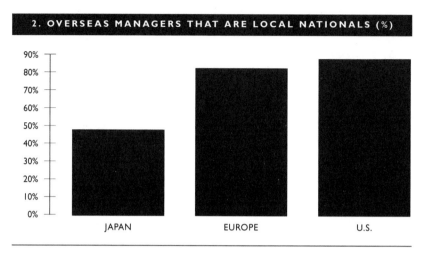

2. OVERSEAS MANAGERS THAT ARE LOCAL NATIONALS (%)

in Japanese organizations, because on average they fill more of their managerial positions with Japanese.

Less Use of Progressive International Personnel Policies

Japanese companies are less likely than western multinationals to use personnel policies that promote the international development and deployment of human resources within the firm. The survey asked whether companies used five specific international personnel policies.

1. *"Performance evaluation measures are the same in every one of our international operations."* Implementation of a standardized performance evaluation measure suggests that the head office is concerned with consistent human resource policies across its overseas operations, and that it is interested in the ability to compare managerial performance across countries.

2. *"A training program has been put in place to groom local nationals for advancement in our company's managerial ranks."* A company that implements such a training program views local nationals as candidates for management.

3. *"Local nationals are often transferred to headquarters or to other international operations so that they can gain experience and learn*

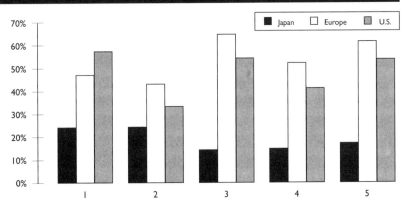

3. TYPES OF PERSONNEL POLICIES AT INTERNATIONAL FIRMS (%)

1. Performance evaluation measures are the same in every one of our international operations.

2. A training program has been put in place to groom local nationals for advancement in our company's managerial ranks.

3. Local nationals are often transferred to headquarters or other international operations so that they can gain experience and learn more about the company as a whole.

4. International work experience is an important criterion for promotion for home-country nationals who wish to advance into top management in our company.

5. At headquarters we maintain a centralized roster of all our managerial employees (both home-country nationals and foreign nationals) throughout the world in order to facilitate worldwide managerial development.

more about the company as a whole." Implementation of this policy suggests an even greater commitment to utilization of local nationals in management than does the implementation of a training program. This is because transferring local nationals requires greater planning and commitment of resources. Also, implementation of this policy suggests a broad view of the capabilities and role of non-home-country nationals that goes beyond their usefulness in their country of origin.

4. *"International work experience is an important criterion for promotion for home-country nationals who wish to advance into top management in our company."* Implementation of such a policy will

promote international awareness among the company's top management, which will presumably increase the company's sensitivity to international human resource issues. Also, implementation of such a policy would mean that the company's most highly capable and well-connected managers are the ones who are sent overseas, leading to better management of the overseas operations.

5. *"At headquarters we maintain a centralized roster of all our managerial employees (both home-country nationals and foreign nationals) throughout the world in order to facilitate worldwide managerial development."* Implementation of such a policy suggests that the head office is actively keeping track of local national employees and is better able to consider them when planning for international management needs as well as activities such as training programs.

Japanese firms are far less likely than U.S. or European firms to have adopted any of these policies, despite an emphasis on human resource development activities for Japanese employees. (See Chart 3.) This suggests that they have less interest than U.S. and European firms in expanding their definition of key human resources beyond home-country nationals.

Greater Susceptibility to International Human Resource Management Problems

Higher reliance on home-country expatriates and lower use of progressive international human resource policies create an environment where international human resource management problems are more likely to occur. One would expect that Japanese companies, which use many Japanese expatriates and few progressive policies, would be more prone to experience difficulties in their international human resource management. This is borne out in the results of the third portion of the survey: Japanese companies are more likely to report international human resource problems than are western multinationals, especially those problems concerning local employees. This pattern of problems closely matches that seen in recent discrimination suits against Japanese firms

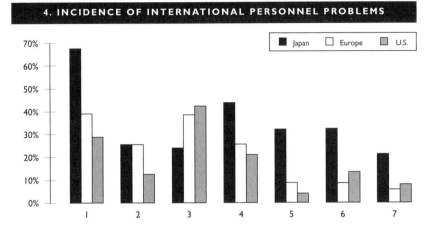

4. INCIDENCE OF INTERNATIONAL PERSONNEL PROBLEMS

Japan ▢ Europe ▨ U.S.

1. Lack of home-country personnel who have sufficient international management skills.

2. Lack of home-country personnel who want to work abroad.

3. Expatriates experience re-entry difficulties (e.g., career disruption) when returning to the home country.

4. Difficulty in attracting high-caliber local nationals to work for the firm.

5. High turnover of local employees.

6. Friction and poor communication between home-country expatriates and local employees.

7. Complaints by local employees that they are not able to advance in the company.

and in the Lantos hearings, media accounts, and various academic works. (See Chart 4.)

The following paragraphs discuss the individual problem issues included in the survey:

1. *"Lack of home-country personnel who have sufficient international management skills."* This was the most difficult problem facing any of the three nations' companies— international management skills are relatively rare among businessmen in any country. Japanese companies reported an especially high incidence of this problem. The relatively low number of Japanese businessmen who are fluent in foreign languages and the fact that international business is a relatively new area for many Japanese companies may contribute to this phenomenon.

2. *"Lack of home-country personnel who want to work abroad."* This issue was equally as problematic for European firms as for Japanese firms, while it was less problematic for U.S. firms.

3. *"Expatriates experience re-entry difficulties (e.g., career disruption) when returning to the home country."* This problem was the one most often cited by U.S. firms and was a significant difficulty for European firms as well. In contrast, Japanese firms reported a relatively lower incidence of expatriate re-entry difficulties. The more active role of the Japanese personnel department in coordinating career paths might be behind Japanese firms' lower level of difficulties in this area. In contrast, the decentralized structures of many U.S. and European firms may serve to isolate expatriates from the home-country headquarters, making re-entry more problematic. Also, recent downsizing at U.S. and European firms may reduce the number of appropriate management positions for expatriates to return to, or sever expatriates' relationships with colleagues and mentors at headquarters.

4. *"Difficulty in attracting high-caliber local nationals to work for the firm."* Multinationals in general often face greater challenges in hiring high-caliber local employees than domestic firms due to lack of name recognition and fewer relationships with professors or others who might recommend candidates. However, the survey results suggest that this issue is significantly more difficult for Japanese than for American and European multinationals.

5. *"High turnover of local employees."* This issue was significantly more problematic for Japanese firms than for U.S. and European ones.

6. *"Friction and poor communication between home-country expatriates and local employees."* This issue was also significantly more problematic for Japanese firms.

7. *"Complaints by local employees that they are not able to advance in the company."* This issue was also significantly more problematic for Japanese firms.

ETHNOCENTRISM AND BEYOND

What is the explanation for the differences that surfaced in this survey? What causes Japanese firms to manage international human resources differently from American and European firms, and to experience a higher level of problems in doing so? Insights can be gained by examining the four different international human resource management paradigms that have been identified by scholars.[3]

Ethnocentric.   An ethnocentric firm is highly centralized and focused on the home-country culture. Parent company employees hold all key positions at overseas operations. Decision-making is controlled by the head office. The assumption is that parent company employees are more suitable than local managers and that the company can manage overseas operations using methods that have been successful in the home country.

Polycentric.   A polycentric firm is decentralized. Local nationals hold all key positions and handle all decision-making at the overseas operations. The assumption is that local nationals are best qualified to respond to the unique business conditions in each country. Each subsidiary is in a sense an island and may be virtually indistinguishable from a local firm in many respects. The parent company assumes a holding-company attitude and permits local management to do whatever seems best for that particular country.

Regiocentric.   In a regiocentric firm, regional headquarters (e.g., for Asia, North America, or Europe) handle much of the decision-making in each region. The various subsidiaries in each region work together closely and trade personnel among one another. Few parent company nationals hold posts in overseas operations.

Geocentric.   Geocentric firms attempt to strike the delicate balance between centralized, coordinated decision-making and significant input from each overseas operation. The organization is characterized by much interchange of information between the various international operations. Personnel are considered for management positions regardless of their nationality, so many key overseas posts are filled by local nationals. There is also a significant transfer of employees from country to country, and third-country expatriates who work in a country that is neither their home country nor the parent company's country are not unusual.

Of course, these are ideal types, and any one firm may exhibit the characteristics of more than one type. However, the first type, ethnocentric, is generally mutually exclusive of the others. This is because ethnocentric management is centered on the home country and home-country nationals, while the other types rely more heavily on decentralization and local nationals.

Although twenty to thirty years ago the majority of U.S. and European multinationals had ethnocentric international management styles, they have moved away from the ethnocentric approach in recent years. Thus, when the average American businessperson conjures up the "normal" or "proper" multinational, he pictures a firm that is managed in a polycentric, regiocentric, or geocentric way, putting local nationals in positions of responsibility. Yet most Japanese multinationals seem to be stuck either in the ethnocentric mode or in an awkward compromise somewhere between a pure ethnocentric approach and a pure polycentric approach. Only a handful of the most progressive Japanese multinationals have adopted or come close to adopting truly polycentric, regiocentric, or geocentric approaches.

This difference is what accounts for the survey results reported above. The greater use of expatriates for overseas managerial positions and lack of "internationalizing" policies are consistent with the ethnocentric approach. The survey results also confirm what scholars have already predicted: an ethnocentric international personnel policy contributes to problems such as limited promotion opportunities for local nationals, low productivity and increased turnover of local nationals, and frictions between expatriates and their local subordinates.[4] In fact, one could take sections from twenty-year-old articles describing the problems faced by ethnocentrically managed American multinationals, substitute "Japanese" for "American," and produce something that would look like an excerpt from the Lantos hearings. What appears to be a "Japanese" pattern can therefore be thought of as a generic pattern. While this generic pattern has largely been cast off by American and European multinationals, it is still retained by Japanese multinationals.

The argument has been made that Japanese companies have less internationalized personnel practices because their international expansion has been relatively recent, and that as time passes they will begin to act more like western multinationals.[5] This argument rests on the assumption that Japanese multinationals will naturally follow the path of western multinationals in moving from ethnocentric policies to polycentric, regiocentric, and geocentric ones. Although this may be true for certain Japanese multinationals that have made significant investments of money and effort in adapting their policies to the international environment, the mere passage of time does not guarantee that a company's practices will change, and it may even serve to solidify current practices.

WHY JAPANESE COMPANIES CLING
TO THE ETHNOCENTRIC APPROACH

Japanese firms have certain characteristics that make it difficult (although not necessarily impossible) for them to abandon the ethnocentric approach and internationalize their human resources. These factors are not ones that will simply dissolve with time or with the growth of a company's international business. Change will only take place when Japanese companies develop a greater awareness of the obstacles that hinder their internationalization and devise strategies to overcome them.

Control Structures

A major factor influencing the ability of Japanese companies to internationalize is the type of control structure that is common to them. Scholars have identified two major ways in which companies institute internal control: output-oriented control systems and culture-oriented control systems.[6] An *output-oriented* control system focuses on objective, measurable data such as financial results and profitability indices. The managers' actions are controlled by the fact that they must act in such a way that their output matches the performance goal expected of them. In contrast, a *culture-oriented* control system is less clear-cut, being based on socialization of employees so that they understand the company's culture and goals. The managers' actions are controlled by training that leads them to act in accordance with accepted standards of behavior within that company.

All firms have control systems that combine both output-oriented and culture-oriented elements, but western (and especially American) firms tend to have more output-oriented control systems while Japanese firms tend to have control systems that are extremely culture-oriented. These tendencies are linked to the difference in employment customs. Output-oriented control systems are well suited to an environment in which managers move from firm to firm. The financial and other performance measures are generally standardized across firms. On the other hand, the lifetime employment system of Japanese companies is the perfect environment for carefully inculcating culture-oriented controls. From the point of view of the company, the effort expended in such training will not be wasted because its workers will not leave to join other firms. From the point of view of the employee, it is worthwhile to master the intricacies of the company's culture because he expects to remain there his entire career. The result is the fabled "Company Man" who knows instinctively what his company expects of him.

The type of control system affects a company's ability to delegate authority to local nationals. The output-oriented controls which American and European multinationals tend to rely on are well defined and easy to communicate to employees from other cultures. When such measures are used, locally hired employees can be given significant autonomy and extensive authority to meet the output goals as they see fit. This has enabled American and European multinationals to decentralize their management processes and put local nationals in management posts at their overseas operations.

In contrast, the culture-oriented controls of Japanese companies are a barrier to decentralization because they are difficult to transmit to local employees. Since Japanese companies indoctrinate their new employees into company cultures informally over a period of years, they are often at a loss as to how to train local employees in the culture quickly. Also, the training of an employee in a firm's culture traditionally takes place in Japan. Anyone who has not worked for a period of years in the head office will probably not be recognized as having adequately absorbed the culture. Finally, because Japanese companies' corporate cultures are firmly embedded in the Japanese language, culture, and labor practices, it is difficult to transmit them to local employees who do not have significant prior knowledge of Japan. Given the difficulties of immersing local managers in their culture, many Japanese companies feel that only the thoroughly company-integrated Japanese employees can be entrusted with important managerial posts.

Employment and Decision-making Systems

Ironically, the lifetime employment system that has proven to be one of Japanese companies' greatest strengths at home is another major obstacle to their personnel internationalization. First, it is difficult to integrate non-Japanese into the rigid lifetime employment hierarchy. This leads many Japanese firms to treat them as a separate category of employee and deprive them of access to the high-level posts that are reserved for lifetime employees. Second, Japanese managers who are unfamiliar with the workings of a labor market have difficulty understanding the local employee's motivations and attitudes toward job content, career paths, and compensation.

A final obstacle to the greater use of local nationals in positions of responsibility lies in the decision-making processes prevalent in Japanese firms. Japanese social structure and corporate organization are centered on group processes, while western social and corporate cultures commonly emphasize individual autonomy and responsibility. It is often difficult for non-Japanese to comprehend and learn to participate in these group processes. Furthermore, the consensus building needed for Japanese-style decision-making frequently extends across national borders to include extensive consultations with the head office. Local employees are often unable to participate in this process because they lack the personal contacts, knowledge of company culture and politics, and Japanese language ability that facilitate this sort of consultative decision-making.

THE COST TO JAPANESE MULTINATIONALS OF THE ETHNOCENTRIC APPROACH

American and European multinationals have largely abandoned the ethnocentric approach because they discovered that it was not the most effective way to manage international human resources. Similarly, many Japanese multinationals are experiencing the downside of the ethnocentric approach in their U.S. operations.

The ethnocentric management style leads to a combination of short-term cultural misunderstandings and the long-term effects of limited advancement opportunities for Americans. The result can be a variety of personnel management problems for the U.S. affiliates of Japanese firms, which can ultimately have a negative impact on their performance. These personnel problems impose costs and decrease productivity, although often in ways that are difficult to measure. An inability to integrate and utilize talented American staff may also prevent an organization from managing effectively in the American environment.

Although many Americans believe that Japanese companies are turning in stunning business performances at their U.S. operations, reality does not necessarily match this image. Recent surveys indicate that many Japanese operations in the United States are plagued by low profitability. For example, a 1992 *Nihon Keizai Shinbun* survey of 264 Japanese firms' U.S. affiliates found that 80 percent weren't returning profits to the parent company, and 63 percent cited earnings as their biggest concern.[7] Similarly, the U.S. Commerce Department reported that American subsidiaries of Japanese companies posted net losses of $2.3 billion in 1992, larger losses than the U.S. subsidiaries of firms from any other foreign country.[8]

Of course, there are many potential explanations for this evidence of

WAITING ON DECISIONS FROM TOKYO

An American employee of a Japanese construction firm is the project manager for the development of a large resort facility. Trying to keep the project on time and on budget is complicated by the fact that all decisions are made at the firm's headquarters in Tokyo. All his communications with the decision-makers must be written in Japanese by his supervisor. He finds this very frustrating because he is never sure how his supervisor will perceive a given situation, or the substance of what is reported to Tokyo. He often discovers that what's been told to Tokyo is 180 degrees from what actually happened.

Tokyo's insistence on making decisions by interdepartmental committees is a further source of frustration. For each matter to be decided, it takes several months for the fifteen or twenty people in Tokyo to gather their input and make the decision jointly. At that point construction has often progressed so far that the issue has become a moot point. In some cases, money is wasted because things have to be torn out and redone.

---

low profitability, including the U.S. recession, tariffs on certain imports from Japan, the costs associated with building up new U.S. operations, the interest payments on loans made by the parent company, and the alleged propensity of Japanese firms to depress their reported U.S. earnings through manipulation of transfer pricing. However, it seems likely that the problems resulting from an ethnocentric management style are a contributing factor in the low profitability of many Japanese firms' U.S. operations. U.S.-Japan business consultant Masazumi Ishii sums up this theory when he observes, "There are a few Japanese organizations where senior Americans have autonomy or influence, but in the majority [that's not the case]. That's why so many Japanese firms fail in the U.S."[9]

Below are some of the significant ways that personnel problems can damage the effectiveness of a Japanese organization in the United States.

Recruiting, Motivating, and Retaining High-Caliber American Employees

The high costs of keeping expatriates in the United States, the difficulty of obtaining U.S. visas, the limited number of Japanese employees with sufficient international management and English skills, and the need to meet U.S. legal requirements all preclude staffing a U.S. operation solely with expatriates. Japanese companies need to access American managerial talent to help run their U.S. operations, but their current practices and structure may prevent them from attracting the most qualified and ambitious American managers available. Says one headhunter, "Sometimes the best candidates turn up their noses at a Japanese firm."

Once someone is brought on board, the company's personnel policies and managerial style may make him or her less motivated. Exclusion from Japanese-only meetings and social events, lack of integration into the decision-making process, clashes with Japanese expatriates, and/or a lack of positive feedback can make an employee feel unneeded and less likely to give his or her all. Lack of opportunities for advancement or a lack of correlation between performance and compensation can also make employees less enthusiastic about turning in a stellar performance.

Employees who are frustrated with a company's atmosphere or who do not perceive that attractive future opportunities are available to them will often leave. The company loses the investment in training that it has made in a departing employee and must incur additional costs to recruit and train a new one. It will also suffer decreased productivity until the new employee "gets up to speed" in his job. Even if a qualified person is found, there will be an inevitable loss of continuity with respect to key projects or customer accounts. Furthermore, when someone quits, office morale can slip, especially when that person is high-ranking or well liked. Companies with high turnover also risk becoming recruiting pools for their competitors and miss out on the opportunity to develop American managers who have in-depth experience in the firm's operations.

Insufficient Adaptation to the Local Market

Firms that fail to fully utilize their American staff are likely to miss business opportunities in the United States and make decisions that are out of step with the demands of the local market. As Henry DeNero, a McKinsey and Company consultant to Japanese companies operating in America, puts it, "In almost every case in my experience where a product was not quite right or where marketing policies did not quite add up, someone in the United States who was close to the customer knew bet-

FRUSTRATED LOCAL MARKETING MANAGERS

A Japanese consumer products firm recently decided to introduce a new product in the United States with two brand names. Its American marketing manager, George, strenuously objected, arguing that it is expensive and difficult to establish even one new brand name in the United States, much less two. He was especially concerned that since both words were Japanese they would be difficult for American consumers to remember. However, the Japanese managers insisted on using both names, pointing out that this was how the product was marketed in Japan. A year later the product launch was far below expectations, and the company decided that one of the names should be eliminated. George can only wonder, "Why didn't they just listen to me in the first place?"

Tom, a marketing manager at a Japanese electronics firm, questions his company's ability to succeed in foreign markets. Whenever his U.S. office makes proposals, the response from Tokyo is "This might be interesting, this might be a good idea, but we want to wait awhile." Tom senses an underlying lack of trust: "They're Americans, they really don't know what they are doing." Meanwhile, the tight control from Tokyo prevents the U.S. operation from being innovative and seizing new opportunities.

ter—and said so. The managers in Japan just did not understand or chose not to listen."[10] Locally hired executives naturally are better able than expatriates to formulate and implement strategic plans in the U.S. environment, follow U.S. market trends, deal with local customers and suppliers, and manage local employees. When Japanese companies do not utilize these strengths of local managers, either by relying primarily on Japanese expatriates or by failing to capitalize on the input of the American managers they do have, they will have difficulty building an effective U.S. operation.

Impracticalities of Using a Large Expatriate Staff

A heavy reliance on expatriates is a significant cost drain, since it is expensive to maintain an expatriate in the United States. When special benefits are included, each expatriate can cost significantly more than a locally hired employee. Also, there is a dearth of Japanese managers who have sufficient international management skills. Whenever the company sends an expatriate abroad, it is removing another manager who could be more useful in Japan.

Strain on Japanese Expatriates

Not only do workplace frictions sap the motivation of American employees, they are also a severe strain on Japanese expatriates. Problems managing American employees are wearying for Japanese expatriates, leading to fatigue, stress, and culture shock. The result is poor morale and reduced effectiveness. It's difficult to make good decisions or work efficiently when your energy is sapped by clashing with and trying to understand your American employees. Also there are personal costs to the employee and his family. Either the employee must leave his family at home in Japan and endure the loneliness of the separation, or bring them along and subject them to the stresses of life in a foreign country. In addition, Japanese expatriates and their families frequently experience readjustment difficulties when they return from overseas assignments.[11] Coworkers who remained in Japan may regard the former expatriate as somehow tainted, while his children may have fallen behind their peers in Japan's regimented and competitive educational system.

Legal Issues

A lawsuit is the most visible way in which personnel management problems can adversely affect a Japanese company's U.S. operations. It is one of the worst nightmares for any Japanese manager in the United States: a disgruntled American employee sues your company for employment discrimination. You face a long, expensive legal process and the potential for negative publicity. Unfortunately, it is a scenario that is taking place at many Japanese companies in the United States

Perhaps, as Japanese firms hired more employees in the United States, it was inevitable that the number of lawsuits against them would also rise, given the litigious nature of American society. Some plaintiffs may also see Japanese firms as "deep pockets," ripe targets for litigation. However, some Japanese firms unduly expose themselves to potential litigation through ignorance of U.S. employment laws or the naive application of certain Japanese practices. In numerous cases, American employees have prevailed or obtained settlements in suits against Japanese employers. Because these suits often involve elements that appear to be common to many Japanese firms in the United States, they suggest that Japanese companies need to take seriously the possibility of legal action concerning their U.S. personnel practices.[12]

The Cost of Being an Outsider

To the extent that Japanese firms become hotbeds of antagonism between Japanese and Americans, they will not be able to blend gracefully into the American environment. For the individual firm, a reputation for being a bad place for Americans to work will jeopardize the company's goodwill and image in the community. Also, companies that fail to integrate American managers into their power structure will always be regarded as foreign outsiders. On the macro level, failure to adapt to American society will only make Japanese companies more susceptible to being singled out in the media and by lawmakers.

THE CHALLENGE FOR JAPANESE MULTINATIONALS

Numerous Japanese companies have begun to understand these costs and are starting to take action to improve their management of American employees. The combination of lawsuits, media attention, poor corporate performance, and individual executives who see the need for change are lending impetus to this trend. However, many Japanese firms seem to lack a road map of how they will manage non-Japanese employees throughout the world. Their efforts at improvement in the United States sometimes seem stopgap or piecemeal and usually are not integrated with policies at other overseas operations or headquarters. For example, the U.S. subsidiary may overhaul its job descriptions, compensation system, and career paths for American employees, yet neglect related issues such as the number of Japanese expatriates and their role in the U.S. operation. To the extent that Japanese are managed solely by Tokyo and Americans are managed solely by a separate local system (no matter how sophisticated), an ethnocentric management style is still in place.

Leading management scholars now believe that the rapidly changing, competitive global marketplace dictates a more complex set of relationships between headquarters and overseas operations, and among the overseas operations themselves.[13] Neither the dependent subsidiary relationships of the ethnocentric model nor the completely independent subsidiaries of the polycentric model are appropriate. From a purely strategic perspective, each has its own weakness. Although the subsidiaries of an ethnocentrically managed firm are able to implement global strategies, they often lack the ability to meet the differentiated needs of the local market. The independent subsidiaries of a polycentrically managed firm are responsive to the local market, yet lack the advantages of global coordination because they miss out on economies of scale in production and other functions and are prone to costly duplication of effort. The competitive environment faced by multinational firms demands that they simultaneously combine the ability to meet the needs of local markets, coordinate on a global scale, and fully exploit innovations and resources from anywhere in the firm, not just the home country.[14] This difficult balancing act requires "collaborative information and problem solving, cooperative resource sharing, and collective implementation," which involve a complex relationship of interdependence between the various subsidiaries.[15]

If it hopes to develop such a global network of interrelationships between operations, a multinational cannot depend on its home-country nationals alone. Not only is it costly and politically risky to do so, but there will not be enough home-country nationals who possess the relevant skills and insights. This is particularly true of Japanese multinationals, who cite the lack of Japanese staff who have sufficient international management ability as their biggest international personnel challenge. In order to be successful in the competitive global arena, a multinational must be able to incorporate the input of its employees no matter what country they are from or where they were originally hired by the company. Employees need to be valued according to the contributions they are able to make to the firm, not by the status (or lack thereof) of the partic-

PERFORMANCE GAPS AT JAPANESE COMPANIES IN THE U.S.

A recent McKinsey and Company report[h] noted that while Japanese companies' American operations "do have real competitive advantages in terms of product quality and cost, [they] succeed *despite* performance gaps in other areas." The report described six gaps in Japanese companies' U.S. management:

- Weak or under-resourced sales and marketing organizations

- Failure to tailor marketing approaches for different U.S. market segments

- Lack of product fine-tuning for the tastes and needs of the U.S. market

- Inefficient management of U.S. operations

- Lack of speed, flexibility, and responsiveness

- Unwise investment decisions and poor management of acquisitions

These weaknesses could all be addressed by more effective utilization of American managers.

ular unit in which they work. To the extent that a Japanese company ignores the potential contributions of its non-Japanese employees, it is crippling its ability to thrive in the global marketplace.

Japanese companies' difficulties in international personnel management are ironic given that human resource management is one of the traditional strengths of Japanese companies that is consistently lauded by academics and the media. In their ideal form, as compared with those of the stereotyped western firm, Japanese human resource management techniques effectively develop employees who have high levels of company-specific skills and knowledge. The rotational process molds employees into well-rounded generalists who have the flexibility to adapt to the changing managerial needs of the company. Furthermore, the Japanese management style in its ideal utilizes the talents of these employees and encourages them to take initiative through a middle-up, rather than top-down, managerial process. Decisions are thus made by those with direct knowledge of the situation rather than being dictated from the top. However, most Japanese companies have excluded their non-Japanese employees from the human resource management system that promotes these benefits.

In order for Japanese companies to become truly global entities, they need to extend their traditional competitive strength in the management of human resources to their non-Japanese employees. They need to involve non-Japanese employees in the "middle-up" management process and allow them the decision-making authority appropriate to their position on the front line. To do so involves overcoming the cultural barriers to trust, cooperation, and effective communication between Japanese and American colleagues. It also involves overcoming the Japanese company's institutional handicap in managing independent-minded employees who are aware of their value in the wider labor market. Furthermore, many Japanese companies will need to shed the ethnocentric biases of their existing international human resource management systems.

These will not be easy tasks for Japanese companies, nor can they be completed quickly. The necessary changes will require much research, experimentation, and investment. But in the long run, globalization of human resources is the only way for Japanese companies to insure their international competitiveness. Individual American employees can help to speed this process in their firms, and can make themselves suitable candidates for positions of increased responsibility, by learning to work more effectively with Japanese colleagues. However, the potential success of such efforts differs from firm to firm. Individual Japanese companies vary widely in how they have responded to the challenges of international personnel management. Some have chosen to muddle along with an ethnocentric approach, ignoring its drawbacks. Others have realized that in order to succeed overseas they need to utilize local employees effectively. The following chapter describes some of the differences among Japanese firms in terms of the atmospheres and opportunities they offer to American employees, and how a potential employee of a Japanese firm can evaluate them.

3

Checklist: Evaluating a Potential Japanese Employer

I've worked at two different Japanese firms. The first was an assembly plant in my hometown in downstate Illinois. The Japanese there were all from rural Japan, real down-home types. They made an effort to keep the American workers happy. The Japanese and Americans went out drinking together and had all sorts of group social activities. When it was his birthday the plant manager threw a party for the whole plant. Later I worked at the branch of a big Japanese bank in Chicago. The Japanese there were all from Tokyo. They were graduates of Japan's most prestigious universities. There was no emotion, just straight finance, just work and that's it. They were very stiff, rigid. The two places were like night and day.

AN AMERICAN BUSINESSWOMAN

There is a common tendency in the United States to stereotype all Japanese and all Japanese companies as being alike. The media speak of "Japan Inc." as a homogeneous monolith. Yet there are tremendous differences among the numerous Japanese companies in the United States. Different sizes, locations, and industries lead to large variations in office atmosphere and personnel management style. Comments Alex Warren, Senior Vice President of Toyota Motor Manufacturing USA, "If someone asked you what it is like to work for an American company, you'd ask 'Which one?' and 'Doing what?' The same differences apply to Japanese firms."[1]

Since the work atmosphere, future opportunities, and other factors vary widely among different Japanese companies in the United States (and even among offices or departments of a given firm), one should thoroughly investigate any Japanese firm being considered as a potential employer. Of course, this sort of "due diligence" is required when one considers any job opportunity. However, in the case of a Japanese company one should ask additional questions and consider different issues from those one would in the case of an American company.

This chapter will begin by discussing some general patterns that I have observed in my research. Then I will suggest specific issues that should be considered by anyone applying for a position at a Japanese firm.

PATTERNS

On the basis of my research and interviews with employees of Japanese companies, I believe that some general observations can be made about certain types of firms: small companies vs. large companies, small offices vs. large offices, manufacturing firms vs. service sector firms, and acquisitions and joint ventures vs. new startups. Admittedly, there is some danger in making broad generalizations because there are, of course, many exceptions. The following discussion is intended to illuminate some of the factors that might determine which firms are successful in managing their American employees and which are most likely to experience personnel-related problems.

Small Companies vs. Large Companies

Some large Japanese firms have become so well-established in the United States that at first glance they appear indistinguishable from American firms. This skillful adaptation to the U.S. environment has contributed to the growth of such firms.

Yet size alone does not guarantee that a firm has developed a successful human resource management formula for its U.S. operations. A firm may have had a relatively long presence in the United States and have achieved a sizable market position but may continue to keep positions of power exclusively in the hands of Japanese expatriates. Or, a large firm may be dominant in Japan but a relative newcomer to the United States and may still be working out the kinks in its U.S. personnel management.

In fact, there are certain characteristics of large Japanese companies that can inhibit their ability to skillfully integrate Americans into their managerial processes. One such characteristic is the bureaucratic, elitist mind-set of many large-company employees, which may put them on a collision course with American employees. On the organizational level, a large company will be more concerned than a small one with maintaining the sanctity of existing management and personnel systems which would be threatened by any adaptations to accommodate overseas employees. A large company may also have a more complex and ingrained corporate culture that is harder for outsiders to understand and penetrate.

In contrast, a midsize or small company may be more flexible, innovative, and open-minded in the management of its U.S. operations. In a sense these are qualities that smaller firms have had to cultivate in order to survive in the competitive Japanese marketplace. Their overseas expansion is often a new experiment, not a matter of established policy. This seems to give smaller firms a willingness to adopt progressive policies that many larger firms would not have the stomach for, such as naming an American to the top post right away. A smaller company is also more likely to have an entrepreneurial leader who sets the tone for the entire company. A leader with a clear vision for the firm's international expansion may inspire expatriates to understand and adapt to the local way of doing things. Smaller companies are also frequently constrained by their lack of talented managers, especially those who can speak English. More willing to admit the limitations of their own stock of human resources, these firms often seem more comfortable giving top posts to Americans. This is in contrast to larger firms, which, due to the lifetime employment custom, often have excess managerial staff that they may want to foist off on the U.S. operation.

Although the absolute amount of its investment may be relatively small, the amount of money that a small firm sinks into its U.S. operations may be a proportionately large part of its overall investment budget. A small firm may have a large stake in making sure that its U.S. operation succeeds and will be motivated to eradicate any internal friction that threatens the project.

These positive characteristics of midsize and small firms should be balanced against their potential pitfalls. For example, a lack of international experience and sophistication may cause a small firm to blunder in its management of American employees. Headquarters employees may not be oriented toward international markets, and they may lack the language skills needed to interact effectively with non-Japanese employees.

Small Offices vs. Large Offices

Smaller offices, regardless of the parent company's size, may be more prone to problems and frustrations than larger offices. This pattern may even emerge within a single company. For example, at one service sector firm, the large New York City office has hired an experienced American personnel manager and has begun to adapt its personnel policies to better meet its American employees' needs and expectations. At the same company's smaller office in another city, the personnel policies are primitive by American standards, and the American employees are frustrated and dissatisfied. In another example, a large subsidiary of a major manufacturer has filled most of its management positions with Americans and grants them a great deal of independence and authority. At a smaller subsidiary of the same company, located elsewhere in the United States, meetings are held only for Japanese employees, and the American managers feel excluded from decision-making.

What factors might lead to fewer personnel management problems at larger offices? For one, large offices tend to be better established, have more solid policies and operating procedures, and have a full-time human resource manager. A large office is also associated with a greater absolute investment in the U.S. market and a greater market share that needs to be protected. It also attracts greater scrutiny of its practices from headquarters, as well as from the community in general.

On the other hand, small offices are often dominated by Japanese expatriates. The rice-paper ceiling is lower in these offices, and many of the American employees are hard-pressed to see a clear career path. Furthermore, in a small office there is no layer of American middle management to insulate lower levels of American staff from having to interact with the Japanese expatriates. This means that a much higher level of synergy between the two groups is necessary in order to get anything accomplished. If the interaction is positive, the office can be quite productive. If the interaction deteriorates, the office situation can become very strained, and employees will not be productive. In this setting the personalities of the one or two Japanese expatriates in charge has an overwhelming influence on the atmosphere of the office. If their attitudes are not good or they do not have the ability to work well with Americans, the office is likely to experience problems. For example, at one manufacturing firm's ten-person administrative office, the two highest-ranking expatriates set a negative tone that permeates the entire atmosphere. The general manager cloisters himself in his office, refusing to talk to any of the American employees. The deputy general manager is clearly unhappy about his assignment to the United States and manifests his feelings by barking orders at everyone. The rest of the staff—both Japanese and American—are so uncomfortable that they can barely do their work. There is no way for them to escape the influence of the top two people; every action or decision must be scrutinized by one or both of them.

Placing the firm size effect and the office size effect together, small outposts of large firms have the potential for particularly severe personnel management problems. Because the office may not be of great strategic importance to the company, headquarters may be especially lax in monitoring how it is managed. The Japanese managers may be bitter at being relegated to an insignificant outpost and may be extra conservative so as to stay in the head office's good graces. There is also an inherent clash between the risk-averse outlook of the typical large-company manager and the small office's typical mission of building something from scratch in the United States. This clash can be exacerbated by the entrepreneurial personalities of the Americans attracted to work in such ventures.

Manufacturing Firms vs. Service Sector Firms

Manufacturing firms tend to be more successful than service sector firms in managing American employees. At the most basic level, this has to do with the nature of the work involved. A business that deals with physical things translates better across cultures than a business that deals with intangibles. It's easier to monitor the quality of a manufactured product than to evaluate the quality of a decision or a customer relationship. Thus, manufacturing firms may feel more comfortable in giving responsibility to American managers because they are more comfortable with their ability to monitor and measure the result of their work.

Another factor that accounts for this difference is the relative degree of independence given to the subsidiary. In comparison with manufacturers, service sector firms such as trading companies and financial institutions tend to have more Japan-oriented decision-making systems. This leads to a large need for interaction with head office staff and a heavy reliance on expatriates to fill managerial roles. The result is a

THE PRODUCTION SCHEDULER

Four years ago, Steve joined a Japanese automotive parts maker in his rural Indiana town. He started as press operator and now is a production scheduler for the entire press shop. "When I came here, I didn't have a totally open mind. My family has a strong UAW background, and I'm the only one who's crossed the fence. But things are definitely working out well."

Steve feels that it takes at least six months to adapt to working with Japanese. "It's like a marriage—you never really know each other until you've been together for awhile. You have to take away your stereotypes about the Japanese." He enjoys the company's egalitarian touches—the president's open door policy, the identical uniforms for all employees, and the first-come, first-served parking. Steve also has grown to admire the Japanese work ethic and thinks it has rubbed off a bit on himself. "Last Friday I was in Chicago all day on business. I didn't get back until nine p.m., but I stopped by the plant to check on things. I wouldn't have done that before."

Steve sees his company as providing good opportunities to its American employees. "A young person could come here, raise a family, and get along well."

structure which sets the stage for internal frictions. A goodly proportion of the recent well-publicized discrimination lawsuits against Japanese firms in the United States have involved service sector firms.[2] Manufacturers' affiliates that are primarily sales and marketing operations for products manufactured in Japan or other non-U.S. locations also tend to have a pattern of problems similar to service sector firms.

In contrast, Japanese firms that have set up manufacturing operations in the United States frequently have better management integration and more harmonious atmospheres. This is in part because Japanese companies in general have been more successful in managing American blue-collar workers than in managing white-collar workers.[3] Many Japanese manufacturing operations in the United States have made great efforts to skillfully manage production workers by purposefully establishing egalitarian work environments, empowering workers, and carefully selecting and training their employees.

Firms that have manufacturing facilities in the United States often see their success in managing blue-collar workers carry over to their managerial workers as well. In part, this may be because it is impractical to import enough people from Japan to run an entire factory and its supporting operations, so firms establishing manufacturing facilities must come to terms with a certain degree of management localization. Also, some Japanese manufacturers have striven to break down blue-collar/white-collar barriers, and follow a hire-from-within policy at their U.S. operations, so that management is not necessarily easily distinguishable from nonmanagement.

A firm conducting manufacturing in the United States will also have sufficient volume to warrant a well-developed and localized sales and marketing organization. In comparison, a company that imports rather than manufactures products locally will often feel that it needs a large contingent of expatriates within the U.S. operation to manage the interface with the Japanese factory and the highly centralized international marketing function at headquarters. Furthermore, companies that are only doing marketing and sales in the United States may have just one or two small offices, while companies that have invested in manufacturing facilities here are likely to have built large organizations in the

United States, so the effect of office size discussed above is also present.

The final difference is that manufacturers' U.S. operations, even if they are only marketing offices, naturally focus on adapting to local conditions. This is because they are making or selling things in America for American consumption. On the other hand, many service businesses in the United States are oriented toward Japanese clients. Many Japanese financial institutions, construction firms, real estate brokers, travel agencies, etc. established their U.S. operations because they want to provide services in the United States for their existing Japanese client base. This orientation to Japanese customers tends to diminish the role of their American employees and strengthen the company's identity as a Japanese entity. For example, an American marketing officer at a Japanese bank commented: "The heart and soul of our branch is our business with Japanese customers, which is a continuation of relationships in Japan. Any non-Japanese business is just icing on the cake. The bank isn't really here to establish business with U.S. companies. They 'cherry pick' choice American deals when they can, but they're not that concerned about problems with American clients and American employees as long as their core Japanese business is stable."

Acquisitions and Joint Ventures

The foregoing discussion has for the most part focused on companies that were established as fully owned subsidiaries of Japanese firms. American companies that have been purchased by Japanese companies, or are joint ventures between Japanese firms and American firms, are subject to somewhat different circumstances.

In many cases, American companies purchased by Japanese firms do not see their management styles altered significantly by the change in ownership. The management team, management structure, policies and procedures, and corporate culture that were already in place are often left largely unchanged. The majority of the interaction, and thus any potential friction, with the new Japanese owners takes place only at the uppermost management levels. The Japanese owner may have a fairly hands-off approach, a holding company attitude. Only a small number

TAKEOVER OF A COMPUTER FIRM

Jim's company was an independent firm until it was purchased by a major Japanese computer company three years ago. "Before the ownership transition, we were a ragtag, maverick cowboy-type outfit. The acquisition was a big shot in the arm financially, and it caused the market to view us as more stable."

Immediately after the acquisition, a flood of Japanese from the new parent company descended on the firm. "There were two ways of looking at it. Either they were just observing, or they were looking over our shoulders." However, once the transition was completed, most of the Japanese returned to Tokyo and only a handful of expatriates were left in departments such as finance and corporate planning.

Jim feels that "for the most part, we are left to operate independently. Since we act as a sales arm for our Japanese parent, there is constant negotiating with them on the cost of goods, volume, and product features. But we are not dictated to—they expect us to know the marketplace better than they do. And they realize that they need to have locals in key decision-making posts."

of Japanese employees may be sent, and they may only be in an observer or trainee capacity. In fact, overall conditions for American employees may improve due to an influx of capital from the acquirer. In reality, such firms can hardly be said to be Japanese companies, but rather American companies that happen to be owned by Japanese.

On the other hand, some firms that have been taken over by Japanese companies are rife with internal frictions. This usually occurs when a large number of Japanese expatriates are sent from the new parent to manage the acquired firm. The clash between how the company did things before the takeover and how the Japanese delegates intend to manage the operation can be extreme, resulting in severe conflict.

As for firms that are joint ventures between American and Japanese companies, there are a large number of variables involved, such as the ownership structure, the corporate cultures of the parent firms, and the skill of the managers assigned to the venture. There are many complex issues involved in the management of a joint venture that are outside the scope of this book. However, since the Japanese managers assigned to the subsidiary will bring with them the personnel management paradigms from the Japanese context, employees of joint ventures will find that many of the potential sources of friction discussed herein are applicable.

THE MOST IMPORTANT VARIABLES: PERSONALITY AND ATTITUDE

Although all of the above patterns have emerged in the course of my research, a Japanese company's size, its parent company's scale, and its industry and customer base do not automatically determine whether an office atmosphere will be harmonious and productive or strained and unpleasant. A more important factor that overshadows these variables is the personality of the Japanese expatriates in the office, especially the highest ranking expatriate. A strong manager with good communication skills and a genuine interest in understanding American employees can make great strides in building an effective organization. On the other hand, a manager who displays a contemptuous or indifferent attitude will quickly alienate American employees.

The following example demonstrates how the most senior expatriate's attitude can make a significant difference. Morale among the American employees was poor at a Japanese high-tech company on the West Coast. All the department manager positions were held by Americans, but the Japanese president would consult only with the Japanese expatriates. On the organizational chart these expatriates held lower-level positions, but they were given significantly more power by the president. He would call them all into closed-door meetings without inviting any of the American department managers and make decisions affecting the entire company. According to one of the American employees, "People felt they didn't have control, that everything was controlled by Japan. They thought that no matter what they did, it didn't matter." The American employees had unhappily resigned themselves to their lack of input.

The sudden arrival of a new president from Japan changed everything in the eyes of the American employees. The closed-door, Japanese-only meetings ended. The president made a point of calling the American department managers into his office to ask them questions, listening carefully and responding to what they said. He communicated that he believed the Americans were capable. This, of course, was the opposite of the previous president's stance, which was to assume that the Americans were incompetent no matter how hard they tried to prove themselves. The change resulted in a "complete difference" in the company atmosphere and a big increase in the motivation of the American employees. The organizational structure and personnel policies were unchanged and not a penny had been spent! The only change was in the attitude of the man at the top, how he related to Americans and utilized the human resources that were already in place.

This story shows that, while the generalizations above may be useful, a detailed understanding of a specific firm and the personalities of its managers is essential in evaluating the likelihood of its success in utilizing American employees. The following sections suggest ways to go about exploring the atmosphere if you are considering employment with a Japanese firm.

HOW YOU CAN INVESTIGATE A JAPANESE FIRM

A useful first step if you are going to interview with a Japanese firm is to do an extensive publication search. Searching a database of news articles through a computer service or at your local library is the most efficient method. Major newspaper indexes and the *Reader's Guide to Periodical Literature* are also useful. Also check back issues of local publications and industry trade journals. Not only will learning more about a company prepare you for the interview, the media coverage may give you insight into the company's personality and its utilization of American employees, including any past pattern of discrimination lawsuits. Sometimes, however, you may need to take media accounts with a grain of salt, since some journalists approach Japanese companies with a negative or sensationalist attitude. Look for patterns rather than a single critical article.

In your background research, don't ignore information about the parent company in Japan. During the 1980s, the rapid pace of Japanese investment in the United States caused Americans to view all Japanese companies as rich and stable. Yet many Japanese firms have been severely weakened by the crashes in the property and stock markets, a fall in consumer spending, and the aftereffects of overly aggressive hiring and capacity expansion during the '80s boom years. You should find out how the recession has affected a firm's parent company, as well as its plans for restructuring its Japanese operations. Is it taking the painful steps necessary to cut overhead and change inefficient practices, or is it dragging its feet?

If the position you are seeking reports to a Japanese manager, try to find an opportunity to speak with him at leisure. (I say "him" because Japanese expatriates are almost always male.) If possible, have lunch or dinner with him so that you can talk in a more relaxed setting. This is the best way to get a feel for him as a person. If you will be working for a Japanese boss, his personality and outlook will be the most important factor influencing your job satisfaction, so it is important to evaluate how you feel about him. Although a superior's poor English skills can make your life quite difficult, try to get beyond English ability and get a feel for character and attitude. Don't assume that someone is "Americanized" or "thinks like an American" just because his English is smooth. An international, open-minded attitude may lurk behind awkward English, while someone who speaks English fluently may not necessarily have an affinity for non-Japanese.

Also, if possible, try to get some time alone with one or more non-Japanese employees of the firm, particularly those who would be your colleagues or are at a comparable level. Ask them about their opinions and experiences. If you are lucky, they will share some candid observations; if not, try to read between the lines.

The following is a checklist of some of the issues that you should attempt to investigate in discussions with both Japanese and American employees of the firm:

- *What is the makeup of the management team (proportion of Japanese vs. proportion of Americans)?* Firms where management positions are dominated by Japanese expatriates are more likely to experience internal frictions, and advancement opportunities for American employees may be limited. On the other hand, a significant number of Americans in managerial positions is a positive sign.

- *Are the American managers primarily in staff positions (e.g. legal, accounting, administration, personnel)?* In some Japanese organiza-

IF YOU ARE A WOMAN . . .

Although Japanese society does not give Japanese women equal status in the workplace, these attitudes are not always carried over to American women. Furthermore, Japanese men vary widely in terms of their progressiveness. While some have attitudes that are archaic by American standards, others are quite accepting of working women. It goes without saying that you should watch carefully during the interview to determine the stance of the individuals you will be working with.

Your experience working with Japanese managers may depend on your age, position, and qualifications. Young-er women and those in clerical and administrative roles might be viewed as analogous to Japanese "office ladies." However, if you are going into a professional or managerial position, you may have few difficulties other than some initial awkwardness. Comments a senior female executive at a Japanese bank, "Initially I was apprehensive—I didn't know how they were going to react to me. But they have gone out of their way to make me feel at home. In fact, the attitude of the Japanese managers here is better than the American managers I encountered in my previous jobs."

tions, the only Americans in managerial positions are those in staff functions. These are generally the first types of managerial positions that a Japanese firm will give to Americans. If there are Americans in line managerial positions, such as operations, sales, marketing, and production, it can be an indication that localization of management has taken deeper root.

- *How far from the top is the highest-ranking American? Who is that person and how long has he or she been in that post?* Learning about the highest-ranking American in the firm, including his or her function, job history, and degree of power in the organization, can provide significant insights into the firm's overall atmosphere and utilization of Americans. Is the president of the firm an American who is running the firm in a largely American manner? Is the highest ranking American an "advisor" hired from a prestigious U.S. firm who has little involvement in day-to-day decision-making? Is the most senior American employee three or four levels down from the top?

- *Are the American managers perceived to have power and authority comparable to that of the Japanese managers?* To what extent are American managers able to exercise autonomy? Are they perceived as tokens or are they respected as having true importance and influence in the firm?

• *Are there posts that are reserved for Japanese expatriates only? What types of posts are they? Are they ones that could reasonably be filled by Americans? If the company feels that a post cannot be filled by an American, what reason is given?* If all or many of the upper-level posts in an organization appear to be reserved for Japanese nationals, it is a clear sign that advancement prospects for American employees are limited.

• *Are there any junior Japanese expatriates reporting to Americans?* Many Japanese organizations are characterized by a dual structure in which no Japanese expatriates, no matter how inexperienced, report to American managers. A senior American banker at a Japanese institution comments that "the thing that drives me most wild is the parallel structure. The Americans do the work, analyze it, write it up

IF YOU ARE A MEMBER OF A MINORITY GROUP . . .

The well-publicized racist comments of certain Japanese politicians have made many American minorities think twice about pursing opportunities at Japanese companies. Paige Cottingham, Director of the U.S.-Japan project at the Joint Center for Political and Economic Studies, an African American think tank, responds to such concerns by saying, "The Japanese business community recognizes credentials. If you have a particular set of skills or experience that give you credibility, whether from the business world or academia, the Japanese are more inclined to treat you the same as anyone else with those credentials and give you a fair shake." To the extent that some Japanese subscribe to racist stereotypes, it is a cause for concern. Yet it is important to keep in mind that the comments reported in the media were made by older, conservative politicians, and do not necessarily reflect the views of all Japanese. Many Japanese companies in the United States have demonstrated a commitment to minority recruiting and devote a considerable amount of time and energy to philanthropic activities that benefit minority communities. Rather than assuming that all Japanese will have negative attitudes toward minorities, explore the record and atmosphere of the particular firm that you are considering.

and hand it off to a junior Japanese person who checks it, translates it into Japanese, and sends it up the system. The Japanese guy may be only three months on the job and have less knowledge and training than the American who wrote it, but he questions the assumptions. It makes me wonder, why do I have to answer to this junior guy?" In some companies, American and Japanese employees are segregated into different sections, or are listed on two different organization charts. Such situations suggest that there are two different classes of employees, one of which is subordinate. In contrast, a firm in which younger Japanese employees report to American managers has put real authority in the hands of Americans and has transcended the division of status on national lines.

- *What is the personality of the general manager of the office or department that you will be joining? How long has he been in this post? Is he likely to be rotated out of this position soon?* The personality, outlook, and communication ability of the general manager sets the tone for the other expatriates and for the organization as a whole. As one American at a Japanese bank described it, "the whole attitude and atmosphere of the office is dictated by who sits in the big seat." Also be aware that if the general manager seems to be on the verge of being rotated out, the one who comes to take his place could have a significantly different style. Transitions from one general manager to the next are often quite stressful periods for a Japanese firm.

- *How much interaction is there between American employees and Japanese management?* A manager at a Japanese bank comments, "Upper-level Japanese managers are always communicated with through lower-level Japanese managers. There is no direct communication between Americans and the upper-level Japanese managers. Most of them want nothing to do with us." This type of situation is a sign of potential danger, signaling a lack of openness in the office and that the Japanese managers may consider the Americans in the office to be unimportant.

- *How much social contact is there between Japanese and American*

IF YOU SPEAK JAPANESE . . .

A Japanese company is a natural choice for someone who has taken the time and effort to learn the language. Japanese firms are more likely than American ones to be able to appreciate or utilize your skills. Your language ability may enable you to develop better relationships with coworkers, have greater contact with the head office, obtain access to a wider range of information, and increase your potential for training in or assignment to Japan.

However, there are potential sensitivities to be aware of. In a company that is trying to wean itself from overreliance on Japanese in its everyday activities, your desire to use your language skills may provoke irritation, especially from American coworkers who do not speak the language. Furthermore, make sure that your desire to speak Japanese is not interpreted as an implicit criticism of your Japanese colleagues' ability to communicate in English—many are quite sensitive about this.

Your level of Japanese ability may also be an issue. Unless you are truly proficient, your language skills may be looked on as cute but useless. Also, overly blunt Japanese can be truly irritating to a native speaker. Take the time to learn polite expressions.

employees outside of the office? In many companies, Japanese and American employees seem like strangers to each other— there is little social contact or development of friendships between them. This type of social stand-off signals, and also exacerbates, general frictions between the two groups. On the other hand, friendships and socialization between American and Japanese employees is a positive sign that the office has a cooperative atmosphere.

- *What is the representation of women and minorities in the organization overall? In management?* The representation of women and minorities in the company overall and especially in management signals how well the organization is adapting itself to the current norms and goals of American society.

- *Are there meetings to which American employees are not invited?* Frequent meetings that exclude American managers are a sign that the decision-making process is being kept in the hands of Japanese personnel. It is also likely to reduce the morale among the American employees. One banker says that "the fact that a meeting is held every week just among the Japanese really bothers the Americans.

IF YOU ARE A JAPANESE AMERICAN . . .

Working for a Japanese company as a Japanese American can have certain advantages but also potential disadvantages. Japanese Americans who are familiar with Japanese language and culture may find it easier to understand Japanese expatriates. Says one Japanese American at a Japanese bank, "I can recognize some of the cultural traits from my parents. In my family, we don't say 'no' directly either."

A Japanese appearance may mean that you are expected to act in more Japanese ways. An electronics industry employee comments, "I think that they are shocked when blunt American-style remarks come from my Japanese face." The banker above noted that "It seems like they expect me to stay later than others." Japanese American women, especially those in lower-level positions, may need to guard against being put into the same mental category that Japanese managers reserve for Japanese-born women. (The particular issues faced by women in Japanese firms are discussed more fully in subsequent chapters.)

The different expectations for Japanese Americans can have positive aspects as well. Comments a Japanese American woman who worked in Japan for several years, "Being of Japanese heritage is an opportunity to be accepted into their realm and gain their confidence. If you put in the effort, you can become a bridge between the two cultures."

There's always some rationale, like 'it's in Japanese' or 'it's just stuff concerning Tokyo,' but we all suspect that they are discussing things that we should be aware of." The frequent occurrence of such expatriate-only meetings is an extremely negative sign.

- *What language is generally used in meetings—English or Japanese?* Extensive use of Japanese in internal meetings in front of Americans may be a signal that Americans are not fully integrated into the company's decision-making process. A manager at a consumer products company reports that "At the staff meeting every week, everything said is prearranged. They will discuss something in Japanese and then move on to the next topic. I ask 'What's the result?' and they say 'Don't worry, it's taken care of.' When I ask them 'But what happened?' they tell me 'You'll find out when the time comes.'" Obviously, American participation is impossible in such an environment. On the other hand, strict protocols mandating the use of English in meetings (or a sufficiently large number of American managers that this becomes a moot point) are a positive sign.

- *What language is used in internal memos (within the U.S. operation and for communication with the head office)?* When internal communication, either within the U.S. operation or with the head office, is conducted in Japanese, it is difficult for American employees to fully participate in management. The need to use Japanese for written communication also entrenches the role of the Japanese expatriates. In contrast, where American employees are able to communicate in English with the head office it implies a willingness on the part of the head office to make the necessary effort to work directly with non-Japanese employees.

- *Are language lessons for American employees encouraged?* Encouragement of Japanese lessons for American employees indicates a willingness to develop their broader exposure to the company's overall culture. On the other hand, active discouragement of Japanese-language study can be a negative symbol—either of stinginess with regard to educational expenditures for American employees or, more seriously, of a desire to keep Japanese-language conversations off-limits to Americans.

- *Are there any American employees who speak Japanese?* If there are, try to get an opportunity to speak with them. Are they encouraged to use their Japanese? Do they feel included or excluded? Due to their language ability they may be able to offer interesting insights into the corporate culture and the personalities of the Japanese expatriates.

- *Are there opportunities to go to Japan for training?* The availability of training opportunities in Japan signals that the organization is willing to make significant investments in its non-Japanese employees.

- *What kind of training is available to American employees?* Is there reimbursement for outside study such as professional seminars and evening classes? Again, the greater the training opportunities provided to American employees, the greater the commitment the company displays toward them as important human assets of the firm.

- *What is the company's record of bringing in people at the lower levels of the organization, training, and then promoting them?* This question will be particularly apropos to those seeking midlevel or junior posts. One banker recounts an interview with a Japanese firm in which his question, "What can I expect from a career path here?" was met with a response that "was almost comical. They had these dumbfounded looks on their faces. They were totally baffled." If you get a similar reaction to this type of question, it is definitely cause for concern. A large number of Japanese firms in the United States have not yet developed the internal structure necessary to develop young managers and move them into increasingly higher posts.[4] In such firms, either there are few Americans in upper-level positions, or those who are there have been recruited from outside.

- *Is there high turnover?* Many Japanese companies in the United States experience a high level of turnover, especially among managers and young white-collar employees who become frustrated with limited opportunities for advancement and cultural friction within the organization. High turnover is a signal of an imbalance in the company's personnel management.

- *How clearly is the job defined? Has the company prepared a written job description for the position?* If the job tasks are not defined with sufficient clarity, is the supervisor willing and able to elaborate? If the company is not able to clearly discuss your job responsibilities, it may signal potential problems; Americans who join Japanese firms often encounter difficulties when they discover that their tasks are not well defined. It may be possible to avoid such problems if in the recruiting stage you stress the issue and obtain a written description for future reference. Be aware, however, that many Japanese managers are uncomfortable with job descriptions because they want to maintain flexibility in their use of employees.

COMPENSATION AND PERKS

Salaries, benefits, and perks at some Japanese firms may differ significantly from those at American companies, while at others they match the American norm. The degree of contrast will vary greatly depending on how the company goes about its hiring, and also the type of position.

For firms that have American personnel managers, hiring and salary negotiations will generally follow the American pattern. The same is usually the case if an executive recruiter is being used—they will often advise the firm on the appropriate market rate and help to conduct the negotiations. However, if a Japanese expatriate is doing the hiring (or has more power in the process than American line or personnel managers), Japanese attitudes will come into play. In general, Japanese are not accustomed to the workings of a free labor market and are unfamiliar with how salaries are set and negotiated in the United States. In Japan, salaries are largely determined by one's age—only for baseball players is compensation linked solely to one's skills. The American approach to salary negotiations is regarded by many Japanese expatriates as crass and unseemly. In their mind, a manager is not a star baseball player.

SALARY NEGOTIATIONS—HANDLE WITH CARE

Japanese misunderstanding of American-style salary negotiations can sometimes lead to reneging on agreements once an employee has entered the company. Such shenanigans occur primarily in Japan, or at smaller operations in the United States that do not have American personnel managers. For example, in more than one case a highly paid American was induced to enter the company at a salary lower than he had previously been earning, with a promise that he could receive a salary review and significant increase within six months or a year. But, as time passed the company conveniently forgot its promise and the increases never materialized.

If a company is hesitant to pay you what you are worth, it's a bad sign. And if you do make any verbal agreements, put together a written memorandum of understanding. However, keep in mind that such behavior is not directed only at non-Japanese. Comments an American employee who saw the substantial starting bonus promised by a major electronics manufacturer evaporate, "It's no different from how they treat their Japanese employees, unilaterally changing salaries. They are used to having employees under their thumb."

In many cases, salary scales at Japanese firms will be higher than at comparable American firms. At higher levels this is because many Japanese firms feel that they are at a disadvantage in recruiting top American managers. At lower levels, and especially in manufacturing positions, higher salary levels may reflect greater expectations for flexibility and overtime. On the other hand, some Japanese firms have salary scales that are significantly below the norm. This may be the result of tight cost controls or unfamiliarity with the concept of a market rate. Lower-level positions are especially likely to be at low pay, reflecting the custom in Japan.

The *Wall Street Journal* recently began an article on executive compensation this way: "Congratulations. The Japanese-owned company down the street has offered you a big job at a big salary. It seems too good to be true. It probably is. When you tally your total compensation package, you may discover that you would be better off at a U.S. firm."[5] The article attributed this difference to the fact that Japanese companies usually do not offer American-style, long-term incentives for managers. These long-term incentives, commonly in the form of stock options, performance plans, or restricted stock, are offered by 89 percent of U.S. companies but only 33 percent of Japanese companies' U.S. affiliates.[6] Often Japanese companies do not offer long-term incentives because they are unaware that this form of compensation exists, since it has no parallel in Japan. Many Japanese firms will also resist such plans because they do not want their U.S. compensation systems to diverge too far from what is available to Japanese employees, and because they feel, in general, that executives at U.S. firms are overpaid.

Another way in which total pay packages may be lower than those of U.S. firms is in the area of incentive compensation. The concept of linking pay raises and bonuses to individual performance has only recently begun to be discussed in Japan. At many Japanese firms raises and "bonuses" are uniform or near-uniform across the board. A banker comments, "There are no individual bonuses: 'bonus' is a function of rank, a certain percentage of your salary," and an industrial firm's employee reports that "Everyone gets a 5 percent raise. It's companywide, based on profits." Many employees of Japanese firms report that there is

WHY AMERICAN MANAGERS JOIN JAPANESE FIRMS

Professional opportunity (34 percent)	Impressed by Japanese executives (4 percent)
Chance to join a start-up team (21 percent)	Acquired by Japanese company (4 percent)
Growth potential (12 percent)	
Interest in Japan (11 percent)	General reputation (3 percent)
No choice after restructuring (6 percent)	Other factors (5 percent)[i]

resistance to commission compensation plans (which are uncommon in Japan). One manager at a consumer products company proposed a commission plan for the sales staff, but was told, "It's their job to sell. They shouldn't need a special commission plan—they should always be selling their best."

Benefits and perks at Japanese firms may also be less generous than those available at American companies. Japanese companies report frustration with the complexity of benefits management in the United States, primarily because the regulations are more elaborate and companies have more choices and responsibilities.[7] Many benefits that are common in the United States, for example 401K plans or family-support programs such as flexible scheduling and childcare aid, may be perplexing to Japanese expatriates. Larger firms, especially manufacturers, are the most likely to have benefits packages that are similar to those of U.S. firms.

Although corporate executives in Japan receive lavish perks such as golf club memberships, enormous expense accounts, and chauffeur-driven rides to work, Japanese firms are not likely to provide these perks to the top American executives of their U.S. operations. In fact, Japanese companies in the United States often purposefully downplay executive privileges in the interest of equality and cost savings. In particular, the elimination of executive perks such as separate dining rooms and parking spaces has contributed to good relations with blue-collar workers at Japanese-owned manufacturing plants in the United States.

Even those who are not top executives may be uncomfortable with

WHAT KINDS OF AMERICANS SUCCEED IN JAPANESE COMPANIES?

Here is a list of personality traits that may predict your ability to succeed in a corporate culture dominated by Japanese managers:

Flexible: Willing to try new ways of doing things.

Forward-thinking: Anticipates needs and issues.

Organized: Stays on top of information and details.

Even-tempered: Able to deal with stress and communication difficulties.

Patient: Prepared to work toward goals one step at a time rather than in giant leaps.

Self-motivated: Brings enthusiasm to the job and doesn't need a lot of coaching.

Persuasive: Able to convince colleagues and management to adopt recommendations.

Curious: Interested in learning about Japanese culture and business practices.

Diplomatic: Diffuses potential misunderstandings before they escalate.

---

the typical Japanese company's Spartan management style. For example, many Japanese companies do not provide managers with private offices; everyone sits at desks in a large open room. Although many Americans find such a setup to be distracting and resent the lack of privacy, Japanese believe that it facilitates the flow of communication. Also, many types of positions that typically have dedicated support staff in American companies do not in Japanese companies. Japanese firms expect that each employee will handle his or her own clerical matters, such as filing and copying.

LOOK INWARD BEFORE YOU LEAP

If you are an American considering taking a job with a Japanese employer, you should ask yourself if you are really suited to join a Japanese company. You will need to consider more than whether you fit the stated job requirements. The working environment is almost certainly going to be different from an American firm. Anyone considering working for a Japanese company should ask themselves whether they are willing to make the necessary effort to understand a very different culture, because this willingness will affect their ability to succeed. As an employee of a Japanese chemical company advises, "Working for a Japanese company is a good opportunity to learn another culture and a way of doing business. The only way to do it is to get immersed. But if someone doesn't have a true reason for working for a Japanese company, I would tell them not to do it." (However, you should not assume that every Japanese company will pose an equal challenge in terms of cultural adjustment. As discussed earlier in this chapter, there is a wide variation among them in terms of corporate culture and the sophistication of their personnel policies for American employees. Some Japanese affiliates are virtually indistinguishable from American companies in terms of corporate culture and management style, while others are like transplanted bits of Tokyo or Osaka.)

One question that potential employees of Japanese companies should also ask themselves is whether they can leave their politics at the door. Of course, if deep in your heart you feel that Japan Inc. is the biggest threat to American society since the Red Menace, you simply shouldn't join a Japanese company. But even Americans who don't think they have strong feelings about the Japanese may be more opinionated than they realize. Over the past decade American politicians and the mass media have spent so much energy stressing Japan's closed markets, collusive business practices, and supposed quest for worldwide economic dominance that adult Americans can scarcely help but carry some intellectual baggage on this subject. Furthermore, many businesspeople are old enough to remember World War II and the wartime propaganda vividly, and even if they aren't they are certainly aware of the facts of history. You don't need to think that every aspect of Japan is saintly in order to work for a Japanese company, and working for a Japanese company should not mean that you need to become an apologist for the Japanese. However, you should be careful to examine your own feelings and make sure that you do not bring them into your interactions with Japanese coworkers.

You should also ask yourself about the attitudes of your friends and family. Some Americans who join Japanese-owned firms experience family tensions, particularly from relatives who are staunch union members or WWII veterans. There may also be insinuations from neighbors

WHAT THEY'RE LOOKING FOR

The over four hundred large Japanese firms surveyed by Professor Hideki Yoshihara of Kobe University identified the following as desirable characteristics for locally hired upper-level managers of overseas operations[j]

- Ability to get things done: 85%

- Personality (trustworthiness etc.): 81%

- Understanding of Japan: 50%

- Devotion to the company: 30%

- Japanese-language ability: 13%

and acquaintances that you have somehow sold out by going to work for "the Japanese." Such negative attitudes shouldn't prevent you from taking a good job at a Japanese firm, but it's a potential issue you should prepare yourself to face.

Another important issue is your own personality and work style. The traits that can make one successful in an American firm—shoot-from-the-hip aggressiveness and directness—can be a recipe for disaster in a Japanese firm. Executive recruiter Christine Houston of TASA International observes, "In this country, we equate A players with aggressiveness, but Japanese want to hire people who are smart but not me-oriented." A human resource manager at a Japanese company notes, "We need people who are open-minded, flexible, resourceful, and looking for opportunities to learn. We don't need solo performers with sensitive egos. A person used to a heavily bureaucratic environment and not comfortable defending themselves in meetings or taking questions from junior Japanese staff in their twenties will not be comfortable here. Our employees must be able to cooperate with their colleagues." For these reasons, a Japanese company may be a particularly good choice for people who are looking for a change from the typical American corporate environment. If your personal style is more collegial, this trait can be quite beneficial in a Japanese company atmosphere. The ability to work in a team is of the essence. If you are not willing to adjust your working style to a collaborative approach, a Japanese firm may not be the right choice for you.

TWO

Coping with the
Japanese Company
Environment Day to Day

4

How You Can Succeed at a Japanese Company

An American branch of a Japanese company is not a Japanese company, and not an American company. It's a strange hybrid between the two. This definitely creates issues, some positive and some negative. There's an odd mixture of things to deal with.

AN AMERICAN MANAGER AT A JAPANESE ELECTRONICS FIRM

It is unrealistic for Americans to expect that Japanese firms and individuals will simply drop their culture and operating style when they come to this country. Would you be able to stop acting like an American if you went to Japan? Although Japanese companies and individuals that come to this country do make efforts to adapt to American business and social practices, as a matter of practicality American employees will need to meet their Japanese employers halfway by learning to adapt to certain aspects of the Japanese work style. Americans who read this and think, "I shouldn't have to change," are not only likely to be unhappy in a Japanese company, but are ignoring the fact that working with Japanese can be a tremendous learning experience.

Much of the advice in this chapter also applies to work situations at American companies. New employees of a firm, whether it be Japanese-owned or not, will always need to adjust to an unfamiliar corporate culture. This involves learning to understand the expectations of superiors and coworkers as well as building credibility by being productive. The difference in the case of a Japanese firm is simply one of degree—the corporate culture of a Japanese company may be more difficult for an American to understand initially and may require a greater amount of adaptation. As one trading firm executive puts it, "You need to be mentally prepared for a different experience. Be flexible, and maintain a sense of humor." An open-minded attitude will also help you determine whether any difficulties you encounter are simply minor issues, or larger problems in your company's management of American employees of the type discussed in Part 3.

CONCENTRATE ON
GOOD WORKING RELATIONSHIPS

Japanese businesspeople place an extremely high value on good personal relationships in the workplace. This is because the consensus decision-making style and team organization require that everyone cooperate closely. Also, Japanese want to form strong bonds with their colleagues because Japan's low job mobility means that they expect to work with the same set of people for extended periods, perhaps even their entire careers. Japanese society also places a higher value than American society on subtlety, nuance, and formality in communication. Since a harmonious work environment is valued, Japanese managers will be sensitive to the perceived attitudes and interpersonal styles of American employees. As a manager at a small manufacturer comments, "They have evaluated me on how I have interacted with them, not on the content of my job."

In order to work well in a Japanese environment, many Americans will need to hone their interpersonal skills. This means becoming more conscious of nuances in your own and in others' communication. Japanese antennae are highly attuned to interpersonal signals. Americans may not even realize what signals they are giving off or how they might be misinterpreted and may ignore the ones they are receiving.

Many basic aspects of subtlety in communication are the same in both Japanese and English. For the speaker, this involves care in the choice of your words, as well as in the tone of voice and body language that accompanies them. As a listener, it involves being aware of subtle cues from the person speaking. You can benefit greatly from making an effort to be more observant.

"It's Difficult"

There are also characteristic Japanese communication codes that need to be learned. One of the most confusing to Americans is "it's a bit difficult," which is a literal translation of the Japanese expression *sore wa chotto muzukashii desu*. In Japanese this is understood to mean "no way," usually due to an obstacle external to the speaker such as budget constraints or internal politics. Given the arduousness of the internal decision-making system (see Chapter 7), a manager has to pick his projects and battles carefully. His perception of "too many difficulties" signals that he is unwilling to expend his personal capital pursuing the issue or is advising that you not do so. This phrase may also be accompanied by non-verbal cues, such as sucking air through one's teeth with a hissing sound or scratching one's head. Unfortunately, Americans often interpret "it's difficult" the way one does in English—as a sign that something is possible but that more effort is needed. The result is that the American wonders why he is beating his head against the wall, while the Japanese manager wonders why the American didn't get the hint to give up and try something else.

This example typifies the Japanese tendency to express negative things indirectly, so as not to unduly damage another's feelings. Those subtle markers that exist in Japanese for this purpose do not translate well into English. Few Japanese managers will ever tell you "no" directly, so interpret what you do hear accordingly. On the other hand, many statements that will seem like "yes"—even, in many cases, the word "yes" itself—should be interpreted as "maybe." If this all sounds ambiguous, that's because it is! Communication in a Japanese context means that very little will be black or white—shades of gray are the rule.

Disagreements

Enhancing one's interpersonal skills also involves being calmer, cooler, and more collected—not raising your voice, eschewing table pounding and other aggressive gestures, and avoiding conflict when possible. While Americans tend to believe in airing disagreements openly, Japanese see the avoidance of confrontation as a sign of emotional maturity and respect for others. In the American context, "putting your cards on the table" and "getting things out in the open" is considered to be constructive and any ruffled feathers can be smoothed over with an apology. In contrast, direct confrontations and arguments are considered unacceptable by Japanese, and even one uncharacteristic outburst may remain a permanent blot on one's record. This is important to keep in mind when the inevitable frustrations of working with Japanese begin to accumulate. One trading company executive, who has a private office, says, "Some days I just have to close my door so I don't say something I shouldn't." Other strategies may be necessary for those who work in a Japanese-style, open-plan office. A woman who works at a high-tech firm in Tokyo says, "Once every two months or so I get so frustrated that I just leave the office and go for a walk. I only come back after I don't feel like I need a gun to shoot everyone!"

In the Japanese context, openly disagreeing with one's superior or colleague is considered disrespectful and may be interpreted as hostility even if that was not the intention. This doesn't mean that you should become a yes-man and avoid all discussion and debate. It just means that you should be sensitive to the Japanese distaste for open conflict and carefully consider how to present your opinions.

Socializing

Getting to know Japanese colleagues on a personal level, for example by having lunch with them, playing golf together, or going out for drinks at the end of the day, will enable you to improve your communication. Socializing with business colleagues is common among Japanese businesspeople. It provides an opportunity to develop the close personal relation-

GETTING TOGETHER AWAY FROM THE OFFICE

Examples of social activities that your company could organize to promote interaction between Japanese and American employees:

- Golf tournaments

- Charity walkathons

- Community volunteer work

- Organized outings to restaurants

- Apple or berry picking

- Spectator sporting events such as baseball, football, and basketball games

- Cultural activities such as plays, concerts, and art exhibits

- Hiking, canoeing, fishing, or simply picnicking at a beach or park

- Participatory sports such as bowling, softball, and 10-K races

ships that are essential to Japanese-style management. It is also a way to iron out interpersonal tensions that develop at work. Unfortunately, many Japanese expatriates are hesitant to interact socially with their American coworkers. Taking the initiative in this respect can be useful, particularly if you coordinate with other American employees and plan a group event.

Getting to know people on a personal basis can also help you stay away from the "us versus them" mentality that is all too common among American employees of Japanese firms. It is important to judge people on their own merits rather than solely by their nationality. For example, consider the case of Suzuki, a Japanese expatriate who is rude and arrogant. He rubs the American employees at his trading company the wrong way with his bad temper and bossiness. All the Americans assume that Suzuki acts this way because he is Japanese. They attribute his behavior to his nationality, not to his individual quirks. The possibility that Suzuki just happens to have a bad personality never seems to be raised. Interacting with the Japanese expatriates in your office and getting to know them as individuals will help you to avoid this trap.

Lay Low

New employees should give themselves time to learn the ropes. Just as in any job, it is important to understand the way things are done and who makes decisions. This is especially true in a Japanese company because procedures are often unwritten and actual power relations may be very different from what appears on the organizational chart. As one banker comments, "You have to be here a few months to understand what's going on." A trading company executive recommends ". . . getting to know the lay of the land. I see so many people come in who are brash and disruptive. You need to find out who's doing what, and how to best approach them." You may also need to be careful about internal politics. A banker warns that "When I first joined, my immediate superior had been branded a troublemaker, and everyone who worked for him was persona non grata, including me. It took me too long to realize that this was happening. I should have distanced myself from him more quickly."

While you are getting to know the company, the company will be getting to know you. Japanese feel that they need time to develop a relationship with a new employee to understand how he ticks and to become comfortable with him. This is often difficult to understand for Americans, who place a high value on developing working relationships and getting down to business quickly. New employees often have to go through a fairly explicit testing period before Japanese superiors and colleagues are ready to trust them. According to an American senior manager at a Japanese securities company, "After you join the company, the first six to twelve months are all about people establishing a personal relationship with you and deciding whether they can trust you. It doesn't matter who you are, what your background is, or if you have the greatest deals on earth, personal relationships and trust are the most important. For the first six or nine months, you've got to answer a lot of questions at a level of detail that you think you shouldn't have to answer. After that, they assume you did it right." An American working at a Japanese bank has similar advice: "Trust is an important thing anywhere but it's especially true of the Japanese. The onus is on you to show that you should deserve respect and that the things you say are in fact true."

This testing period is in some sense analogous to that said to have been employed by Middle Eastern merchants of old, who would take up an extended residence in someone's tent to find out what sort of person they were before doing business with them. Americans, on the other hand, may be offended when they aren't trusted immediately. "They saw my resume, interviewed me, and checked my references, isn't that enough?" is the common reaction. The key here is to accept this as a cultural difference, not to take it personally, and to work at proving that you are sincere, competent, and trustworthy. Once you have done so, a Japanese manager will give you more latitude in how you do your work. The same banker who warned of the need to develop mutual trust comments: "My manager gives me a lot of flexibility to try new products. They give you a lot of leeway if you can prove yourself."

During the initial "breaking in" period, you may not receive much direction about what you should be doing. In fact, you may be asked to do tasks that are not in your job description or that you consider to be below your level. This is particularly true for junior-level employees. Generally, it is a good idea to perform these tasks cheerfully, while looking for improvements that could be made or other ways to add value. This is a way to demonstrate your cooperativeness, a quality highly valued by Japanese managers. In fact, that is usually the purpose of such tests. Once the manager has become comfortable with you he will assign more responsible tasks. If he doesn't, after having demonstrated your cooperativeness and flexibility for several months, you will be in a better position to ask for more challenging assignments.

For managers who have been brought in with a specific goal, it is also a good idea to "lay low" for the first few months. Charging in with a premade plan and trying to change everything all at once is a recipe for disaster. It is better to slow down, learn about the organization and its needs, and cultivate support for proposals and changes. An excellent example of this approach is the new personnel manager at a Japanese bank's New York branch who, rather than immediately producing a thick policy manual, spent the first several months on the job getting to know everyone in the branch, asking questions, and doing a lot of listening. Not only did this enable her to learn the lay of the land, but it enabled her to demonstrate her earnestness and develop the trust of her Japanese colleagues. After conducting an active dialog with the branch's managers about what policies would be applicable to the bank's situation, a two-year plan was developed, translated into Japanese, and sent

FINDING A MENTOR

As in any organization, finding a mentor can be valuable at a Japanese firm. In my own personal experience, having a mentor was a way to learn more about the company and develop a new perspective on my job.

My mentor took it upon himself to alert me to various nuances of the corporate culture, such as the traditional greeting made on the last day of the fiscal year. He also gave me suggestions on whom I should approach when I was trying to gather support for a new project proposal.

Perhaps most importantly, because he was in another part of the organization, my mentor was able to give me objective advice on how to handle difficult interpersonal situations that I encountered in my department. In talking things over with him I also discovered that my own frustrations with some of my department's policies were often shared by people in his department as well.

I got to know this particular individual because he had a crush on the pretty secretary who sat next to me and was a frequent visitor to our area. In general, Japanese gravitate toward mentoring relationships, and derive great pride from being good *senpai* (senior colleagues) and taking younger employees under their wing.

---

to headquarters for approval. Although time-consuming, the six-month process of reaching this consensus proved to be valuable. Because all the top managers of the branch were involved in the process, they understood the policies and supported the plan's implementation.

MEETING JAPANESE EXPECTATIONS

A Japanese employee of an electronics firm notes that "When a Japanese manager who has worked at the company for thirty years and been very successful comes to the United States, he can't imagine that other ways of conducting business exist. So he expects employees, customers, and suppliers to act as they do in Japan." It is inevitable that Japanese expatriates will judge their American employees by the standards of Japanese business culture and expect them to behave in familiar ways. To the extent that American employees' behaviors do not match what a Japanese expatriate thinks is appropriate, the Japanese will be tempted to evaluate them negatively. This is just a simple fact of human nature in cross-cultural situations. Of course, Japanese expatriates coming to the

United States should learn to understand and appreciate American customs and ways of doing business. Americans working for Japanese firms should not be expected to act exactly like Japanese. However, it is useful for Americans to understand what the Japanese are likely to expect so they can modify their actions to the extent they feel is appropriate without compromising their identity and effectiveness.

Details

One area where Japanese expectations differ from American ones is in detail orientation. Japanese are trained from childhood to be extraordinarily fastidious, so be prepared to pay enormous attention to details. Even the most minor spelling mistake or arithmetical error will be viewed as unacceptable. You can improve your image in the eyes of Japanese colleagues by simply being more careful about the little things. One common complaint of Japanese managers is that their American subordinates are not sufficiently meticulous. Also be aware that a command of detailed information is expected from subordinates. As one American working at a Japanese bank puts it, "One of the most shocking replies you can give a Japanese is 'I don't know, but I'll find out and get back to you.' In the Japanese world, the junior person has to have all the answers." Being able to answer detailed questions is seen as a sign that you are on top of your work. Furthermore, your Japanese colleagues will want to obtain from you a full understanding of the details so that they can answer similar questions from their superiors.

Quality

Japanese tend to value quality over speed. In most cases, it's better to take a longer time to make something as polished as possible than to do something quickly but have it be rough around the edges. Japanese managers don't want to see rough drafts; usually they would rather wait an extra day to get a finalized product. You are less likely to score points for how fast you work than for the carefulness and quality of your output. The extra time you take to refine something will seldom be counted against you. As U.S.-Japan business consultant Elizabeth Andoh explains, "Americans are highly focused on efficiency. Our use of phrases such as 'spend time' and 'waste time' suggest that time is a precious commodity that must be used appropriately. The Japanese see time as a continuum, the end result of which is effectiveness. Things 'require time' (*jikan ga kakaru*), a phrase which doesn't indicate the intrinsic value of time itself." This attitude carries over into the Japanese approach to decision-making, which often seems glacially slow by American standards. Japanese will focus more on whether a decision is appropriate and whether all the affected parties support it than on how long it takes to reach it.

Overtime

Japanese concepts of time are also related to the famous Japanese penchant for putting in long hours at the office; one should put in as much time as necessary to get something right. The tendency to work late also has a lot to do with the Japanese concept of group solidarity. A Japanese TV variety show recently posed the following question: "How does a worker in Spain respond when asked to do some extra work after five?" The panel was stumped, and when it was revealed that he would call his wife to ask her permission, the result was gales of laughter. In Japanese society it is most important to display commitment to one's group, which for a worker is his company. Displaying less than perfect loyalty to the group by blatantly putting the wishes of one's spouse first goes so deeply against an important Japanese cultural value that it seemed surprising and humorous to the Japanese panel. As an American manager at a Japanese bank puts it, "They are married to the bank. That's the only way I can describe it. They need to prove their loyalty, their love." In fact, although this banker was unaware of it, the Japanese term for company loyalty, *aisha seishin*, uses the written ideograph for "love."

Putting in long hours at work is viewed as an expression of one's commitment to the company. It also can be viewed as a display of personal commitment to members of one's immediate work group. Many Japanese will not leave until their coworkers, superiors, or subordinates are finished

NEAT, PRECISE, AND ORDERLY

Many Americans at Japanese firms wonder "Why does every calculation have to be balanced literally to the penny, every typographical error pointed out with glee, and trivial rules enforced with vigor?" Neatness, promptness, and precision are highly valued in Japanese culture in general and also in Japanese corporate culture. Because American culture does not value these traits to the same extent as Japanese culture, it is natural for Americans to chafe when Japanese managers dwell on them. By the same token, Japanese will tend to view American employees as uncommitted, even insubordinate, when they do not exercise the same attention to details as a Japanese would. This extends beyond the work at hand to the general office environment. Many Japanese managers are extremely irritated by what they perceive as American sloppiness. "Why is the coffee cup just left in the sink, why are newspapers left sitting on the lunch table, why doesn't anyone pick up the papers on the floor?" To Japanese, trained since their school days to clean communal places (Japanese schools have few janitors—the students do most of the cleaning) American inattention to such details is a glaring shortcoming.

for the day, even if this means sitting around and twiddling their thumbs. This practice is so widespread that there is even a word for it, *tsukiai nokori* (staying late to keep someone company). Those who do leave before their coworkers make a ritual apology of *osaki ni shitsurei shimasu* (literally, "Excuse me for leaving before you"). The tradition of long office hours is so deeply embedded in Japanese business psychology and business culture that entire volumes have been written on the subject by Japanese scholars. Furthermore, at Japanese companies in the United States there is an additional pressure to work late because the evening here corresponds to the start of the business day in Japan. Being in the office after hours makes one available for consultations with headquarters.

Given these expectations, the American tendency to wrap things up quickly and leave in time to have dinner with the family or pursue other personal activities may be perceived by Japanese as evidence of selfishness, laziness, or lack of commitment to one's job. A senior banker at a Japanese institution comments that: "Americans who leave at 6 p.m. are considered slackers. A Japanese asked me how one of my subordinates was doing. I replied that he's doing a good job. The response was 'Oh, but he leaves so early.'" In companies where the Americans go home promptly and the Japanese stay late, the difference in quitting times serves to reinforce the stereotype that the Japanese are the ones who are really doing the work and are more committed to the company. When American employees are willing to stay late, it enables them to break down that stereotype and develop a better rapport with their Japanese colleagues. As one banker puts it, "If you are willing to stay later it may make you seem more part of the team . . . When you leave at five o'clock every day, that subtly plays into their minds." A woman working at a trading company voices a similar sentiment, "No one who doesn't like to work should join a Japanese company. I rarely leave at five o'clock. I stay late while the other American staff goes home. This makes me closer to the Japanese."

How Much Is Enough?

While Americans should be aware that putting in longer hours will help them to get into the good graces of Japanese employers, there is a question of how much one should have to adapt to Japanese expectations. This is especially true because how late one stays at the office affects not only oneself, but also one's family. Japanese wives expect that their husbands will spend a lot of time at the office and socializing after-hours with their colleagues. Americans' spouses and children don't generally view that kind of schedule as legitimate. This issue exemplifies the different role of work in Japanese and American culture. Japanese expatriates should respect American culture and learn to evaluate employees' performance by results rather than by "face time" after five. However, American employees should be aware that how late they stay may affect the way their Japanese colleagues view their level of commitment.

Of course, the symbolic importance of this issue can vary from company to company. It will be less important where the proportion of Japanese employees is smaller. Alternative approaches are also possible. For example, one morning person working at a large company in Tokyo was able to avoid the pressure to stay late by arriving every morning before any of her Japanese coworkers. "They were so impressed by my promptness that I was able to leave at a reasonable hour each night with-

CONTRASTING WORKSTYLES

It's eight fifteen in the morning at the U.S. marketing operation of a major Japanese electronics manufacturer. The American managers have already arrived at their desks and begun the day's work. The Japanese managers arrive just in time for the official start of the workday at nine o'clock, still bleary-eyed from the previous evening's overtime work or the occasional Japanese-only carousing. Throughout the day, they hold meetings among themselves. In the eyes of the Americans, who work pretty much steadily at their own desks from the moment they arrive, the Japanese managers are just lounging around and chatting, doing very little "real work." Meanwhile, the Japanese view their conversations as essential consensus-building activities.

By five forty-five or so, when the American managers are getting ready to go home, the Japanese managers are on the phone to Japan, preparing to settle in for an evening of work. The Japanese at this company resent the fact that the Americans go home promptly every day and conclude that they do not share the same company loyalty. On the other hand, the Americans are bewildered by the seeming inefficiency of the Japanese and their willingness to spend late nights at the office rather than at home with their families.

out any criticism." Major Japanese companies' recent reduction of working hours (*jitan*) and curtailment of business entertaining may also be changing expectations. In addition, younger Japanese are beginning to place a higher value on their leisure time and many admire Americans' ability to balance business responsibilities and personal lives. Some expatriates who return to Japan even find that they have grown uncomfortable with the expectations for long hours and late-night partying.

GET INVOLVED WITH THE OVERALL COMPANY AND ITS CULTURE

A Japanese company's culture and way of doing business are inextricably linked with the overall Japanese culture. Even if the company doesn't provide classes, all employees of a Japanese company should spend some time on their own studying Japanese culture and business practices.[1] Also, studying the Japanese language should be a priority for anyone who is serious about pursuing a long-term career at a Japanese company.[2] Japanese-language classes are often offered at local colleges or at the local Japan Society or Japan-America Society. There are specialized language schools (like Berlitz) and self-study tape programs as well. Also, many Japanese living in the United States, particularly students, are willing to work as private tutors.

Language

Although learning the Japanese language is admittedly difficult and time-consuming, its long-term usefulness cannot be stressed enough, even if it is not necessary for one's day-to-day job functions. Even if you do not become fluent enough to use Japanese in your work, learning some of the language may enable you to develop a better rapport with your Japanese colleagues. Comparing herself to two Americans in her company who can speak Japanese but not fluently, a manager at a manufacturing company who does not speak any Japanese notes with a touch of envy that "Even if it's not perfect, their conversational ability helps in their interaction with the Japanese managers. They can chat, talk about their golf game or what they did on the weekend. It's a great relationship builder." Even a quick exposure to the language will also provide valu-

---

WHY ARE YOU STUDYING JAPANESE?

Your Japanese colleagues may react oddly to your Japanese studies because:

- Many Japanese businesspeople are very sensitive about their English language ability (or lack thereof) and may perceive your language study as a sign that their ability to communicate is inadequate.

- Some—but certainly not all—Japanese expatriates enjoy the fact that Americans cannot understand their conversations and may view your studies as an unwelcome encroachment on their second communication channel.

- If you are at a beginning level, your fledgling Japanese may sound very awkward to a native speaker's ears—don't practice with your coworkers until you reach an intermediate level, unless they specifically encourage it.

Even if a particular individual discourages your language studies, don't take it as company policy—it's likely just his personal opinion. Emphasize your belief that studying Japanese will help you to further contribute to the company.

---

able insights into Japanese behavior. An effort to study Japanese will also demonstrate your commitment to the company and increase your potential for training opportunities in Japan.

The Company As a Whole

Japanese managers often complain that their American employees are focused solely on the local subsidiary where they are employed and don't understand the company as a whole. In order to learn as much as possible about overall company operations, ask your Japanese colleagues questions about the company, its activities outside the U.S., and the current challenges it faces. Get as many internal publications produced in English by the head office as possible (e.g., the parent company's English-language annual report) and follow your company's activities in Japan as reported in the *Wall Street Journal*, the *Nikkei Weekly*, and other publications. If your company is listed on a Japanese stock exchange, try to obtain analyst's reports produced by the Japanese branches of American investment banks; these can be a gold mine of information about your company and its industry. These suggestions may sound rather basic, but many employees of Japanese companies' U.S. subsidiaries do not follow the wider activities of their organizations. Japanese companies often cite this as a reason why they have trouble promoting locally hired employees: their focus is too narrow in comparison with that of Japanese employees. Learning as much as possible about the company shows your commitment, helps you to understand the perspective of the head office and your Japanese colleagues, and may help you to identify new opportunities for yourself.

The Head Office

Employees who envision building a career at a Japanese company should also try to develop relationships with people at the head office. This should be one of your main goals whenever traveling to Japan on business or meeting people from the head office who are visiting the United States. Part of what makes Japanese managers effective is their network of personal relationships with people throughout the company. As a locally hired employee you are at a disadvantage in forming such relationships, so extra effort is needed in this respect. A senior executive at a Japanese securities firm describes how he went about building a network of relationships at the head office that helps him to do his job more effectively: "After I had been with the firm for two months, I went on a business trip to Tokyo. My one agenda item was establishing relationships. Even though I had seven deals under my arm, they weren't the main thing. The point of the trip was the beginnings of personal relationships, personal trust and respect. After I got back, for the ten guys important to me, I have a relationship in some form with each of them. We either had drinks, dinner, or meetings or a combination. Now we can deal with the most complicated and difficult things over the phone."

Even if a business trip is unlikely, a trip to Japan for training may be possible. Such training trips are a perfect opportunity to learn more about your company and to start building an internal network. If your company has an established training program, express interest in participating. If it doesn't have an established program, the possibilities become a matter of your personal initiative. The firm may be willing to create something for you if it views you as an employee with long-term managerial potential. For example, Julia, a woman working at a Japanese chemical company, was developing relationships for her company in a new field and had to describe her company to many people. "I told them that if they want me to represent the company I need to know more about it. I can't learn what this company's all about from just reading the annual report. My boss approved, so I was sent over." Before going, Julia told the head office what she needed to learn about, and they scheduled the appropriate itinerary of meetings and plant visits for her. The trip greatly improved her ability to represent her company to American firms.

Don't expect to go to Japan for training until you have already made a contribution to the company. You will also need to make a legitimate business case for how a visit to Japan will enable you to do your job better; don't ask for it as a reward. Also, it is inappropriate to request a trip to Japan if you are not planning to stay with the firm for a long period of

OUT OF SIGHT BUT NOT OUT OF MIND

Maintaining your network within the company is important, but how do you keep alive a relationship with someone halfway around the world?

One useful habit is to become *fude mame na hito*—a good correspondent—which is something held in high esteem by the Japanese. Go ahead and add company contacts to your holiday card list (Japanese also have a tradition of sending year-end cards to business associates). If you have established a particularly good relationship with someone, you can also send postcards from your summer vacation, which is analogous to the Japanese custom of summer greeting cards. Another occa-

sion for keeping in touch is when you run across a newspaper or magazine article that your colleagues in Japan would be interested in.

Suggested people to add to your list:

• Everyone at the head office you have frequent contact with by phone or fax

• Anyone you have met on a trip to Japan

• People from Japan who have visited your office

• Japanese expatriates you have worked with who have rotated back to Japan

---

time afterward. Abandoning your firm after you have coaxed it into making a large investment in you is, in the Japanese context, viewed as unacceptable behavior. If you leave the company soon after it has sent you on an expensive training trip, the company will be bitter about its lost investment and potential leakage of valuable knowledge. It will also cause great embarrassment for your boss, and the negative stereotype of Americans as mercenary job-hoppers will be reinforced. Future training opportunities in Japan could then become more difficult to obtain for the other American employees in your company.

You should also consider the possibility of a long-term assignment to Japan. Some of the more progressive Japanese firms are establishing formal programs to rotate overseas staff to positions in Japan. A company that does not have such a program may still be open to the possibility if your interest is genuine. A long-term stint working for your company in Japan is an excellent opportunity to understand the company's overall business, develop an internal network, and increase your understanding of Japanese language and business culture—all of which will facilitate your career development.

KEEP IN MIND WHAT YOU CAN LEARN

One of the most important things to focus on when working for a Japanese company is what you can learn from the experience. Even if the rice-paper ceiling seems unbreakable, the insights and experiences you gain can be extremely valuable. Working at a Japanese company is an opportunity to observe firsthand the management techniques behind the famous "economic miracle." Some aspects of the Japanese management style may seem unjustifiable from the American perspective (especially when transplanted to the American context), but the rapid postwar growth of the Japanese economy is due in part to Japanese companies' management methods. Although Japanese business practices such as attention to detail, penchant for consensus decision-making, distaste for quick decisions, and emphasis on teamwork over individual recognition may be a source of frustration, they also represent areas where American businesspeople have something to learn. On the other hand, don't fall into the trap of expecting a Japanese company to match American business's idealized impressions of Japanese management. Not all Japanese firms are the ultraefficient, long-term-oriented dynamos portrayed in the U.S. media.

You don't need to become exactly like the Japanese in order to utilize the encounter with their management techniques as an opportunity to reflect on your habits and assumptions. Most of the people interviewed for this book, including many of those who were unhappy with their employers, described how they had grown as a result of their experience working with the Japanese. For example, one manager at a small manufacturer cites improved communication skills and a newfound ability to orchestrate consensus decisions. She notes, "I have gained the ability to bring more people into the decision-making process. I'm more able to stop and think: 'Who else is this going to affect? I need to talk to them. I need to get their input. I need to be able to explain clearly why I have made this proposal.'" An employee at a Japanese chemical company comments, "I have more patience than I ever dreamed I would have. I tend to look at things from two sides of the coin, not just my own perspective. That's personal development." John E. Rehfeld, who spent eight years as vice president and general manager of Toshiba America's computer business and is now president and chief operating officer of Seiko Instruments U.S.A., recently wrote an article for the *Harvard Business Review* about what he has learned from his experiences at Japanese companies.[3] He cited a continuous improvement orientation, a stick-to-the-knitting approach to strategy, and a customer-focused operating style as some of the practices he had learned from working with Japanese managers.

In addition to these potential lessons, as business becomes more international, experience in cross-cultural situations will become increasingly valuable. Not only is knowledge of Japanese business practices useful, but many of the skills involved in dealing with situations that crop up in a Japanese workplace will also be applicable to interactions with people from other cultures as well. In the words of an employee at a Japanese industrial firm, "People ask me why I work for the Japanese. I tell them that I feel that those of us who are ignorant of international business will lose in the future, and those of us who understand how other people think will get ahead."

Finally, working with people from another culture is an opportunity to grow and learn about oneself, although not necessarily in the ways you initially anticipate. Being open to questioning your assumptions and growing in unexpected directions is one of the best ways to get the most out of working in a cross-cultural environment.

5

Understanding
the Japanese Expatriate

You have been assigned to a country where you are not fluent in the language, and whose cultural, legal, and business environment is radically different from your own. You are required to do a job you have not been prepared to do, at a new and daunting level of responsibility. The actions of your colleagues seem strange and confusing. You are under a great deal of pressure to help improve the local operation's flagging profitability. You are very concerned with maintaining your relationships with colleagues at the head office because you want to make sure that there is a good position waiting when you return home. Many of the people who come back from overseas see their careers derailed, and you don't want that to happen to you as well. On top of these stresses, much of your personal time is devoted to helping your wife and children adjust to the new environment. Their language skills are even worse than your own, so your wife is unable to run the household the way she did at home, and your children are having trouble in school. You are far away from your usual support network of friends and relatives, and you miss little things like your favorite foods. You wonder, When can I go home?

The situation above describes a typical Japanese expatriate assigned to the United States. Frequently, coming to the United States was not his idea, and it is very disruptive to his professional and personal life. (Again, I use "his" here because virtually none of the expatriates sent by Japanese companies are women.) The expatriate is likely to be experiencing a high level of stress, if not near paralysis, due to culture shock. Furthermore, he has incentives and goals that are different from what Americans might expect based on either their concepts of managerial behavior or stereotypes about Japanese management. These different incentives and goals frequently cause expatriates to behave in ways that puzzle and frustrate their American colleagues. This chapter explores how Japanese expatriates are assigned to the United States and the attitudes and goals they bring with them. Hopefully, this information will make their actions more understandable, enabling American employees to anticipate and avoid potential conflicts.

SELECTION AND TRAINING OF JAPANESE EXPATRIATES

For the most part, Japanese expatriates sent to the United States are unilaterally assigned by the personnel department—usually they have not asked to come here. Regardless of whether or not they wish to be transferred to the U.S. operation, they will probably agree to come because rejecting such a marching order could be career suicide. Japanese personnel managers are accustomed to this unquestioning obedience, so when selecting expatriates they tend to place low priority on whether someone actually wants to go abroad.[1] It may not even cross their minds to ask.

This means that many Japanese expatriates are not particularly happy about being in the United States. Their personal lives have been involuntarily disrupted, and they may feel that their careers have been sidetracked. In some firms, a transfer to the United States may be the equivalent of banishment to Siberia, reserved for those who have somehow fallen out of favor. Even if it does not carry such a harsh connotation, the expatriate may be fearful for his future career because he will be far from the company's nerve center. Unfortunately, someone who doesn't want to be in the United States, for whatever reason, will resist making the necessary adjustments to American culture, and may let his unhappiness sour his ability to work with American employees.

SPEAKING ENGLISH YOUR COLLEAGUES WILL UNDERSTAND

Many Japanese expatriates are ill prepared to use English intensively in an everyday context. You can make things easier for them by communicating as clearly as possible:

- Avoid slang and unusual vocabulary.

- Enunciate clearly, and slow down (although not too much or you will sound condescending).

- Avoid humor, especially sarcasm, that is likely to be misunderstood.

- Don't be afraid to grab a pencil and paper to draw an explanatory diagram if it seems helpful.

- Prepare a simple agenda even for informal meetings—this can help structure your interaction with someone whose spoken English skills are imperfect.

- Write up a memo after any conversation in which decisions were made, to confirm and clarify everyone's understanding of the situation.

Poorly Prepared

In addition to a less-than-enthusiastic attitude, many expatriates are also burdened by inadequate preparation for working in the United States. As an American manager at a Japanese consumer products company comments, "Japanese companies who have sent people over are doing them a terrible disservice by not teaching them English and introducing them to American life." While some larger Japanese companies have developed extensive training programs that are models for western multinationals,[2] many Japanese firms provide their expatriates with little or no predeparture training or orientation. Those that do tend to concentrate on English skills and offer little or no cultural training.[3] The lack of preparation afforded Japanese expatriates tends to worsen the inevitable culture shock and impairs their ability to communicate with American colleagues.

Many Japanese expatriates are also inadequately prepared for the specific work that they will be doing while in the United States. The details of American market conditions and legal structures are naturally new to someone who has never worked in the United States. In addition, some expatriates also find themselves assigned to activities in which they have no experience. This may be because the activities of the U.S. operation are different from the company's activities in Japan. It may also be due to Japanese companies' tendency to view their Japanese employees as interchangeable parts. As long as someone is a good worker, it is reasoned, he can jump into any position and succeed if he learns quickly and tries hard. As one banker complains, the expatriates he works with "have absolutely no training for what their position will be. A teller from Japan may be assigned to run credit approval or become a trader—their background has little relevance to the job at hand." Expatriates thrust into these difficult situations need their coworkers' understanding. Remember that it usually wasn't their idea in the first place. Even a bright and energetic expatriate will find it extremely difficult to learn a new type of work while at the same time adjusting to unfamiliar language and surroundings.

Stressed Out

On top of these issues, most expatriates sent to the United States are dealing with personal challenges. When moving abroad there is the added stress of leaving one's support network of family and friends.

HOW TO MAKE YOUR REPORTS READABLE

Most Japanese businessmen are more comfortable reading English than speaking it. Nevertheless, they find reading significant numbers of documents in English to be time-consuming and tiring. You can make it easier for your Japanese colleagues to digest your written output by following these guidelines:

- Organize documents so that they can be perused quickly.

- Divide anything over three pages into sections and add section headings.

- Keep sentences short and straightforward. Use two or three sentences instead of one long one.

- Always include an executive summary, or, for shorter memos and reports, a summary sentence at the beginning.

- Avoid flowery language.

- If a point is particularly important or difficult to get across, restate it again in a different way.

- Use lists and charts to clarify and organize data.

- Use metaphors to convey points that are complex and abstract.

- When in doubt, err on the side of over-communicating by adding more explanations.

Those who are single may be nervous about being out of the running in the marriage sweepstakes back home. Those who are married may decide to leave their wives and children in Japan so as not to disrupt their children's education, and end up suffering the inevitable loneliness. Furthermore, most Japanese men have no experience living on their own—they have always had their mother, company dormitory, or wife to take care of them. An assignment to the United States may be their first time living on their own, and this factor complicates the difficulties of adjusting to a foreign environment. Those who do bring wives and children may find themselves overwhelmed by family responsibilities. In Japan, wives generally manage all household affairs, including finances and the children's schooling. However, when the couple comes to the United States, the wife's English skills are likely to be far less developed than those of the husband, and he must take on unaccustomed tasks at home. Also, in many cases Japanese expatriate wives become isolated and lonely due to their lack of English and driving abilities, and their children experience difficulties adapting to American schools. Such personal issues make many expatriates' adjustment to life in the United States more difficult.

THE "UGLY JAPANESE"

Japanese expatriates may also be carrying intellectual baggage that makes it more difficult for them to adapt to working in the United States. Some American employees report that the Japanese they encounter seem to feel superior to Americans. In some cases this may be just a vague feeling due to the Japanese managers' general attitude. For example, an employee at a manufacturing firm comments: "We feel like they treat us as outsiders. In their actions that's very clear . . . The Japanese executives order people around. They are unfriendly and arrogant and it leaves a bad taste in the mouth of the average American employee. It doesn't engender warm fuzzy feelings." In other cases, Americans report more direct signs that their Japanese colleagues feel superior. It may come in the form of comments, similar to those made by Japanese

CONSIDERATE EXPLANATIONS

Due to the tremendous differences in the legal, social, and business environment between the United States and Japan, things that seem elementary to you may be completely new material for a Japanese expatriate. Be ready to do a lot of explaining, and don't get huffy when basic explanations are met with blank stares. (Keep in mind that if you went to work in Japan, your coworkers would have to explain very elementary things to you too!) Also, remember to explain *why* something is the way it is in the United States. Just as it's annoying to be told, "We should do it this way because that's how it's done in Japan," it is equally unpleasant to Japanese to be told, "We have to do things this way because this is how it's done in America." Taking the time to explain things thoroughly and respectfully will be appreciated. It will also give the expatriate additional insight that he can use the next time he meets with an unfamiliar American practice.

politicians, that Americans are lazy or uneducated. One woman who works in a Japanese service sector firm says, "I don't know why my colleagues would speak so negatively about Americans when I am there. All three Japanese men I have worked with have always done this. I find it quite offensive."

Much of what Americans may perceive as arrogance is pride in Japan's economic success. This attitude is akin to the "ugly American" syndrome of the 1960s, when many Americans felt that the American system was unquestionably the best and that other countries were backward. In the Japanese case, the success of the country's economic miracle of rapid development from the ashes of war, as well as the strength of Japanese companies in the global marketplace, have given Japanese well-deserved pride in their country's accomplishments. However, this pride sometimes transforms itself into an attitude of superiority. A related factor is the popularity of theories that extol the virtues of Japanese management. Western works on Japanese management (e.g., Athos and Pascale's *The Art of Japanese Management*) have been translated into Japanese and have received an enormous amount of attention among Japanese businessmen. Native Japanese scholars have naturally offered their own theories explaining Japanese management. In a kind of business-world counterpart to the anthropological "theories of Japanese uniqueness" (*Nihonjinron*) that sell so many books in Japan, Japanese management (*Nihon-teki keiei*) has become a kind of "theory of Japanese business uniqueness." In the words of Kunio Odaka, a Japanese expert on management theory, "Over the last twenty years, the myth [of Japanese management] has escalated and proliferated to create a dangerous situation, especially in Japan. Originally couched in a foreign language, deviating from the reality of Japanese management in several particulars, and tending to praise the good side and ignore the bad, the myth is today finding eager converts among Japanese who use it to justify exaggerated displays of national pride. This situation tends to hide the true nature of Japanese management and to interfere with efforts to correct its by-now-conspicuous defects."[4]

Since "Japanese management" has taken on so many *Nihonjinron*-type nationalistic trappings, Japanese companies' conviction that they are practicing Japanese management affects how they frame conflicts with non-Japanese employees who might criticize or fail to understand their methods. Non-Japanese who question how things are done may be told sharply, "We've been so successful because we've been using Japanese management." This type of comment ignores the possibility that successes might have been due to factors unrelated to the use of Japanese management, or even *in spite of* using Japanese management.

Many Japanese businessmen also hold negative stereotypes about American managers, which are heavily propagated by the Japanese media. Unfortunately, these stereotypes of Americans and American workers seem to have become ingrained beliefs among many Japanese. For example, in a 1989 poll one thousand Japanese adults were asked to choose two or three reasons for America's economic problems. The most common responses were "Too many different minorities" (42 percent) and "Lazy work force" (35 percent), while "Incompetent management" was mentioned by 11 percent.[5] Many Japanese businessmen bring these attitudes to the United States and allow them to influence their dealings with Americans. Fortunately, the recession that began in 1991 has shown that Japan is not immune to the economic forces faced by the rest of the world, and there are signs that such attitudes are softening.

ATTITUDES TOWARD WOMEN AND MINORITIES

Many Americans are aware of the unequal status of working women in Japan and of Japanese politicians' repeated derogatory comments about American minorities—these topics have been widely reported in the U.S. media. There is no denying that these underlying attitudes have led to some troubling examples of discrimination by Japanese companies against women and minorities in the United States. These have come out in lawsuits and in the press, and they have surfaced in interviews for this book. The manager who refused to shake the hand of a new African American employee, the company that decided not to hire an African American candidate for a receptionist position because "the receptionist is the face of the company," the managers who ask an American woman with multiple graduate degrees to type and run errands, the coworkers who openly trade pornographic videos and magazines in the office—all these incidents are examples of how some Japanese can act in blatantly prejudicial ways that are repugnant to Americans.

However, there are also many cases of women and minorities who are happy in their positions in Japanese companies, and there are Japanese firms that go out of their way to hire and promote women and minorities. To cite some prominent examples, Susan Insley of Honda is likely the highest ranking woman in automotive manufacturing at *any* auto company, and Norah Hughes is the president of an important Sumitomo Bank subsidiary. Toyota Motor's manufacturing operation in Kentucky received an award from the National Conference of Christians and Jews for its success in hiring and promoting minorities.[6] With numerous such examples, it is inaccurate to label all Japanese managers and companies as prejudiced. In fact, where opportunities for women and minorities in Japanese firms are limited, it often seems to be due to the individuals not being Japanese rather than to being female or nonwhite. As a woman who is a manager at a Japanese bank puts it, "In general the line is drawn much more harshly between Japanese and non-Japanese than between men and women. I know I'll never be general manager or deputy general manager. It's not because I'm a woman, but because I'm an American and I can't speak Japa-

MAKING A PROFESSIONAL IMPRESSION

If you are a woman working for a Japanese company, you will need to be extra careful to signal that you are a serious professional. One important way to do this is through your dress. Although American businesswomen's fashions have become less rigid in recent years, when working with Japanese it is best to stick with the classic dress-for-success look: dark-colored suits with conservative blouses. Japanese men will be more likely to regard you as a professional if your attire matches their image of how a professional woman should look.

When you first join the company, or a new colleague is rotated in from Japan, you can expect some initial awkwardness. This may be the first time that they have worked with a woman in a professional position. You should maintain a professional demeanor, politely overlooking their awkwardness. Also, resist the temptation to put your colleagues at ease with humor, since it may be misunderstood and worsen the situation.

One female executive who joined a major Japanese manufacturer encountered resistance at first, because "Not only was I a woman, but I had not yet demonstrated what I could do for the company." She plunged into her work, and found that the awkwardness disappeared once she had begun to produce concrete results.

---

nese." Furthermore, the generally small number of women and minorities in managerial positions at Japanese companies should be viewed against the background of American business's generally dismal record on this subject. In some cases, a lack of women and minorities in managerial positions at a Japanese firm may reflect the entrenched attitudes of that company's white male American managers. As one female manager at a Japanese electronics firm comments, "I find I have more problems with some of the American managers than I do with the Japanese ones."

Nevertheless, societal conditions in Japan do not predispose Japanese businessmen to understand American expectations of fair treatment for women and minorities. Japanese society has very different standards on issues of equality, and thus the words and actions of some Japanese expatriates can upset their American employees.

Japanese Views on Women in the Workplace

Japanese women are commonly relegated to second-class status in the workplace. For the most part they are limited to clerical positions and are generally expected to quit when they marry or have children. In fact, many companies see their female workforce as a stock of potential brides for their male employees, who are working so hard that they may not have time to meet anyone outside the company. The years of work after a woman graduates from high school or college are often viewed as a time to learn about the world before settling down to one's real purpose in life as a homemaker and child rearer. The underlying assumption is that business is for men and the home is for women.

Some Japanese see this rigid division of labor as one of the strengths of the Japanese economy. Dedicated full-time housewives manage the affairs of their households so that their husbands can devote all their time and energy to their jobs. Stay-at-home mothers can also spend hour upon hour coaching their children's educational progress, a factor behind the success of the Japanese educational system that is often overlooked by western observers.

While it is tempting to project American values onto Japanese women and imagine that they are all chafing under male domination and champing at the bit to gain greater roles in society, that is not necessarily the case. There are many Japanese women who are battling social stereotypes to establish themselves in the business world and are having a difficult time. There are others who, while they pursue traditional roles, are deeply unhappy with the status quo. But there are also many Japanese women who accept and relish the traditional homemaker role, which includes power in the form of complete control over the family purse strings and the freedom to pursue hobbies. Many Japanese working women seem just as happy to serve tea to their male coworkers and perform clerical tasks that don't involve heavy responsibility. Given that the typical Japanese salaryman's life is so demanding and regimented, it is hardly surprising that many Japanese women look at the male rat race and say, "no thank you."

The status of women in Japan *is* changing, if slowly. Younger women are becoming more interested in having careers. The enactment of an equal opportunity employment law in 1986 meant that companies could not be as blatant as they once were in discriminating against female employees, although the law lacks the punch of enforcement provisions.

Sexual harassment has recently become a hot social issue in Japan as women begin to stand up against mistreatment in the workplace.

Given this background of change in Japanese society, it is difficult and risky to stereotype all Japanese men in terms of their attitude toward women. Some are quite traditional and vehemently oppose giving responsibility to women, while others are very progressive and support women's equality. A still larger group is somewhere in the middle, clinging to some traditional ideas while accepting that the role of women is changing. And even those with flexible views may be perplexed when faced for the first time with American career women who expect to be treated just like the men at their level. In some ways, the situation is analogous to what the atmosphere was for working women in the United States in earlier decades. As an American female executive at a service sector firm describes it, "It's deja vu. I find myself going through experiences I went through twenty years ago when the American male was being enlightened."

In some cases, Japanese will display different attitudes toward American women than they do toward Japanese women. Some Japanese businessmen are so dumbfounded by the mere concept of a businesswoman that they will treat American businesswomen as a sort of "third sex." Being a female may also give an American businesswoman an edge in dealing with those Japanese who are uncomfortable with American men, because they perceive women as less confrontational. Furthermore, sophisticated Japanese businessmen are aware that American women often hold positions of responsibility.

One significant difference between Japan and the United States in attitudes toward women is the fact that in the United States sexually discriminatory comments are looked upon with disfavor. An American man who is uncomfortable with women holding managerial positions may hesitate to verbalize his opinions due to social pressure and fear of litigation. There is no such taboo in Japan, and Japanese expatriates may bring this lack of inhibition to the United States.

The open expression of sexist opinions by Japanese is often shocking to Americans. For example, one Japanese bank recently started adding more women to its marketing staff. When a client commented on this

ARE THINGS GOING TO CHANGE AROUND HERE?

Jane recalls when she and her colleagues found out that their employer was being acquired by a Japanese rival. "We were really worried. There was a packet of articles that got passed around—clippings about how Japanese have negative attitudes toward women and minorities, how they rule companies with an iron hand."

Much to her and her colleagues' surprise, these fears proved to be unfounded. "Before the acquisition, our company had been bad at promoting women and minorities. That hasn't necessarily improved, but it certainly hasn't gotten any worse. I haven't seen any overt actions that are negative to women, and personally I've had no problems." Jane has also been encouraged by the appointment of an Indian immigrant to her department's top post. "It certainly wasn't what we had expected. It really allayed our concerns when they did that." The work environment has not been adversely affected by the takeover either: "There's freedom to talk about things, criticize ideas. It's a very open environment."

As for the issue of control, Jane feels that "while there are some Japanese here, they defer to the American managers. There is never anything to indicate that they are trying to run the show."

---

fact during a meeting, the general manager of the branch replied, "It's because women don't demand as high a salary and their expectations are lower." The conversation stopped in stunned silence, and the general manager's comments spread all over the office as soon as the meeting was over.

Another American taboo which Japanese may not appreciate is in the area of sexual harassment. Although sexual harassment has recently become an issue in Japan, sexually oriented speech and actions are tolerated in Japanese offices to an extent that is now unthinkable in the United States. For example, desk calendars featuring nude women and embossed with the company logo are distributed by major Japanese corporations and shamelessly displayed on desks. Unaware of the different standards on this subject in the United States, Japanese expatriates may say or do things that are unacceptable in the American context.

Japanese Attitudes on Race

There are relatively few ethnic minority groups in Japan as compared to America, and those that do exist—the descendants of Koreans who were forcibly brought to Japan as laborers, the descendants of feudal period lower castes (*burakumin*), the native Ainu people of Hokkaido in the north, Okinawans, the few non-Japanese who live in Japan—are often the subject of blatant discrimination. Popular *Nihonjinron* (Japanese uniqueness) theories have imbued many Japanese with the sense that they are somehow special and different from other races. Also, official government policy has portrayed the country as a racially homogeneous entity, despite the existence of these minorities and the influx of Korean and Chinese blood in preceding centuries.[7] Looking at the racial strife that occurs in the United States, many Japanese believe that their country's economic success is related to the fact that they are a harmonious, homogeneous society.

As for their views about specific races outside Japan, Japanese stereotypes result from ignorance. The average Japanese has had few opportunities to meet any non-Japanese, much less representatives of American minority groups such as African Americans or Hispanics. Sadly, many Japanese seem to have picked up the worst aspects of American stereotypes and prejudices. And again, Japanese expatriates sometimes do not hesitate to voice their opinions on racial matters, unaware that such comments are offensive to Americans. For example, a former employee of a Japanese construction firm reports that "My administrator's bigotry was really bad. He told us that he didn't like Koreans or Hispanics."

In an incident of this type, Japanese Prime Minister Yasuhiro Nakasone made headlines in the United States in 1986 when he suggested that minorities were pulling down American educational levels. Two years later, in mid-1988, tensions rose again when politician Michio Watanabe implied that African Americans have no qualms about going bankrupt. Meanwhile, reports surfaced in the United States that black mannequins with exaggerated racial features were being used in Japanese stores and that a major Japanese company was marketing a line of "Sambo" products. Soon afterward, a study was released which charged that Japanese auto companies were locating most of their new American plants far from African American communities and were hiring African Americans at rates well below their representation in the population of nearby areas.[8] African American leaders threatened a boycott of Japanese goods, and the Japanese embassy in Washington recommended to Tokyo "that they not take cosmetic measures, but real actions to deal with this."[9]

The following year, Japan's Federation of Economic Organizations (the leading Japanese business association, known in Japanese as the Keidanren) set up a Council for Better Corporate Citizenship to help Japanese companies better integrate into overseas communities. This Council took as one of its goals raising Japanese companies' sensitivity to minority issues in the United States.[10] At the same time, some of the larger Japanese firms operating in the United States began to consult with prominent African American lawyers on how they could improve their ties with the African American community, and Representative Mervyn Dymally (D-California), then the chairman of the Congressional Black Caucus, circulated a model code of conduct that called on Japanese companies in the United States to engage in affirmative action programs, underwrite scholarships for minority students, and actively recruit employees from minority population centers.[11] Many companies seem to have taken this advice, since Japanese philanthropy to minority organizations has ballooned.[12] Initiatives to improve communications between Japanese and American minority communities have continued, such as the establishment of a U.S.-Japan Project by the African American think tank the Joint Center for Political and Economic Studies and the formation of a Japan-Hispanic Institute.[13]

These activities, combined with the quiet efforts of American personnel specialists and the impact of discrimination suits, have prompted many Japanese companies in the United States to become more sensitive to American standards on racial issues and to improve their relationships with American minority communities. Individual minority Americans working at Japanese firms have also found that Japanese are able to shed their stereotypes. A supervisor at a small Japanese manufacturing plant in the Midwest states that "As the only black American working here, I found it tough to overcome the stereotypes of the Japanese along with the U.S. stereotypes of the Americans in the company. It was like fighting two uphill battles simultaneously. But now, the Japanese have accepted the fact that people are people and can do the job well—more than the Americans have."

PLEASING THE HEAD OFFICE

American employees at Japanese companies typically complain about the inordinate role that the head office plays in the day-to-day activities of a Japanese organization. While this can in part be explained by the desire of the head office to closely monitor the overseas operation, the countless faxes and late night phone calls are also a way for individual expatriates to avoid being out of sight and out of mind. Since the head office personnel and their subjective opinions carry the greatest weight in one's future advancement, expatriates often feel that they must expend a great deal of effort maintaining their profile in Japan. Keeping the head office informed of a subsidiary's activities and seeking the head office's input is a way to maintain one's visibility.

Expatriates may also frame their business decisions to please the head office rather than to promote the long-term interests of the subsidiary and the American employees. This can take the form of avoiding risk, sweeping problems under the rug, and making short-term-oriented decisions.

Risk Aversion

The lopsided mechanism for reporting expatriate performance back to the head office leads many Japanese expatriates to avoid risk. Performance evaluation in Japanese firms often relies more on politics and reputation than rigorous analysis, and it is difficult to play the political game over a long distance. An individual expatriate's successes while overseas may be overlooked by managers at the head office, or not be attributed directly to him. On the other hand, if something goes wrong, blame is quickly attached to an individual. The news travels back to the head office, where it will undoubtedly hurt his future prospects. In terms of the expatriate's advancement, it is more important that he avoid mistakes that would attract head office censure than take risks and make progress that may go unnoticed.

Due to these imbalanced incentives, many Japanese expatriates try to avoid risk. Any major change or new initiative is perceived as some-

KEEPING A DISTANCE FROM AMERICA

An expatriate's lack of interest in socializing with American colleagues may represent a conscious or subconscious desire to withdraw from American culture. The wish to retreat to a familiar language and interaction style is a symptom of the culture shock that many Japanese expatriates undergo when they come to the United States. The result can be a resistance to becoming involved in and adapting to American culture.

Expatriates may also avoid contact with American employees due to a fear of becoming too Americanized. When an expatriate returns to Japan, the very adaptations that would enable him to fit in well with Americans are likely to become significant handicaps in the parent organization. Talking too loud, talking too much, expressing oneself too directly, getting into confrontations with coworkers, laughing and smiling too much—all these brand a returned expatriate as having lost his "Japanese-ness." The conformity-minded Japanese organization will reject those who have been transformed by their foreign experience the same way a body will reject a transplanted organ. The result is career disaster. Many expatriates who have seen this scenario before resolve that they will not sully their Japanese-ness by unnecessary immersion into American culture.

thing that could backfire and damage their career, while doing things as they have been done in the past is perceived as safe. A missed opportunity is not cause for great concern, while an opportunity seized incorrectly can be dangerous. This orientation is often in direct conflict with the full-steam-ahead attitude of American employees, who want to build the business in the United States and generate personal accomplishments. An American manager at a trading company comments, "Cautiousness and risk-averseness are the source of many of my problems. There is a reluctance to take up new business. It is very difficult for me to convince them that something new is worthwhile." A banker tells of Tanabe, a Japanese manager in his office who was so petrified of making a bad decision that he "analyzed every proposal to death." Tanabe would spent weeks looking at a potential deal, by which time the business opportunity had vanished. The Americans he worked with were aggravated because they felt that their hard work was being wasted, but Tanabe was glad because he was relieved of the necessity of making a final yes or no decision that could come back to haunt him later.

Expatriates also have an incentive to maintain the status quo within the office and downplay any problems until they are reassigned and can wash their hands of their responsibilities. As one banker complains, "They have not discovered that not making a decision *is* a decision. It doesn't seem to matter because of the way they rotate personnel. A new manager comes in, looks at problems, and blames them on the previous person. He's only responsible for what goes on during his watch." As a result of this mentality, problems snowball as they get handed down from manager to manager, or simply fall through the cracks.

Short-Term Decisions

The desire to please Tokyo can also become the cause of short-term-oriented decisions. Given the purported Japanese tendency to look long term, this phenomenon is particularly surprising to Americans. For example, a trading company employee tells the story of a department that needed high-powered computers to be able to participate in a new companywide information network. The American staff asked their Japanese manager, Nakanishi, to purchase new computers and arranged for a special discount to obtain them cheaply. However, Nakanishi insisted on upgrading the old and unreliable computers that had been giving the department headaches for years, even though upgrading was only slightly less expensive than buying new ones. The American staff was furious that their manager had disregarded their request and had sentenced them to continuing to use the obsolete computers. Meanwhile, Nakanishi felt that he was able to look good in Tokyo's eyes by avoiding the purchase of new computers and saving a little money. Since he would be returning to Japan within a year or two anyway, the possibility that the American staff would resent his decision for years to come was probably not a priority in his mind.

Since many Japanese companies' U.S. operations have profitability problems and their parent companies are suffering from the recession in Japan, expatriates are likely to be receiving pressure from the head office to cut expenses, and to be frugal in whatever new expenditures they make. This pressure may explain why a woman at a Japanese company asked in frustration, "Why is it that when you give a Japanese manager more than one alternative, he always goes for the cheapest one?" Unfortunately, just as in American firms that undertake costcutting, the long-term good of the organization may be sacrificed in the interest of short-term cost savings.

FOUR TYPES OF EXPATRIATES

There are four prototypic positions for expatriates at Japanese firms' U.S. operations: the top manager, the workhorse manager, the coordinator, and the trainee. These four categories are described below. Recognizing which of these four categories applies to a particular manager may provide clues to understanding his outlook and behavior. However, depending on the organization and its size, some expatriates' positions will combine aspects of more than one of these categories.

The Top Manager

An assignment to a top post in a U.S. office is often an expatriate's first opportunity to test his leadership skills. Some individuals bloom into excellent managers and enjoy the relative freedom of action that a post far from headquarters affords. Others don't seem to know what to do when the reins of power are put in their hands and are at a loss without consulting headquarters.

At some Japanese firms, top managers don't seem to be managing at all, in the American sense of the word. Some Americans complain that their top managers are not really engaged in the nitty-gritty of the operation's activities and appear to make little effort in that direction. One banker describes her branch's general manager as thinking of himself as royalty. "He wants to go to ceremonies but he doesn't want to know what's going on." Such comments reflect in part the different role expectations that Americans and Japanese have for senior managers. Japanese see senior managers as figureheads and facilitators, in contrast to Americans, who expect the top person to do the leading and give the orders. These situations may also reflect the frequent tendency of Japanese companies to view senior posts as semiretirement, honorary positions.

Under such a view, the senior manager can enjoy the prestige of rank while the middle managers get the actual work done. This mentality can sometimes even result in the feeling that an overseas office is a good place to banish a disliked senior manager, because it is presumed that he can do little harm there.

Workhorse Managers

Workhorse managers are the second tier below the top manager, although in smaller operations the workhorse manager and top manager role may be merged. In traditional Japanese organizational style, these are the deputy managers who are expected to carry out the bulk of the work. This arrangement is reflected in the fact that Japanese top managers (*bucho, shacho, shitencho,* etc.) are described as being like "husbands" and deputy managers (*jicho*) as like "wives"—a reference to the traditional division of labor in a Japanese household, where the husband is nominally in charge but the wife holds the purse strings and makes all financial and purchasing decisions. The workhorse manager may be under a great deal of pressure from headquarters to establish a thriving new operation or to improve the lagging performance of an existing operation. The overseas assignment may be the test that will make or break his career. Or, in other situations, the workhorse manager may be in an operation that is perceived as unimportant, and thus he is very concerned about getting back into the mainstream of the company at this crucial stage in his career. In either case, the workhorse manager is likely to feel that he has a lot at stake.

Coordinators

As the term implies, the coordinator's main function is to act as an interface between the U.S. operation and the company's operations in Japan. The coordinator role is ambiguous, but it will always involve extensive communications with personnel in Japan. There are generally three coordinator roles. The first is rather passive, acting as a quiet observer of the U.S. operations and reporting back to Tokyo. Such coordinators are often regarded by American colleagues with curiosity because they seem to be doing very little, or because their activities are unexplained. The second type of coordinator is an intermediary between American employees and those in Japan when headquarters input is required for U.S. activities. In this role, the coordinator is a combination translator and cross-cultural negotiator. The third type of coordinator has a de facto decision-making role—he either makes decisions himself or acts as a conduit for decisions made in Japan. This third coordinator role in particular can lead to misunderstandings and friction, which will be discussed further in Chapter 8.

Trainees

Trainees are young (i.e., under thirty-five) employees who have been sent to the overseas operation to gain experience. This is generally part of the typical Japanese human resource development practice of rotating employees through a large number of areas for on-the-job training in order to create well-rounded generalists. "Overseas" has joined the list of "Sales," "Administration," "Product Development," and other areas that young fast-trackers are expected to experience in order to become promotable. Although in some companies these employees are clearly identified as being there for the purpose of learning, in others they are given operational or managerial positions. The latter category can be problematic, as inexperienced young expatriates may be thrust into management positions beyond their capabilities and may expect the American employees to act as their teachers. A banker complains that "our managers are our link to Japanese culture and the bank's credit approval process, but they usually don't understand what they are doing. We have to spend a lot of time just teaching them about our work. It's very difficult and frustrating." Another banker who commented, "It seems like our role is to educate the Japanese managers for a short period of time so they can move on to something else" may have hit the nail on the head. This "trainee" mentality can extend beyond younger expatriates to older ones as well, especially since many expatriates are unfamiliar with the specifics of their assigned U.S. position.

FREQUENT ROTATIONS CAUSE DISRUPTION

It is standard practice for a multinational to rotate its expatriates periodically. Although the disruption that ensues is a problem for any multinational, it is particularly difficult for Japanese firms, since a larger proportion of their managerial slots tend to be filled with expatriates. With some Japanese companies rotating expatriates as often as every two years, long-term American employees feel that they are witness to a continual stream of new people. As one banker observes, "You never know what you are going to get. We joke that if you don't like them, don't worry, they'll leave soon."

The training issue complicates the transition process. Many American employees of Japanese companies complain that just when they have brought a Japanese expatriate up to speed, he is sent back to Japan. A green new manager takes his place, and the training process must begin all over again.

Because many Japanese-run offices lack set procedures, the way things work is very dependent on the judgment of the individual Japanese expatriates. The numerous policies and thick procedures manuals that are fixtures of many large American companies are virtually unheard-of in Japanese firms. Instead, each expatriate manages according to his personal compass. Since expatriate managers tend to vary greatly from person to person in terms of attitude and ability, a changeover can mean a 180-degree difference in the way things are done in an office, department, or section. This is extremely destabilizing to local employees who may find their job responsibilities unilaterally redefined and their role in the organization completely changed. Women seem to be particularly vulnerable to this phenomenon because Japanese men vary widely in their attitudes toward women in the workplace. A capable woman who has been given responsibility by a Japanese boss with a progressive attitude may find her activities curtailed by a new Japanese superior with more conservative ideas. For example, Cathy, a woman in an office management post at a service industry firm, went from a "more Americanized" superior to a "more traditional Japanese" superior. The old supervisor had made sure to explain the scope and

BRIEFING YOUR NEW SUPERIOR

If your superior is rotated back to Japan or to another area, the transition between him and his successor can be a critical inflection point in your career. Many employees of Japanese companies find that a job they enjoy suddenly deteriorates when a new supervisor arrives. On the other hand, if you handle the situation skillfully, a transition to a new boss can be an opportunity to improve your job content.

Soon after your new superior arrives, sit down with him to probe his objectives and expectations. What are his plans, and how do you fit into them? This will give you important information. If his view of your role is consistent with your goals, you are already on the same wavelength. If there is a mismatch, you will need to point it out—but gently, and not all at once. As you work together, gradually point out what your activities have been in the past. Bring to his attention examples of your past work. You should also suggest any ideas you have for improvements or new activities that are consistent with his goals.

---

limits of Cathy's duties to his successor. But as soon as he returned to Tokyo, the new superior started asking her to type and file letters—secretarial activities which weren't in her job description. When Cathy asked about the possibility of a promotion, the new superior told her that it was out of the question. This was the complete opposite of what Cathy's first boss had told her: "Anything is possible if you work hard." A job she had been led to believe had growth potential had suddenly turned into a dead end. While such discontinuities are to some extent unavoidable, it helps to be aware of the potential for difficulties when a key manager's transfer is imminent.

PROSPECTS

The difficult issues involving expatriates are problems for multinational companies of any country, wherever in the world they are operating. The uncomfortable expatriate described at the beginning of this chapter could be of any nationality, assigned to any country. As demonstrated by the survey results presented in Chapter 2, United States and European multinationals also use expatriates from the home country to fill managerial positions, and also experience international human resource management problems. This observation is also confirmed by anecdotes of American expatriates' experiences in Japan and other countries, and by reports of frictions at German, British, and other foreign firms in the United States. To some extent, clashes between expatriates and local staff are inevitable. Expatriates naturally have incentives and viewpoints that are different from those of local workers due to their different relationship to the company. Linguistic, cultural, and social differences will come between the two groups. Expatriates who are experiencing culture shock will also be likely to stick together and attempt to insulate themselves from the local culture.

Nevertheless, frictions between expatriates and locally hired employees are more prominent in Japanese firms than in other multinationals because Japanese firms follow an ethnocentric management model and tend to staff their overseas offices' managerial ranks with greater proportions of expatriates. The particularly large gaps between Japan and the United States in terms of language, culture, and corporate structure also exacerbate the situation. Since these differences are unlikely to evaporate, and Japanese firms are likely to continue using significant numbers of expatriates, American employees of Japanese firms will need to develop an ability to work closely with Japanese. Coming to terms with their different work habits, incentives, and outlooks is necessary in order to have a good working experience at a Japanese company.

6

Strategies for Coping with the Karate-Teacher Manager

It was a good chance to learn to work with people from diverse cultural backgrounds. It wasn't like working with other Japanese, where you seldom have to explicitly ask others to do things. I learned to become more attentive about getting my messages across. When I had an opinion, I had to say it. Otherwise, no one would know what I was thinking.

JAPANESE FILM DIRECTOR SHIMAKO SATO
COMMENTING ON HER EXPERIENCES WORKING OUTSIDE OF JAPAN[1]

A common complaint among Americans working at Japanese companies is that Japanese managers are not good communicators. They feel like they are in the dark about what they should be doing, how they should be doing it, and how well the Japanese managers think they have done it. This is primarily a result of the differences between typical management styles in Japan and the United States. Unfamiliar with traditional Japanese managerial methods and the philosophies that underpin them, they can only judge their managers' actions by American standards. In the American context, lack of communication from Japanese expatriates is interpreted negatively as showing lack of management skills, unfriendliness, and even secretiveness. The aloof posture of the traditional Japanese manager often leaves American subordinates dissatisfied. Meanwhile, Japanese managers often express dissatisfaction with

BAFFLED BANKERS

Some of the most clear-cut examples of lack of direction and feedback come from American loan officers at Japanese banks. One such banker, Scott, recently attended a business function with some of his counterparts from a major American bank in the same city: "They were talking about how their bank planned to allocate their capital, what industries they planned to stress. I realized that I had no idea what my bank's policies are in that respect. They asked me what my bank was doing and I had to answer 'I don't know.'"

The biggest problem Scott and his colleagues face is not knowing "what direction to take with our calling efforts. We figure out what the policy is by throwing things against the wall and seeing what sticks. If we try four loans in a certain industry and they all get turned down, we know to stay away from that industry." Sometimes this lack of knowledge can be embarrassing. "We had been calling on one company for three years, and finally they wanted to start borrowing from us. We had been telling them that they were just the type of company we wanted to do business with. Then, when we sent in the credit application it was rejected. And we didn't know why."

their American subordinates, complaining that they always have to be told what to do and seem to lack initiative. This is because their expectations for subordinates' behavior are shaped by the Japanese model.

Americans expect their bosses to be like football coaches. First and foremost, the football coach is charismatic. He is a leader, and he rallies the team around him by virtue of the strength of his personality. The coach is the one who creates a game plan. He knows the game inside and out, and masterminds the plays. He doles out assignments, giving the players explicit directions. He also provides each team member with individualized attention so that they can improve their performance. Before the game, he gives a peptalk. The coach cheers when the team plays well, and after the game presents the team with an analysis of what they did well and how they can do better the next time. The skill and personality of the coach are what holds the team together, and makes or breaks its performance. The player's responsibility is to carry out the coach's directions as faithfully as possible. The key to a coach's success is to create innovative plays, and to develop a team that can respond independently and creatively to changing conditions on the playing field.

In contrast, the Japanese ideal image of a manager is closer to that of a karate teacher. He is aloof and enigmatic, even stern and gruff. The karate teacher is most appropriately approached with a deference that is perhaps even tinged by a bit of fear. He gives a minimum of instruction, only what the students really need to know at their particular skill level. Students learn by imitation and figuring things out for themselves— they practice what they have seen the teacher demonstrate. They must be self-motivated and have the patience to perform the same moves again and again until they have mastered them. They must also develop for themselves the ability to evaluate their own progress, since little evaluation will be forthcoming from the teacher. The only feedback will be minor criticisms of their style—"kick a little higher," "you need to stand up straighter," or "punch more smoothly." And certainly no praise will be offered. In fact, the better a student is, the more frequent and harsh the criticism. The student becomes proficient in karate by mastering a set repertoire of moves, striving to perform them exactly as the teacher does. There is little room for the creative move or the brilliant play.

How can you cope with this management style? The key lies in understanding the aspects of Japanese culture that underlie the "karate-teacher-style manager" ideal.

SILENCE IS GOLDEN

A former accounting manager at a Japanese software company offers this description of what often occurred when his Japanese boss assigned him a new project: "He would just put it on my desk without any instructions. When I asked him to clarify things, his answers were cryptic. I never felt like I knew what he was looking for. And once I had done it he would evaluate it critically based on whether it was exactly the way he wanted it! If he had just given me five sentences of explanation it would have cleared up half the confusion and saved me a lot of time." Complains a banker, "There are no manuals. Just this past year we started writing them. Before, it was just expected that we would absorb what was expected, how to do things, like an oral tradition. The

Japanese concept is on-the-job training. I don't know how—by osmosis?" A banker at another firm comments, "The Japanese management expects you to know intuitively what you are supposed to do. You are expected to know on your own how to handle situations or set up procedures. Until you have a problem, it's difficult to find out what procedures the Japanese think you should have set up." A manager at a small manufacturer comments, "They don't supervise me. They don't know what I do from one day to the next. There is tremendous freedom, but not much direction. I would like more direction because the way professionals grow is by learning from the people around them who have more experience." These sentiments are common among Americans who work for Japanese managers—they find the lack of direction to be baffling and discouraging. They want to do a good job but are unsure of what a good job is supposed to be. They feel that they waste a lot of time just trying to understand what needs to be done and what is expected of them.

The feeling of pervasive ambiguity continues after the job is done, when substantive feedback—positive or negative—is not forthcoming. One manager at a manufacturing firm reports that "The only way I

DIFFERENT INTERPRETATIONS

Even a Japanese person whose English is excellent may inadvertently phrase something in a way that offends a native speaker. I thought that I had received a tremendous insult when the deputy general manager of my department (an accomplished English speaker) told me that I was "not a professional." Our mild debate about whether or not I needed a bigger desk came to an abrupt halt as I excused myself, too shocked to continue talking. For the next hour or so I wondered what I had done to merit being called unprofessional. After all my hard work, was this what my superiors thought of me?

Finally, I reapproached the manager to ask exactly in what way I was "not a professional." "Why," I was told "it's because you don't have a graduate degree. You're not a lawyer or an M.B.A." My manager had no idea that he was insulting me—by telling me that I was not a professional, he thought he was making a simple statement of fact about my qualifications rather than passing judgment on my job performance. Despite his thorough knowledge of English, he was unaware of why "not a professional" has negative associations to a native speaker.

know I have done something that my boss doesn't approve of is he stops talking to me. Then I know that I've done something wrong, but I don't know what that is." An administrative manager at a Japanese bank comments: "One of the hardest things about working here is that I'm required to give my American staff a seven-page performance evaluation report but I get nothing from my Japanese superiors. The Japanese managers aren't comfortable spending twenty to thirty minutes talking about what I've been doing right or wrong." An employee of a Japanese chemical company says that "With the Japanese, everything is positive, nothing is negative. After I complete a project, I don't hear anything. I go to my boss every other month and ask him how I'm doing. He says fine, and repeats to me something good that someone has said about me. It's so frustrating because I don't know how I'm *really* doing!" An employee of a Japanese manufacturer states that "Performance reviews are only for formality's sake. Nothing negative is ever said, so what's the point? It's not that I want there to be so many negative things, but give me a hint about what I can improve upon."

It is unlikely that Japanese managers are purposefully leaving their American subordinates to drift without their bearings. What reasonable explanations might there be for this lack of direction and feedback from Japanese managers?

One important factor at work is the traditional Japanese preference to leave as much unsaid as possible between two people. This preference is a pervasive cultural phenomenon and a basis for many aspects of typical Japanese social interaction. The Japanese tend to feel that many things are better left unsaid, and may be suspicious of those who are too glib or verbose. This feeling is similar to that expressed in the proverbs "Talk is cheap" and "Silence is golden." Middle-aged Japanese men in particular strive to be strong, silent types. They feel that putting things into words runs the risk of producing misunderstanding and conflict, so it is better to keep things vague and rely on the listener to interpret the subtle nuances of meaning. (Of course, this presupposes a listener who is able to correctly decipher the various verbal and nonverbal cues.) The direct expression of emotions or clear opinions is generally frowned upon. Japanese believe that it is preferable to carefully control what is stated in order to avoid overwhelming or burdening the listener. Undue specificity also leaves less room for later changes of opinions or plans, and Japanese managers place a high value on being able to adapt to "different circumstances." This Japanese approach to communication is in sharp contrast to the direct, detailed communication that Americans are accustomed to, especially from superiors. Thus the comment that may seem perfectly clear to a Japanese subordinate may seem cryptic to an American one. It may be extremely difficult for an individual Japanese, no matter how fluent his English, to communicate in the forthright manner that Americans expect.

The language barrier itself is one additional explanation. Many Japanese managers' English skills are not sufficient for clearly conveying instructions or evaluations of their subordinates' work. Some, self-conscious about their lack of English fluency, may avoid speaking English except when absolutely necessary. This of course cuts down on the amount of communication between managers and subordinates. Even those who speak English well may not be able to express the subtleties of meaning necessary to communicate abstract guidance or to appraise someone's performance. What communication does occur may not always be tactful or diplomatic—such nuances are the most challenging part of speaking a second language. Thus, poor English-language skills can be an alternative explanation for lack of communication or for statements that might seem odd or insulting.

THE ZEN AND CONFUCIAN INFLUENCES

The karate-teacher-style management model is heavily influenced by traditional Japanese concepts of learning, apprenticeship, and the superior/subordinate relationship. The theory of learning in Japan is very different from how we view it in the West. Our ideas of learning date from such sources as the ancient Jews and Greeks and tend to stress intellectual grappling with issues and problems. Questioning—even of one's teacher—is valued as part of the learning process. American students are encouraged from an early age to express their opinions. Class-

SPEAKING UP

Both Americans and Japanese retain school days' habits in later life; while Americans are fond of broadcasting their opinions, Japanese may be very uncomfortable when asked to directly state what they think. A Japanese woman who has worked in the United States offers the following scenario: "When a Japanese manager is in the United States, the American staff may read a newspaper article about U.S.-Japan relations and ask him what he thinks. The Japanese is surprised. There is the English problem, but also his reaction is 'Huh?' We are not accustomed to expressing ourselves. But the American just thinks that the Japanese is cold and unfriendly." A reluctance to engage in the kind of debate and exchange of opinions that often characterizes American conversation may be another reason why some Japanese expatriates seek to minimize their interaction with Americans.

room discussions are a standard school activity and debate is often a popular after-school club.

In contrast, Japanese ideas of learning are rooted in Zen Buddhist concepts such as the strength of the unconscious, intuitive understanding, and Confucian concepts such as complete obedience to one's elders. The key ingredients in Japanese-style learning are unquestioning deference to one's instructor and personal humility. The teacher, rather than a textbook, is the final authority on whether one's performance is correct or not. Instruction comes not from set lesson plans but from constant practice, punctuated by small criticisms from the teacher. Praise is seldom given because it would swell the student's head and interfere with his ability to remain humble and practice diligently. The teacher pays as much attention to the student's efforts and mental attitude as to his technical competence, because they are all part of the same package. This concept of learning pervades formalized schooling in Japan, although the outward forms are similar to those of the West. Students at all levels, from elementary school to college, are expected to sit quietly and attentively in class while the teacher lectures. There is little classroom discussion and no challenging of the teacher, whose position is highly respected. Curriculums generally emphasize rote memorization in preparation for standardized tests rather than the development of individual creativity or critical thinking skills.

Similarly, those who train for traditional Japanese occupations are expected to be deferential assistants to their masters, practically like servants. The master (*sensei*) is godlike, and an apprentice who dared to talk back to his master would quickly find himself out in the street. An apprentice to a famous potter says simply, "I'm always at the bottom . . . *Sensei* is at the top."[2]

Apprentices spend long periods of time meekly performing menial tasks before they are deemed ready to actually learn their chosen discipline, and even that learning occurs in small steps. For example, an apprentice at a sushi shop will grate horseradish, make deliveries, and cook rice for *three years* before being allowed to handle a knife, and even then he will start by peeling cucumbers.[3]

This traditional Japanese method of learning is best described by a detailed example. The example is from my own experience with a traditional Japanese art. I have studied *ikebana* (flower arrangement) for several years and have finally become used to the method of teaching, but for a long time its logic eluded me. The typical Japanese flower arranging class that I attended in Tokyo had the following pattern: At the beginning of each class we would be told what style of arrangement to do and would be given a bundle of flowers and branches. The teacher might draw a quick geometric diagram of the arrangement we would be doing, and give some cursory instructions, but these were often very vague: "The flower should be at an angle from forty-five to sixty degrees away from the main stem" or "the supporting branch may be placed to the left or the right of the main branch at an angle of from ten to thirty degrees." There was no explanation of why one would choose the right side or the left side, forty-five degrees or sixty degrees. We would each then attempt to assemble our flowers as best we could into an arrangement that resembled the teacher's diagram. We all had textbooks, but in terms of practical guidance they were even less helpful than the instructor's introductory remarks.

Instruction occurred when the teacher went around to each student and critiqued his or her arrangement. If you were on the right track, she might rearrange it slightly to make it better conform with the model in her mind. If you had gotten it wrong, she would completely disassemble

ZEN BUDDHISM

Zen is a sect of Buddhism that was brought to Japan from China in the late twelfth and early thirteenth centuries. Its austere character appealed to feudal warriors, who took up Zen meditation as a means to develop self-discipline and strength of character. A major tenet of Zen is the superiority of intuitive understanding over rational analysis—"enlightenment is based on direct, personal experience and not on scholarly achievement."[k] Zen disciples are given answerless puzzles (*koan*) such as "What is the sound of one hand clapping?" that are intended to break down their reliance on conventional logic.

Many traditional Japanese arts, such as the tea ceremony, flower arrangement, and landscape gardening, developed under the influence of the Zen aesthetic of simplicity and naturalness. Zen philosophy also encompasses the ideas of Baigan Ishida, an influential early-eighteenth-century philosopher. Ishida's concept that "all work is the pursuit of knowledge" became the foundation for the Japanese work ethic—industriousness is seen as an end in itself, and as a means to building a strong character.[l]

what you had done and remake it while you watched in silence. Even a beginner could see that her changes improved the arrangements and that the ones she did herself were unquestionably superior to what we produced, so this was how she gained her didactic authority in our eyes. She embodied the perfect method of flower arrangement that we should strive to emulate.

Even if your arrangement was good, there was usually little praise except a curt "That's all right." No explanation was given for what made a particular arrangement better than another one, it just *was*. The only way to know if you were doing well seemed to be if the teacher didn't destroy your arrangements as often as those of your classmates. Our teacher's word was the final say on what was right or wrong, and no one questioned her judgment. If her advice seemed strange, then that was simply a matter of our not having sufficient insight. The only appropriate response to the teacher's critique was a quiet "Yes, I understand." It would be pointless, and certainly improper, to ask, "Why?"—we all already knew the answer: because the teacher says so, and she is right. The only way to improve was to continue to attend class, try one's best, and attempt to deduce what the teacher wanted to see.

Needless to say, I found this method of instruction extremely dissatisfying. I felt as if I had no idea what I was doing, and the weekly destruction of my arrangements sapped my self-confidence. I wondered why I was wasting my time and money. However, after a year or so had passed, I finally began catching on. As I worked, I found myself unconsciously anticipating what the teacher might do to my arrangement, and how she might do it herself. The teacher's alterations to my creations became slightly less comprehensive. She never told me that I was making progress, but I realized that I was, and that was what was important. Also I had begun to internalize the school's aesthetic, so that now I can create arrangements without consulting any text or diagram. Eventually I learned to appreciate my teacher's method of instruction and understood how appropriate it was to flower arrangement.

HOW YOU CAN WORK EFFECTIVELY
WITH THE KARATE-TEACHER MANAGER

The way my *ikebana* teacher taught me to arrange flowers is the same way Japanese managers approach their relationships with subordinates. Vague directions, learning through doing rather than from logical explanations, feedback only in the form of corrections, lack of positive reinforcement, and the taboo about questioning authority—the complaints I had about my *ikebana* teacher are the same complaints that American employees so often make about Japanese managers.

Take Initiative

Japanese companies seldom create job descriptions or detailed written policies, and Japanese managers are not necessarily forthcoming with guidance. The best way to cope with this sort of ambiguity is to ask a lot of questions. A Japanese manager may be unwilling to structure a situation, so it will often be up to you to do so. You will need to be gently aggressive in order to draw out the information you need.

One of the most common complaints of Japanese executives in the United States is that American employees "lack initiative" and "always have to be told what to do." The American style of independently pursuing one's defined job tasks and waiting for direction from superiors is difficult for Japanese to understand. One Japanese expatriate in the United States offers the following opinion: "In the eyes of a Japanese manager, Americans seem lazy, passive, or not having a good attitude toward their work. Americans do well when their work falls within their job descriptions, but when it is unclear whose job description some work falls under, no one will take it on. Then the boss has to do that work himself or tell someone to do it. Americans seem to be waiting to be given directions." A Japanese expatriate manager in a manufacturing firm complains that his subordinates "don't have initiative. They lack a sense of how to point out things that could be improved. It's a matter of changing their way of looking at things. They think it's okay to keep doing the same thing as yesterday." Japanese managers may become disappointed in American workers because they do not act in the way they think good workers should behave.

In the Japanese context, employees are expected to be able to work without much direction or feedback. An employee should be self-motivated and self-regulating and should not expect to be babied. Each employee should think for himself about what needs to be done and go about doing it whether or not it is in his job description and whether or not he has been given an explicit order. A group working under one boss should cooperate as a team to divide up all the necessary work and see that it gets done without the boss giving them explicit directions. Individuals are expected to seek out improvements and make proposals. Alex Warren, a senior manager at Toyota's U.S. manufacturing operations, describes this ethic by saying, "At Toyota, managers aren't the only people who can decide what areas need special attention. We expect team members at every level to make suggestions for improvement that lead to positive action within the company."[4]

In order to meet such Japanese-style expectations, you need to be a self-starter. As an American manager at a trading company comments, "You need an independent spirit. You're not going to be able to help yourself, train yourself, unless you have the wherewithal to search things out. Their idea of training is giving you a desk and a phone." It will likely be up to you to find your own niche, figure out how to do your job, and start making things happen. Another employee of a trading company says, "The philosophy is that anybody can be trained, anyone can learn. They expect you to try to learn what you need to do. They give you the tools, then expect you to make the effort. They're not going to spoon-feed you. I was clueless when I started. I had to figure out how to do things. They assume that if you have come this far in business you must have some sort of intelligence, so you can figure it out." In some cases, the company may not even have specific duties in mind for someone they hire—they will just have a vague feeling that the person will be able to make themselves useful.

However, taking initiative should not be confused with working completely independently. While a Japanese manager will want you to come up with new ideas and find useful activities, he will want you to keep him informed, especially before you involve the company in any commitments or spend any money. Constant communication and keeping people up-to-date are highly valued in the Japanese context. If you make the effort to sit down with your manager frequently and keep him apprised of your progress, he will appreciate it. Nothing makes a Japanese manager more nervous than not knowing what his subordinates are up to—Japanese tend to dislike surprises in business, even happy ones. On the other hand, if you bring your supervisor along carefully and convince him of the merits of the path you are taking, he is more likely to be supportive. Says one manager of her Japanese colleagues at a Japanese electronics firm, "If you let them know exactly what you're trying to do and what is the ultimate achievement, they are very much of the 'yes, let's get it done' variety."

The ambiguity and absence of structure in a Japanese environment is a double-edged sword. You can let it bother you or you can learn how to take advantage of the freedom it can provide. A senior executive at an electronics firm praises the company's management style, saying, "They allow you to do what you're supposed to do. They tell you this is your position, this is what you're supposed to be doing, go ahead and get it done. It's up to you to get it done. I don't have a manager who's on my back every moment wanting to know what's happening, what's the status. It's been an excellent working relationship with my immediate superior, who is Japanese—quite a contrast with many of the American managers I've had at my previous employers."

One of the reasons Japanese managers don't specify job descriptions and don't give specific direction is to allow room for creativity and individual growth. It is expected that employees will be alert enough to propose new and useful activities. The ability to anticipate issues and opportunities as they arise and bring them to the attention of one's superiors and colleagues is one of the most prized skills in the Japanese corporate context. Even if not all of your suggestions are acted upon, your cooperative spirit and positive attitude will be duly noted. The key is to communicate to the organization your ideas and willingness to contribute. In the words of a woman who has been successful in a line position at a Japanese trading company: "I'm open with them. I tell them what I want, what I plan to do, and I give them time to ruminate over it and we go from there. I'm not sitting there waiting for things to happen."

Alertness to new opportunities can also open avenues for growth and advancement. Even if it doesn't mean a change in your job title, the addition to your responsibilities of new activities that you have proposed will increase your value in the organization as well as your own job satisfaction. Because Japanese companies tend not to pigeonhole people as specialists, they will often be open to your undertaking activities that are not necessarily in your area of expertise. This is particularly true in smaller or rapidly expanding offices where employees are expected to wear many hats and where business opportunities are plentiful. Thus, you may be able to develop professionally by extending yourself in various new directions. As an American at a Japanese bank comments, "The Japanese feel that people are competent to do anything and expect them to get up to speed. It can be very refreshing and interesting because you can avoid getting segmented and keep your broad perspective." Japanese companies are not fixated on credentials and will tend to assign new responsibilities on the basis of good work in the past. At its best, this management philosophy enables people to grow faster than they would be able to in a more rigidly managed American company. As another banker comments, "I'm thirty years old, but I have the same responsibility as a lot of fifty-year-olds in this town."

Keeping her eye on new opportunities and being willing to make proposals enabled Sharon, an American working at a Japanese industrial firm, to completely remake her job. After she had been in the company one and a half years as a business development specialist, her supervisor was rotated back to Japan. Leveraging the solid relationship she had built with her supervisor's superior, Sharon took the change as an opportunity and proposed that she lead the development of a completely new business area. She had observed that this area was attractive to the organization and would fit in well with its overall strategy. From a personal standpoint, developing this area would allow her to increase her responsibility and do work that was more interesting to her than what she was doing at the time. Sharon's proposal was enthusiastically received and she has succeeded in carving out a niche for herself in the organization. She had carefully analyzed both the organization's needs and her own skills and interests, and created a proposal that would be attractive to the company. She also took the initiative to bring her idea to management and timed her move carefully to coincide with the management change taking place. And, of course, her performance in her first year and a half with the company was of sufficient quality that management was willing to take her suggestion seriously. Sharon's advice to other Americans in similar positions is "If you see something, go for it. Don't wait for them to hand it to you or you'll wait forever."

Don't Expect Praise

Many American employees of Japanese companies report that Japanese managers never seem to praise them for their hard work, even on occasions when they produce unusually good results. As one banker put it, "getting credit for things a lot of the time won't happen. If something turns out well, the top person in the office will get recognition, because the emphasis is that the office did well, and the top person represents the office. It's up to an individual Japanese manager to say which individual did the deal, to bestow the recognition, but that doesn't happen very often."

This lack of recognition for individual effort is completely at odds with the American outlook. However, it is perfectly consistent with the karate-teacher mentality. Praising someone is considered detrimental to the learning process. If a student has too much confidence, he will lose the discipline needed to learn, and his respect for the teacher may be reduced. This mentality shows up in the grudging compliments some American employees report receiving from their Japanese managers. One high-performing American woman was told by her Japanese boss, "I guess I'd like to tell you that you're doing a good job, but that would just swell your head too much." A Japanese supervisor told one banker, "If I told you that you are doing well, you wouldn't try as hard."

The American penchant for positive feedback may even seem puzzling in Japanese eyes. One Japanese businesswoman who has worked extensively with Americans comments, "Americans are always expecting to get a lot of praise, even if they haven't necessarily done anything above the ordinary. It seems that Americans exaggerate things with too many superlatives. Everything is 'great,' but how can it be possible that so many things are *really* great? I think that this atmosphere of too much praise gives people unrealistic expectations about what they can do in life." Comments Jennifer Crockart, an Australian who has trained Japanese expatriates in cross-cultural skills, "On a corporate level, the Japanese don't expect brilliantly innovative work; they want accurate and well presented work done on time. They take that standard for granted, which is why they do not see the need to give thanks for it."[5]

Given that the gap between Japanese and American sensibilities on this issue is so wide, it seems unlikely that any but the most unusual Japanese manager will give American-style positive feedback. Thus, American employees of Japanese firms will need to accustom themselves to this in order to be happy. You will need to develop your own measures of performance, your own goals, and determine for yourself whether or not you have met them. Deriving personal satisfaction from meeting your own standards is essential, since you may be unlikely to receive any overt praise from external sources.

At the same time, it is also important to realize that while Japanese are unlikely to directly say, "You've been doing a great job!," they will convey their esteem for an employee in more subtle ways. Being assigned more interesting and challenging tasks, having your counsel sought on a wider range of issues, and even the amount of company information you are privy to can serve as signs that Japanese superiors and colleagues value your work.

Be Ready for a Stream of Minor Criticisms

Often, the little feedback that a Japanese manager does give will be in the form of critical comments about relatively minor aspects of one's work. Like the karate teacher, the Japanese manager will point out small aspects of how his subordinate can improve. At some level, this is a manifestation of the Japanese concept of continuous improvement (*kaizen*) and striving for perfection.[6]

Rather than resting on their laurels, Japanese have an attitude of searching for any aspect of the process, no matter how small, that can be improved upon the next time. Furthermore, small, concrete, and obvious criticisms are considered to be more acceptable and less likely to provoke confrontation than general, wide-ranging evaluations, because they are less personal in nature. Thus the Japanese manager who is uncomfortable with the idea of giving extensive face-to-face feedback may nevertheless provide a steady stream of small criticisms. Also, as mentioned earlier, Japanese are highly concerned with neatness and presentation. The slightest hint of sloppiness or a slipshod work product will be taken by a Japanese manager as a sign of insufficient effort and diligence. As consultant Elizabeth Andoh points out, "Americans judge people by achievements, accomplishments, results. The Japanese are focused on process, effort. If a person tries really hard, even if the end result of that effort is not fabulous, the person is still held in high esteem." It seems that the things that strike Americans as superficial are what Japanese use to measure process and effort.

American employees of Japanese firms often feel that these small critical comments are a poor substitute for substantive feedback and expressions of appreciation. One banker commented, "Many times I have been counseled about lateness or the importance of the daily report or the importance of a tidy desk. However, I have yet to receive a review that identifies the aspects of my job that I do well and the areas that need improvement." Another banker notes that "If you bring in a $3 million deal they won't say, 'Hey, great job!' Instead they'll point out a word you misspelled in the proposal." Similarly, a white-collar employee at a manufacturing firm reports that the office manager stands at the door in the morning and tells employees who are as little as thirty seconds late that their pay will be docked. But there is never any mention of overtime pay even if employees work well into the night, a frequent occurrence. Another excellent example of the Japanese manager's tendency to criticize in the face of good performance occurred in the recent movie *Mr. Baseball*, in which an American baseball player portrayed by actor Tom Selleck goes to play for a Japanese team. The coach is a classic example of a Japanese manager in the traditional style. After Selleck's character helps win an important game with an excellent play, the coach merely growls at him: "You *still* have a hole in your swing!"

From the Japanese perspective, a manager wouldn't bother making small suggestions and corrections if he didn't care about the subordinate. The motivation is a desire to help the subordinate improve. Since this low-level negative feedback is a deeply rooted aspect of how Japanese managers view their task, take it as it is intended, and don't allow it to adversely affect your morale.

Respect the Hierarchy

Another facet of Japanese managers' focus on small matters is their expectation that they will be appropriately obeyed and respected in all circumstances. This can combine with Americans' distaste for niggling regulations to sour the atmosphere of an entire office, bringing the general antagonisms between the American and Japanese employees out

CONFUCIANISM

Confucianism is another philosophy that Japan imported from China. It was promulgated by the government during the Tokugawa period (1600–1867) as a philosophical underpinning to the strict social order that was being imposed. Although no one practices Confucianism per se in Japan today, Confucian tenets that continue to influence Japanese society stress the importance of the following:[m]

- Respect toward parents and elders

- Social ritual and etiquette

- Education

- Hard work

- Obedience to the law

- Observance of social hierarchy in all dealings with others

---

into the open. The themes of these heated confrontations over seemingly minor matters often are related to different Japanese and American viewpoints on individualism and deference to authority.

At one Japanese bank, the Japanese managers felt that there was a problem with tardiness among the American employees. The Americans would sometimes walk in five or ten minutes late, but since they usually stayed until six-thirty or seven o'clock in the evening the Americans assumed that the lost time was more than offset. But the Japanese managers felt that this was unacceptable, so they stationed a Japanese manager at the door acting as a guard to monitor and confront latecomers. Often, he would follow the putative offender into the open-plan office and bellow, "Is it your policy to be late for work?" loud enough that the general manager and everyone else could hear. The Americans hated this and the resulting confrontations would be heated, to say the least! The company's next remedy was installing a time clock. This was acceptable to the administrative workers, but the American marketing managers felt that it was degrading to punch a clock. One of them commented, "Every time I punched that clock it was like a slap in the face." Management finally rescinded the time clock requirement for the American marketing managers, but the damage had already been done to office morale.

As this time clock example demonstrates, Japanese managers will attribute a great deal of importance to the symbols of a subordinate's attitude and his degree of respect for superiors. This is partially a reaction to the extreme contrast between the hierarchical society that Japanese managers are accustomed to, and the egalitarian, individualistic nature of American society. Japanese managers may feel extremely threatened by American employees whose motivations they do not understand, whose actions seem unpredictable, and who act in ways that seem disrespectful and insubordinate. The Japanese concept of a good subordinate is one who quietly accepts the manager's superiority, which is due both to the manager's age and to his greater wisdom and experience. One can only learn from a Japanese-style teacher once one has submitted oneself to his will. Strict rules that seem silly to Americans are how Japanese managers monitor their subordinates' obedience. The result is an atmosphere that, in the words of one loan officer at a Japanese bank, "Makes me feel like I've joined the military."

Japanese managers who are operating under the assumptions of the traditional Japanese learning method expect unquestioning obedience from their subordinates and will be offended if they do not get it. This is difficult to accept for Americans, who tend to believe that all ideas are open for debate no matter who expounds them. Americans are taught from childhood to think independently and will not accept the absolute authority of a boss who they know cannot always be right. Before performing a task they want to know the purpose behind it, so that they can make sure that they are in agreement with that purpose.

Clashes often arise from this difference in assumptions. Consider the case of the Japanese manager who tells a subordinate that things will be done a certain way "because I say so" or "because that's the way we do it in Japan." The American subordinate asks why, but the manager does not give any further explanation. The manager perceives the question as an insult to his authority that borders on insubordination. Meanwhile, the American is offended by his manager's lack of a substantive response. In the American context, such explanations are considered sufficient for children, but not for adults. An adult deserves an explanation of the reasoning behind a policy or decision.

STRATEGIES FOR HANDLING
CONFLICTS WITH YOUR BOSS

Developing a good working relationship with a karate-teacher manager shouldn't mean that you need become as meek and nonconfrontational as a Japanese subordinate would be. However, when you are in disagreement with a Japanese superior, you should follow these guidelines:

• Do not contradict or argue with your boss or other superior in public, especially not in a meeting or in front of his superior. In the Japanese context, the duty of a subordinate is to help maintain the boss's "face." Any discussions or exchange of opinions should take place privately, behind closed doors if possible.

• Be careful with your phrasing. Use the classic feedback technique of giving positives before negatives.

• Attempt to discern the real reason behind his stance. Is it his own viewpoint or opinion, is he presenting a consensus that has been painstakingly reached, or is he repeating the official line from headquarters? It will be easier to sway his personal opinion than to counteract something he perceives as having been decided by others.

• Pick your battles carefully. Save your discussions for really important matters, and be more flexible on smaller ones. If you get into too many heated debates you will use up your stock of goodwill.

• In any discussion, be sure to convey that you are motivated by a sincere desire to do your job well and to achieve company goals. Your stance may otherwise be interpreted as selfish uncooperativeness.

• If the differences between you and your superior are particularly sensitive, it is best to avoid a confrontation. The Japanese strategy in such situations is to use a sympathetic go-between to convey the issue in a diplomatic way. This method prevents any embarrassing loss of face by either party. A trusted colleague or the personnel manager are potential go-betweens.

7

Participating in Japanese-Style Decision-Making

Jack had joined the New York branch of a major Japanese securities firm several months ago and was working on a deal with a tight schedule. An important decision needed to be made quickly. Jack approached his boss to tell him about it, but after giving an overview of the situation he was cut off before he could offer his "American-style list of alternatives, pros and cons." His boss called the chairman of the firm to discuss it and a meeting was scheduled for thirty minutes later. Jack and his boss walked into a big conference room filled with people, some of whom he hadn't ever met. There were junior people with only four or five years of experience and a senior person from a totally unrelated department. The American manager thought to himself "What's going on? Why do I have to put up with this? Why can't we make a decision? Why include all these people?" But sure enough, as the discussion unfolded, everyone in the room had a comment that was relevant. They spent several hours discussing the issues. Gradually a consensus began to emerge with some guidance from the chairman. The chairman then summed up the consensus, looked at Jack, and said, "Is that OK with you?" to which he replied, "Yes." And that was that. A $200 million transaction had been approved. Jack was "amazed and delighted." He cautions, however, that "this process doesn't work for Americans if the Japanese don't conclude along the way that they trust you."

This actual incident shows Japanese-style decision-making at its best—input is gathered from a large number of people, the issues are hashed out, and a consensus is reached. The key factors that made this swift and

HAS MY BUDGET BEEN APPROVED OR NOT?

In a Japanese organization, even seemingly clear-cut issues like getting the go-ahead on an annual operating budget can become a source of confusion. The American president of a midsize Japanese manufacturer's U.S. operations describes the following situation: "I went to Japan in February to get my budget approved. April 1st rolled around, the start of the new fiscal year, and there was nothing telling me whether my revised budget was approved or not. I wondered if I should just go through with the budget as I had submitted it—but what if they really wanted something else? Finally in mid-April I went to Japan to get a personal feel. It seemed that it had been accepted, but no one could pinpoint a particular meeting where that decision was made or how it was made. It wasn't a case of 'We'll have your budget review from nine to twelve on Monday and we'll tell you then whether we accept it or not,' the way you would expect in an American company."

favorable decision possible were the good relationship that Jack had developed with his superiors, the decision-making autonomy that had been granted to the U.S. operation, the chairman's ability to skillfully orchestrate the consensus process, and the willingness of the Japanese staff to conduct a long discussion in English. But even when Japanese-style decision-making goes smoothly, as in this case, it can still be bewildering to an American.

TYPICAL JAPANESE DECISION-MAKING

Traditional American organizations cherish the idea of individual authority. You are given a budget and a sphere of operations and you run with it. You make the decisions—if they are good ones you are rewarded, and if they are bad ones you may be shown the door. Successful people are those who lead others by setting clear goals and making sure that they are met. Individual vision, decisiveness, and risk taking are at a premium.

For someone accustomed to this mode of organizational life, the typical decision-making pattern in a Japanese company is bound to be a shock. First of all, it is not always clear who has authority. As an American who works for a midsized manufacturer comments, "I don't see any evidence of a delineation of who decides what sort of issue. Our president never sends decisions down from the top that I know of. That makes it hard to know who to go to in order to get a decision. The president is not the final arbiter of all things. He gives guidance." From the Japanese perspective, the ideal leader creates an environment in which his subordinates can be productive, but does not necessarily "take charge" as an American leader would. As former U.S. ambassador to Japan Edwin Reischauer describes it, in Japan "Leaders are not expected to be forceful and domineering, but sensitive to the feelings of others. Their qualities of leadership should be shown by the warmth of their personalities and the admiration and confidence they inspire, rather than by the sharpness of their views or the vigor of their decisions. What the American might consider as desirably strong leadership causes suspicion and resentment in Japan."[1]

Ringisho

As a result of this different concept of leadership, decision-making in a Japanese company differs from the top-down American model. Instead, middle- and lower-level employees are expected to develop plans that are then fed up through the ranks for comment and approval. The lower layers of the organization make the plans and proposals, while the upper layers provide guidance and oversight. In many firms, any matter to be decided will be written up in a formal document referred to as a *ringisho*. This document passes through various layers of management, and through every area which might be affected. The successful proposal accumulates literal "stamps of approval" (*hanko*) from each person who reviews it. Not until the proposal has been approved by everyone involved will it be implemented. As many observers have remarked, this process is time-consuming but results in a thorough consensus that leads to swift and smooth implementation.

The unsuccessful proposal is another story. It may languish on the desk of someone who is opposed to it until a modified proposal is made or everyone simply forgets about it. This becomes the equivalent of a pocket veto. The reason for rejection of the proposal may never be communicated—by simply sitting on it, the person who is opposed can avoid making explicit his reasons for opposition. While such lack of communication is generally considered by Americans to be poor management, it is an effective technique in the Japanese context. Usually, the person who initiated the proposal is not willing to provoke a confrontation by directly questioning the reason for its lack of progress, and the vetoer succeeds in killing the proposal. This technique of passive rejection is one source of the "black hole at head office" that irritates many American employees of Japanese firms.

In some cases, the proposal document may only be sent upward rather than circulated horizontally. In such cases the manager(s) at each level will take it upon themselves to verify that all interested parties are in agreement before approving it. Even if a proposal is not formally routed throughout the organization, this process ensures that many opinions are taken into account.

Nemawashi

Given the need for consensus, simply launching one's proposals and hoping that everyone likes them is clearly a risky enterprise. Savvy Japanese businesspeople use a technique called *nemawashi* to increase the likelihood that their proposals will be accepted. This term is derived from a gardening technique used in transplanting trees. To suddenly clip all the roots and pluck the tree from the ground can send it into shock. So a Japanese gardener will clip one root a day over the course of a few weeks in order to give the tree an opportunity to adjust. Similarly, in the business context *nemawashi* involves laying the groundwork for a proposal before it is formally advanced. The initiator finds an opportunity to have a quiet one-on-one discussion with each person likely to be reviewing the *ringisho*. His manager will join in this process as well where higher levels of management are involved; no one ever undertakes *nemawashi* without the support of his direct superior. The initiator presents his ideas and judges what kind of reception they are likely to find. He may also receive valuable feedback that can help him to tailor the proposal into a form that is more likely to be accepted. The overall goal

HOW YOU CAN AVOID THE "BLACK HOLE"

Many Americans complain that fax upon fax sent to the head office in Japan goes unanswered. One explanation for this phenomenon is that in Japan mutual relationships, rather than job descriptions, are the impetus for one's activities. In the Japanese context, having a personal relationship implies an obligation. Since the overseas employee is just a name on a facsimile, not a relationship, there is little sense of obligation.

Visiting the head office in person is the best way to develop a relationship. But even if you cannot visit Japan, with some creativity you can find other ways to develop a more personal connection.

For example, through your general and professional reading you may come across articles that would be of interest to colleagues at the head office, but which they would not otherwise have access to. Sending such information as a "favor" can make head office personnel more receptive to your needs.

Another more direct way to avoid the black hole is to include a "copy to" line on any correspondence sent to the head office—either of someone else at the head office, or a colleague at your location. The recipient will be more motivated to respond since he knows that others are aware of the inquiry.

---

is to obtain the buy-in of everyone who will participate in the decision.

The *nemawashi* process can be quite time-consuming. One can't just pop into someone's office and plop an idea down on the table in front of him unless a friendly relationship has already been established. Such relationship creation requires that time be spent face-to-face. Thus, *nemawashi* is one of the activities that happens in those evening drinking sessions. The need for this type of interchange with people in various parts of the company also explains why Japanese businessmen are so intent on bolstering their internal networks and maintaining them even while they are outside of Japan.

Use of the *nemawashi* technique is not confined to formal proposals where a *ringisho* will be written. This habit of quiet discussion and give-and-take with all concerned parties comes into play whenever any sort of decision is made, no matter how small. Americans have a different method for resolving the business issues that Japanese handle through *nemawashi*—the meeting. An item is put on the agenda, and everyone hashes it out together, airing any concerns or disagreements openly. This sort of open debate is extremely unsettling to Japanese, and *nemawashi* is used to avoid it. *Nemawashi* is calm, private, orderly, and conflict-free.

Meetings are used for formal acknowledgment of the results of the *nemawashi* process, not for debate.

This difference in approaches can lead to various clashes. The Americans in a Japanese firm may not realize that *nemawashi* is taking place or even understand why it is necessary. They may not know who are the "concerned parties" who need to be consulted, or what is the best way to approach them. When they want to get something done they may skip this vital procedure and then find their proposals blocked. Or, they will be confused as to what their Japanese colleagues are up to. As a Japanese manager at an automobile manufacturer who has worked in his company's U.S. operations notes, "There is a difference in the basic working style between Japanese and Americans. Japanese do their *nemawashi*, come in with their decisions already made, and will go through the motions during the meeting. Americans come with ideas to discuss. They see the way the Japanese run the meeting as secrecy. They get frustrated and angry."

FACTORS THAT INFLUENCE DECISION-MAKING

Due to the consensus decision-making process described above, the criteria for making decisions do not always seem rational from the American standpoint. Japanese firms do not usually base decisions on the numbers generated through financial analysis the way that an American company would.[2] Decision modeling and strategic matrices are also scarce in Japanese firms. Decisions are more likely to be based on instinct, and whether or not a consensus can be reached. Furthermore, the professional standards that are often used as decision-making guides in America may be unfamiliar to Japanese. Instead, decision-making is likely to be highly influenced by the types of factors described in the following paragraphs. While similar factors also come into play in the decision-making of American firms, the degree of importance attached to them in a Japanese company might be surprising to an American.

Internal politics.   Although all organizations are prone to internal politics, Japanese companies have especially intense political atmospheres. This may be a result of lifetime employment—conflicts and pressures are seldom relieved by departures from the firm. Instead, rivalries develop and grudges are nursed over years and even decades. It is common for competing factions (*habatsu*) to emerge that are similar to those in Japanese politics. Internal power struggles between such factions can become so intense that the participants become more interested in securing their own power bases than in furthering the interests of the company as a whole.

Actions of competitors. Japanese decision-making is often influenced by the desire to emulate one's competitors. Whereas an American firm might view mimicking the strategy of a competitor to be risky, a Japanese firm may feel that it can't afford to fall behind by not doing the same thing.[3] Although Japanese companies naturally compete against American and other firms in the United States, this tendency to match the actions of competitors occurs most often with other Japanese firms. Japanese companies keep a careful eye on what their Japanese competitors are doing in the United States, and rivalries born in Japan are often played out on U.S. soil.

Personal relationships. Decisions in Japanese companies are often influenced by personal relationships. The personal feelings between individuals within the company, or between someone in the company and someone from the outside party involved in the issue, can make or break a project. This applies in particular to the initiator of a proposal; this is one reason why Japanese are so loathe to get on anyone's bad side. Americans will find that making an effort to develop good relationships can pay off when it comes to getting things done. A consultant to Japanese joint ventures and cross-border investments comments, "If they like you, that alone can open doors. If they don't, even the greatest idea won't get you anywhere."

Institutional relationships. Institutional relationships with customers and suppliers are taken very seriously in Japan. In order to avoid disrupting what are perceived to be valuable long-term relationships, Japanese firms will frequently take actions that in isolation seem irrational. For example, one Japanese financial institution uses the outrageously overpriced services of a certain Japanese transport company to move employees within the United States, even though identical services are available from American carriers for considerably less. The reason is that the financial institution felt it might endanger its relationship with this firm, with which it does significant business, if it were discovered that it used another moving service. However, the relationships that really matter to a Japanese company may only be those with other Japanese firms. For instance, one banker related how his branch was forced to take on a questionable transaction from a company that was a major client in Japan, but when he requested that a special arrangement be made in Japan for one of his important U.S. clients, he was refused.

Risk aversion.   For reasons both of organizational structure and personality, Japanese managers in the United States are often quite risk-averse. (See Chapter 5 for further discussion of this topic.) A general preference for incremental improvements rather than splashy ventures also can preclude risk taking.

Difficulty reversing a consensus.   Because reaching a consensus decision is so difficult, once a decision is made it is difficult to alter, even in the face of changing circumstances (or the voicing of second thoughts by American employees). Once a direction has been set, a Japanese organization will frequently plow ahead because no one is willing to attempt the cumbersome process of changing course.

YOUR ADAPTATION TO
JAPANESE DECISION-MAKING

Americans who work in Japanese organizations tend to compare their autonomy with what they would expect in an American firm. In a traditional American company, responsibility and authority are always linked. If a manager needs to do something, the company gives him the tools he needs in terms of staff and budget, as well as the authority to manage them as he sees fit. His sphere of influence will be well defined, and he will have considerable latitude in accomplishing his goals. Having to check every decision with someone else marks one as powerless. However, this is not the case in a Japanese firm. As John Kageyama, a Japanese manager at a Japanese electronics company's U.S. subsidiary observes, "Authority to make decisions is shared in Japanese companies in ways that Americans are not used to . . . [a manager] is rarely given the kind of individual authority that is common in American companies.[4] Virtually no one in a Japanese company can act autonomously. Those who do are criticized as engaging in *wan man kodo* (autocratic action, from "one man," the term used in Japan to denote a bus or train with only a driver and no conductors or attendants on board). A director of a large Japanese manufacturer confides, "One of my greatest problems in dealing with Americans is that they expect me to be able to come to a meeting and make decisions on the spot. But anything I decide on my own is merely tentative. Even though I am an officer, I cannot commit the firm to anything without first obtaining the consensus of my colleagues."

Anyone who works in a Japanese company will need to adjust themselves to decision-making processes that are different than those in an American company. It is usually not possible to successfully bring an aggressive, individualistic working style into a Japanese environment. The ability to persuade, influence, and precipitate consensus are far more important. However, these qualities are not applicable only to Japanese firms. As the "John Wayne" style of management is falling out of favor and more U.S. companies turn toward cross-disciplinary teams, these qualities are also becoming increasingly important at American firms. Thus, learning to work within the Japanese decision-making structure is a way to develop skills that can be useful elsewhere as well.

The following are some guidelines for working in a Japanese decision-making system:

- *Make your supervisor your ally.* Any new proposal should first be discussed with your immediate supervisor. If he opposes it, the idea will probably not get serious consideration. But if you work together with your supervisor you can improve the chances of a favorable decision.

- *Sound out key players.* When an idea is in its early stages, sound out the key players that it will affect. Find out what they think of the idea, while subtly selling it to them at the same time. Incorporate their ideas into your proposal, and ask them to suggest others to consult. This process—in effect, *nemawashi*—will enable you to gather support.

- *Expect things to take time.* The Japanese decision-making process often takes time and much discussion. It's not necessarily quick. Don't get discouraged.

- *Write things down.* A proposal or initiative will get a better reception if you present a well-thought-out written discussion of your ideas. This is true for even minor issues that would seem to require only a quick conversation in the American context. A written document will make it easier for Japanese colleagues to consider your proposal, and they may attach it to a *ringisho* when working to convince higher-ups to back the project.

- *Gather detailed information.* You can speed the decision-making process by anticipating the questions that your Japanese colleagues will have about a proposal. Collect in advance the data that is relevant to likely concerns.

- *Start small.* American culture often predisposes us to creating grandiose plans. We are encouraged to "think big." Japanese, on the other hand, are encouraged to think incrementally. Propose a way to test your idea or start it in motion in a small way, using limited funds. The successes of a small-scale trial can then be parlayed into something bigger.

- *Point to success models.* Having a precedent for your proposal carries a great deal of weight with Japanese. For example, wherever possible try to point to similarities between your proposal and successful projects that the firm has undertaken in the past. Pointing to the actions of other companies, especially your competitors, can also be useful.

- *Being pushy doesn't work.* In American organizations, the person who is loudest or most forceful often gets his way. However, this tactic is dangerous in the Japanese context, because it will call your maturity and competence into question. Being aggressive may sometimes seem to work because Japanese will often give in just to end a conflict. However, the person who "wins" in this way will likely be worse off. The apparent "victory" may actually be a loss—Japanese colleagues may refuse to cooperate, stonewalling or ignoring the project until it dies on the vine. Pushiness can also make you a persona non grata whose every proposal is automatically rejected.

- *Be prepared to discuss and defend your ideas.* "I'm the expert on this so you should just take my word for it" is generally not an approach that goes down well with Japanese. Such statements are only appropriate coming from a superior or teacher to a subordinate—a role that you are unlikely to find yourself in unless you have been with a Japanese firm for decades. "Many heads are better than one" is the hallmark of Japanese decision-making, and each of those many heads will be thinking through the issue and asking you questions. Do not take this as an insult to your expertise.

- *Remember that the end result may be better decisions.* As a senior executive at a Japanese bank comments, "Their style is very deliberative, and they like to get as much input as possible before making a decision. It's definitely not shoot-from-the-hip decision-making here. But I find that good, because then you don't go off on wild goose chases as far as strategy goes. They really make you prove exactly what direction you want to go in and how you're going to get there."

The above suggestions are aimed at Americans who are participating in a Japanese-style decision-making process. However, for many Americans working at Japanese firms, the primary problem is not how the process works, but whether they have the opportunity to participate in this process. In many firms, Americans are completely or partially excluded from the firm's decision-making processes. This issue, and the reasons for such exclusion, are discussed in the following chapters.

THREE

Long-Term Prospects
for Non-Japanese
Employees

8

Out of the Loop

*On the official organizational chart, I'm on the third rung. There's a Japanese
General Manager, a Japanese Deputy General Manager, and then two Assistant
General Managers—myself and a Japanese national. However, my participation
doesn't match my official status. Japanese expatriates who technically are junior
to me get invited to Japanese-only meetings held by the General Manager. There
is never an explanation of why I'm not included. I submit budget proposals for
my area, but I've never seen an overall budget. I have no idea whether we're
operating profitably. Since I'm technically an Assistant General Manager, you
would think I'd know more about what's going on.*

ASSISTANT GENERAL MANAGER
OF A JAPANESE SECURITIES FIRM'S U.S. OFFICE

The previous chapter discussed how American employees of Japanese
firms are often confused by Japanese-style decision-making. Yet at many
Japanese firms in the United States, the most contentious decision-
making issue is: Who will make the decisions, American employees, or
Japanese expatriates and the head office? Japanese firms in the United
States seem to fall into three patterns in terms of the degree to which
American managers participate in decision-making: Japanese-dominated
decision-making, American-dominated decision-making, and shared
decision-making.

JAPANESE-DOMINATED DECISION-MAKING

In firms with this pattern, all decisions are explicitly made by Japanese, either those in the United States or those at headquarters in Japan. Japanese expatriates usually dominate the managerial positions in these organizations. Such companies are the most likely to report meetings that are held only in Japanese, and are likely to receive extensive input from Japan in day-to-day operations.

American staff are usually placed in operations, marketing, and clerical positions. Where Americans do have higher-ranking positions, they are most often in locally oriented staff positions that would be difficult to fill with expatriates, such as personnel, legal, accounting, and administrative. Where Americans are in line-management positions, it is usually in posts that have limited decision-making authority.

The American managers in such organizations tend to have mixed feelings about their positions. On the one hand, they have been hired to provide knowledge and capabilities that the expatriates lack, and as a result their advice is relied upon. This can lead to job satisfaction for Americans, who may address challenging work issues and wield considerable influence within the organization. In some cases, this degree of influence may even exceed what the Americans had enjoyed in previous firms. As one personnel manager at a Japanese bank comments, "I get a lot more respect here than I did when I was working at American banks. Now I can practice personnel management the way it's supposed to be done."

For some, however, being influential is not sufficiently satisfying, and the lack of decision-making authority becomes frustrating. This is particularly true for those who are accustomed to evaluating positions by the size of the budget under one's control or the decision-making autonomy one holds. When judged in such a way, the title "manager" may seem an empty one. An American who has risen to a management position in a Japanese bank comments, "Americans like myself they call managers. We have more responsibility, but not more authority or involvement in decision-making. Even though they give us titles, they don't give us more decisions to make. They are just appeasing us."

In some respects, the situation of American managers in such firms

IF JAPANESE EXPATRIATES MAKE ALL THE DECISIONS IN YOUR FIRM

Even in a firm where decision-making is dominated by Japanese, it is possible for American employees to have challenging, responsible positions by developing their own niches as specialists or advisors. The more experience and expertise you have, the more you will be respected. Also, the better the relationship you develop with your Japanese colleagues, the more influence you will be able to have on their decisions. However, you may need to accept that such influence will not be formally recognized. If you are comfortable measuring your job according to the intrinsic interest of your tasks rather than by the formal authority or rank you hold, the Japanese-dominated decision-making structure may not be a severe difficulty for you. On the other hand, if you aspire to general management posts that are filled by Japanese expatriates, you may find that a company of this type is not the best situation for you.

is analogous to being an external consultant—understanding the situation, doing the legwork, forming recommendations, but not making the final decision. The sense of being an outsider can also be reinforced by other elements of exclusionary behavior by Japanese expatriates, such as conversations and memos that are only in Japanese. In the words of one banker, "My opinion and recommendation is sought and occasionally followed. They take my advice, talk in Japanese amongst themselves, talk with Tokyo, then get back to me with a decision. I don't feel like I'm part of the process." As a result of this type of frustration, frictions can run high in such organizations. So can turnover, as managers become frustrated and lower-level employees decide that their opportunities for advancement are limited. As one senior American in a branch of a Japanese commercial bank comments, "My job is professionally very rewarding. I can make recommendations and suggestions, and I think they are taken seriously. I've built up credibility, but there's no real responsibility for an American. I'm purely a hired gun for advice and recommendations. All decision-making is done by the Japanese."

Complete control of decision-making by Japanese is frequently found in service sector firms (e.g., banks, securities companies, and trading companies) and in the sales operations of manufacturing firms. It may also occur in the operations of smaller companies.

AMERICAN-DOMINATED DECISION-MAKING

These organizations represent the opposite extreme and are the most Americanized. The majority of the management, and perhaps even the top person, is American. Individual Americans have direct contact with headquarters in Japan when input is needed, although this may be infrequent since the U.S. operation has a relatively high degree of autonomy. The proportion of Japanese expatriates is small, and the majority are in technology transfer or trainee positions. Although some level of friction is inevitable, it is significantly lower than in organizations where control is exclusively in the hands of Japanese. The friction that does occur may be concentrated at upper levels of the organization, where the American managers have the most direct interface with the Japanese organization. Friction of this type is not much different from what one would expect at any other multinational—some degree of conflict between headquarters and subsidiaries is par for the course.

Some, but not all, of the Japanese companies with large operations in the United States, such as automakers and electronics firms, have delegated most decision-making to American managers. For these firms, establishing a large, successful organization in the United States would have been difficult without the true involvement of American managers. Furthermore, it is difficult to establish a large organization with solely Japanese management—there are simply not enough qualified Japanese managers to go around. Some medium-sized and smaller firms have also made significant progress in Americanizing the management of their U.S. operations. Also, a preponderance of American managers is often the normal status in companies that have been acquired and whose management teams have remained largely unchanged since prior to the acquisition.

SHARED DECISION-MAKING

Shared decision-making is the most complex of the three decision-making patterns, so I will dwell on it at greater length. These organizations have Americans in managerial positions, but most contact with Tokyo is con-

SOME JAPANESE AFFILIATES WITH AMERICAN PRESIDENTS

Matsushita Electric Corporation of America, Richard Kraft

Mitsubishi Motor Sales of America, Richard Recchia

Nissan Motor Corporation in U.S.A., Robert Thomas

Okidata, Bernard Herman

Okuma Machinery, John Hendrick

Pilot Pen, Ronald Shaw

Sony Corporation of America, Michael Schulhof

Sony Music Entertainment, Thomas Mottola

Subaru of America, George Muller

Sumitomo Bank Securities, Norah Hughes

Zotos International, Philip Voss

trolled by Japanese expatriates. Some aspects of the company may be highly localized (e.g., sales, manufacturing), while many aspects continue to require a large amount of coordination with Japan (e.g., transfer of technical information, coordination of imports from Japan). The question of who makes what decisions and how to balance the opinions of Japanese headquarters, U.S.-based expatriates, and American managers is often a difficult one for firms with this structure.

A structure of shared decision-making may seem to be a logical compromise, but it is extremely difficult to manage skillfully. Continual pressures will stem from the different orientations between Japanese and American staff, and from the lack of clarity in decision-making responsibility. As a result, these firms can be characterized by anything from excellent cooperation to mutual suspicion.

Shadows

"Shadows" are a common feature of firms that are characterized by shared decision-making. The term shadow has come into common use by Americans who work at Japanese companies to refer to Japanese expatriates who gather information and consult closely with headquarters in Japan—like shadows, they are unobtrusive, but always present. Japanese often refer to these staff members as "advisors" or "coordinators," while some Americans simply call them "spies."

George, who was a product manager at an electronics firm, found that one of the most frustrating parts of his job was having a Japanese shadow working under him. Throughout the day the shadow would keep tabs on his activities: which customers he called, what they talked about, etc. At the end of each day or the beginning of the next day there would be a "data dump" from the shadow to George's Japanese boss. The boss would then make decisions based on information from the shadow, without first discussing it with George himself. George would be visited by his boss, who told him what to do based on the discussion with the shadow. In effect, George was bypassed—although he was the one actually doing the work, he was out of the decision-making loop.

Jean, a manager in a high-tech firm, reports that "Some of the Japanese people are here as spies to report back to people in Japan. There are extra eyes watching, peeking at what is on people's desks. We even have a guy who goes through people's garbage. His argument is that he is checking for company confidential things that should be shredded. He stands over people's shoulders while they are working at the computer and will blatantly watch what they are doing and ask them about it. People suspect that he looks at their files when they aren't there, but they can't prove it. He knows everything that's going on. Even if he's a nice guy, it's distasteful." Although most of the top management positions in Jean's office are held by Americans, "There's this feeling that big brother is watching over you. It's really unsettling."

Why do Japanese companies use shadows? Having a Japanese national act as an interface between the head office and American employees is deemed to be an efficient way to prevent misunderstandings. Someone who is familiar with internal politics and has a network of contacts at the head office is more likely to be able to orchestrate a *nemawashi* process or shepherd a *ringisho* through to approval. Also, in companies where products or technology are being transferred from Japan, a Japanese expatriate can play an important role in conveying information to American employees. The problem is not necessarily in having Japanese staff assigned as "coordinators" and "advisors" per se (although in many cases they would be superfluous if head office personnel were more willing to use English and work directly with locally hired employees). The problem lies in the way some of them conceive of, and carry out, their roles.

Working with Shadows

In some cases, American managers work very closely and comfortably with Japanese expatriate coordinators. A senior executive at a Japanese securities company describes his relationship with the senior Japanese he is assigned to: "I don't report to him, I work together with him. We evolve together how to work together. It's one of the best relationships I've ever had with anyone. It's fantastic, we trust each other, we can be open and can argue with each other. It's a terrific, tremendous team effort. I like that system. I work closely with the people in Tokyo, but some things need to be explained to senior management in Japanese and I don't see any problem with that." Clark Vitulli, a Mazda executive who works with a Japanese coordinator, says that "These are nice guys, just like you and me. Their interest in me is warm and personal, not just the cold issues of business. This took my anxiety away."[1]

Skillful cooperation with a Japanese coordinator can enable an American manager to be significantly more productive. The coordinator can help to navigate the minefields of internal politics, and can quickly skirt language and cultural barriers that are likely to trip up Americans.

KUROKO

The desire to maintain control through the use of coordinators is demonstrated by the fact that many Japanese companies think of their Japanese expatriates in the United States as *kuroko*.[n] *Kuroko* are the stagehands used in Kabuki (traditional drama) and Bunraku (traditional puppet theater). Dressed in black with hoods over their heads, they blend into the background during the performance. In Kabuki they handle all the props and make sure that the performance goes smoothly, while in Bunraku they are the ones who control the motions of the puppets. The connotation of *kuroko* is someone who is inconspicuous but, in actuality, is stage-managing the entire performance. The main actors who command the attention of the audience cannot play their roles without the assistance or the total control of the *kuroko*. A desire to use expatriates as *kuroko* shows a company's lack of trust in the ability of American employees to act autonomously. It also shows a discomfort with what Americans consider to be legitimate forms of control: clear job descriptions, explicit directions, open information-sharing, and documentation in the form of detailed files and memoranda.

In fact, one American manager at a medical products firm requested that a Japanese coordinator be assigned to him. "I thought that having a Japanese person would smooth and simplify communication with the parent company. Not only would it be a good developmental position for that individual, but it would be a chance for me to form a close personal relationship with someone from the head office."

The presence of Japanese coordinators can be either positive or frustrating to Americans—it just depends on how they are used. Are the Americans and Japanese working together as a team, cooperating and sharing information openly? Or is the Japanese coordinator quietly monitoring everything an American does while refusing to disclose the content of his communications with the head office and other Japanese expatriates? Does the coordinator report to the head office the decisions made in the United States, or does he impose the decisions made at headquarters on the U.S. organization?

The idea of having coordinators takes on a sinister cast in American eyes when they are perceived as spies or as silent manipulators. Unfortunately, the way that many Japanese companies conceive of the role of coordinators is likely to cause clashes with Americans. In the worst cases, Japanese assigned to be monitors either get carried away with their roles, or are given explicit directions from their superiors to keep the Americans in line. The company may feel nervous about letting its foreign subsidiary be managed by Americans who are an unknown quantity. It may seem safer to construct a parallel underpinning of Japanese expatriates who know what is going on and can make sure that things unfold the way the head office wants them to. As an American manager at a high-tech firm puts it, "The Japanese think, 'We'll let the Americans be managers but we'll have spies to monitor them.' The Japanese look at it as 'It's our deal, we have to do our best.' They don't look at it as a negative, nasty thing. They see it as just carefully keeping track. But it doesn't come off that way to other people."

Why do firms with shared decision-making structures maintain this awkward balance rather than putting either Japanese or Americans completely in charge? In some cases, the large degree of Japanese participation may be a purely practical response to issues arising from the

Hiroshi is a Japanese citizen who has worked at the same Japanese commercial bank for his entire career. A year ago, he was transferred to his company's Los Angeles branch.

"I have to spend an incredible amount of time on the phone with Tokyo. It's unbelievable how bureaucratic they are!" Hiroshi's job involves convincing headquarters to approve the various deals that the American marketing officers have lined up. It's not an easy task. "A few years ago, Tokyo used to give this branch fairly free reign. But then the real estate crisis hit us hard. Now, they won't trust us; they don't want us to do anything the least bit risky."

Hiroshi feels caught between Tokyo and his colleagues in Los Angeles. "I can understand Tokyo's point of view. They think that they are being careful and reasonable. But I have a lot of trouble explaining that to the American marketing officers. They just see how many deals slip by, and wonder why the bank has a branch here if it's going to severely restrict its operations. And deep down, I think they're right."

language barrier. In other cases, it may be a more cynical attempt to place Americans in visible positions as a facade of "Americanization," while decision-making remains completely in the hands of Japanese. In most cases, however, shared decision-making structures exist because the organization has not resolved how to integrate non-Japanese into its internal processes. Sincere-yet-vague good intentions may be paired with inertia and then combined with the mistrust that comes from cultural frictions.

Increasing Your Participation

If your firm is one where there is shared decision-making between Japanese and Americans, try to determine why that structure exists.

• What practical considerations might call for the involvement of Japanese in many aspects of decision-making?

• What is the attitude of the Japanese who serve as coordinators? How open would they be to your participation in communication with Tokyo?

• Is the company in a transition stage, trying to put more responsibility and autonomy in the hands of the American staff? Or is the company trying to reassert Japanese control over an organization that had previously given Americans a greater decision-making role?

• Has the proportion of expatriates to local employees increased, decreased, or remained stable in recent years?

• Has the shared decision-making structure become institutionalized and solidified, or is there a possibility of altering the system to provide for greater American participation?

Next, you will need to consider what efforts you can make to become more involved in the company's power structure and decision-making processes. The first step is to forge a strong relationship with the coordinator. Make him your ally rather than an adversary. He is your link to the information you need about how decisions are being made. To the extent that you can develop a relationship of trust and cooperation, you may be able to increase your participation in the company's management processes.

Opening lines of communication, perhaps over lunch or dinner, is a good first step. Find out what the coordinator does. Who at headquarters does he communicate with? What sorts of issues require headquarters input? What conflicts does he see between the desires of the U.S. operation and those of headquarters? Most importantly, what does he feel you can do to make his job easier? Through such a conversation with the coordinator, you can gain a better understanding of the relationship between your operation and headquarters. Interaction with the coordinator will enable you to determine how to work better with him and thus to increase your participation in the decision-making process.

BARRIERS TO AMERICAN INTEGRATION INTO DECISION-MAKING

The fundamental issue that underlies the situation of firms where decision-making is entirely or partially controlled by Japanese is: Why do many Japanese organizations resist including Americans in the decision-making process? Three types of factors, linguistic, cultural, and structural, are at work.

Linguistic Factors

Linguistic factors arise because greater American participation in the decision-making process requires that Japanese employees use more English. This is problematic given the imperfect English ability of most Japanese businesspeople. Not only is it easier for Japanese to use their own language, but the information content is obviously richer when one is dealing in one's native tongue. When meetings at the U.S. operation are held in English rather than Japanese, it is more difficult for the Japanese to participate. Head office employees also resist having to communicate with overseas operations in English. Furthermore, when decision-making processes are conducted in Japanese, expatriates will need to act as translators and interpreters in order to keep Americans informed and involved. Many of them do not have sufficient language skills for such tasks, and even if they do, they will only view it as extra, low-priority work on top of their ordinary responsibilities.

Although these linguistic factors are formidable, they can be solved through a combination of individual effort and corporate encouragement of language study.

Cultural Factors

Cultural factors are the topics that have been discussed in previous chapters. The ability to meet Japanese expectations and work smoothly in the Japanese corporate context are a prerequisite for inclusion in decision-making processes. Americans who precipitate too many conflicts or do not convey flexibility and sincerity will not be able to gain the necessary trust from Japanese managers. On the other hand, those who can work skillfully in a Japanese company environment have the potential to be included in decision-making.

As the previous chapters indicated, cultural factors are difficult to avoid because they have to do with our basic assumptions and ways of looking at the world. However, if individuals and their companies make an effort to recognize and address these issues, they can be resolved.

Structural Factors

Structural factors are the organizational divisions that separate Americans from Japanese staff, even when Americans have made great efforts to adapt to the Japanese company environment. Structural factors become both a wall and a rice-paper ceiling separating American from Japanese employees. This pattern is so prevalent at Japanese firms' overseas operations that scholars have given it a name, "the dual company."[2]

It is tempting to think of the distinctions made between American and Japanese as a racial or national issue. American employees of Japanese firms often interpret it that way. A former construction company employee commented, "If you don't have a stamp on your forehead that says 'Made in Japan,' you're never going to get anywhere." Some authors have pointed to a supposed Japanese general distrust of foreigners and a national predisposition to distinguish "insiders" (*uchi*) from "outsiders" (*soto*). These factors do exist to some extent—just as there are some Americans who are biased against foreigners, there are some Japanese who want nothing to do with non-Japanese. Yet such attitudes are gradually disappearing as Japan increases its interaction with the rest of the world and as younger Japanese develop an openness toward non-Japanese. Thus, while bias against non-Japanese may be a factor in some cases, a more generally applicable explanation for the tendency to exclude non-Japanese from decision-making can be found by examining the Japanese corporate structure.

In a Japanese company, Japanese who have been hired in Japan are considered "our men" worthy of complete trust. At some level, this is a natural phenomenon in any multinational corporation. The parent company knows the expatriates and has tested them in the home-country environment. The parent company will naturally feel more comfortable with them. When they go abroad, the expatriates are oriented toward the parent company and identify closely with it, while locally hired employees are oriented toward the local market and do not share the same ties with the parent company.

This phenomenon is intensified in a Japanese company, because the testing process for Japanese employees lasts decades. The typical Japanese expatriate will have worked in his firm for at least ten years before his assignment to the United States. The company knows him well, and he has developed an extensive network within the firm. Furthermore, the Japanese lifetime employment system gives Japanese firms a high degree of control over their employees. A Japanese company knows that its employees have little choice but to do as the company wishes and are unlikely to leave.

From the Japanese perspective, Americans are not as easy to manage as Japanese employees because we do not have a custom of lifetime employment. Many Japanese companies say to themselves, We never know when our American employees will quit. How can we risk putting important activities in their hands if we cannot count on them? How can we let them in on important decisions and company secrets if they could leave tomorrow and take that knowledge to a competitor? Also, if they don't stay around long enough, how can we really get to know them, and how can they truly understand our company?

These are powerful concerns for many Japanese companies. They add up to an inability to trust Americans and integrate them into the company's decision-making processes. The result is that many firms end up keeping American employees at arm's length and do not make them a part of the overall "company family."

In order to better understand this phenomenon, it is necessary to take an in-depth look at the Japanese lifetime employment system. What is it about this system that makes it so difficult for Japanese firms to understand and effectively utilize American employees? The next chapter will examine the lifetime employment system as practiced in Japan, while the chapter after that will describe how the existence of such a system can relegate non-Japanese employees to the margins of the corporation.

9

The Japanese Lifetime Employment System

I cannot imagine my life without my company. I have worked here since I graduated from college. When I joined, I had no skills, no knowledge of this industry. Everything I know about business I learned from this company and my senpai *(seniors) here. My best friends are people who joined the company along with me. I even met my wife through the company—she was a secretary here, but she resigned when we got married. And with real estate prices so crazy, the only way I could afford to buy a house was with the generous loan that the company offered.*

A TYPICAL JAPANESE "SALARYMAN"

Most American businesspeople are aware that in Japan there is a tradition of lifetime employment. Against the background of frequent layoffs by American companies, such absolute job security can look extremely attractive in American eyes. However, few Americans know anything about how this system works or the profound effects it has on organizational behavior, corporate policies, or the incentives of individual employees. In order to understand how Americans fit into the Japanese company's overall hierarchy, it is necessary to examine how personnel management works in Japan.

Contrary to popular belief in the United States, not all Japanese companies offer lifetime employment to their employees. Haruo Shimada of Keio University estimates that in the mid-1970s half of Japanese workers were covered by lifetime employment and that the figure today is closer to 25 percent.[1] However, the ideal of lifetime employment and the related policies described in this chapter are standard among the large Japanese companies that are most likely to have operations in the United States. Thus, this account of traditional Japanese white-collar personnel management describes the assumptions held by the Japanese expatriates that Americans are most likely to encounter.[2]

RECRUITING NEW EMPLOYEES

Japanese companies recruit for permanent positions just once a year. At this time they only hire new college graduates. Because they have no work experience, the students are generally chosen based on the school they attended and the perceived fit with the company's personality. For their part, students spend a great deal of time researching potential employers, but not necessarily for information about the specific jobs they might perform. They are choosing a company rather than a job, so emphasis is placed instead on the company's prestige within its industry, its prospects for the future, and its corporate culture. Alumni of the same university who work at the firm also play a large role in influencing students to join, as do professors who may have developed personal ties with certain companies.

When a student chooses a firm, there is no explicit contract in which the company agrees to provide lifetime employment. Rather, there is an implicit understanding that firms will not lay off employees and that employees will not choose to quit. Any company that fired employees for reasons other than severe misconduct would damage its reputation and its ability to recruit new employees. Similarly, any employee who leaves his company would find it difficult to secure a job with another large Japanese firm. This is because other large firms also center their hiring process on new college graduates and are usually not inclined to make exceptions. Also, someone who leaves his company is often regarded as somehow tainted. Even if he finds a job with another large company through one of the rare midcareer hiring (*chutosaiyo*) programs, he may be regarded as something of a second-class citizen by those who joined the firm directly from college. Thus, lifetime employment can best be described as a customary system of mutual obligations that is made tenable by the fact that it is practiced uniformly among major companies. (In fact, the word "lifetime" is something of a misnomer, since most firms have relatively low mandatory retirement ages of fifty-five or sixty.)

A new employee induction ceremony is held each April following college graduations in March. The ceremony is always a solemn occasion marked with a speech by the president or chairman. The new recruits then receive at least several weeks of group training. This training covers topics ranging from an overview of the company's policies and procedures to pointers on business etiquette. The goal is to prepare new employees to be integrated into the company. Many firms also include some sort of arduous event designed to promote group solidarity. For example, every year new employees at the advertising agency Dentsu climb Mt. Fuji together.[3]

The Doki

During their new employee training, recruits get to know the other members of their *doki* (entering cohort). In the hierarchical world of the company, fellow *doki* members are the only ones with whom an employee can interact as equals. Others are either *senpai* (one's seniors), who serve as both teachers, role models, and masters, or *kohai* (one's juniors), whom one should advise and put in their place when appropriate. Throughout their careers at the company, members of a *doki* will often socialize together. On the other hand, the *doki* also becomes the focus of intense competition. This competitive atmosphere is heightened by the fact that all the new employees will be trained as generalists, with achieving department manager (*bucho*) level and eventually director level the measures of success. They are all competing for the same prizes rather than for recognition in particular specialties suited to their own unique abilities.

Initially, the new employee is often assigned to a demanding post that does not necessarily utilize his higher education. For example, manufacturing companies frequently place new employees in assembly line or low-level sales and service positions. Banks assign new recruits to work as tellers, clerks, and door-to-door deposit gatherers. The object of such assignments is for the employees to learn the business from the bottom up and to discourage arrogance by fostering empathy for those performing less prestigious jobs.

The first few years of employment are typically devoted to training and job rotations for the purpose of company-wide exposure. Distinctions will begin to emerge between employees as some are moved to more glamorous departments or given more responsible assignments. However, it is generally not until employees reach the age of thirty or more that they begin to receive promotions to lower-level managerial positions. In many companies there is also an unspoken rule against promoting those who are not yet married. It is assumed that men with wives are more stable and will have the support at home to enable them to take on managerial tasks. Those who are unmarried are assumed to be devoting energy to finding a mate or are deemed to be poorer risks for management jobs due to the suspicion that some character flaw is preventing them from finding a spouse.

CLIMBING THE CORPORATE LADDER

From the time of the first promotion, employees gauge their own progress by monitoring their position in comparison with fellow *doki* members. Everyone closely watches to see who will be the first member of a *doki* to be promoted to the next level in the hierarchy. A considerable amount of energy is expended reading the tea leaves of personnel department announcements in order to determine who is an up-and-comer, as well as less formal signals, such as who is invited to what social functions. Employees in their early thirties have already begun to discuss who in their *doki* might make it to president twenty or more years in the future. (It is inconceivable that anyone in their *doki* would make it to such a high-level position before then due to the emphasis on seniority.)

Hierarchy

The hierarchy itself is manifested in two sets of uniform rankings throughout the company. The first is an internal personnel ranking, which is used for personnel administration and generally appears only on personnel department documents. This hierarchy consists of a finely graded set of levels, and every employee is assigned a rank on this scale. A person's compensation is for the most part based on his ranking, and promotions are upward movement within this ranking. However, ranking in this system, which Japanese economist Masahiko Aoki has termed the "ranking hierarchy," is disassociated from the function that an employee performs in the organization. A person may be "promoted" but still continue to perform the same job function, or may be transferred but not promoted.[4] Two employees with different statuses in the ranking hierarchy may perform similar job functions, while in the context of a work team, more responsibility may be delegated to someone with a lower formal ranking. This tendency to disassociate work content from formal rank is one reason why Japanese companies in the United States often unwittingly frustrate their American employees by granting "promotions" that are not matched by changes in responsibilities.

The second ranking consists of the formal titles that are used on business cards, which indicate functional authority. A typical basic set of rankings would include *kacho dairi* (deputy section chief), *kacho* (section chief), *jicho* (deputy general manager of a department), *bucho* (general manager of a department), *torishimariyaku* (director), *jomu* (managing director), *senmu* (senior managing director), *fuku shacho* (vice president), *shacho* (president), and *kaicho* (chairman). Although there are as many variations on this theme as there are companies, the terms used are always standardized throughout a single company (although at some companies no titles are used except for managerial employees).[5] Thus, someone can look at the title of a person anywhere else in the company and immediately determine whether he is of higher or lower rank. The fact that the relevant levels are similar across companies facilitates comparisons with those in other firms as well. This ability to quickly determine relative rank is especially important in Japan, where different Japanese verb forms must be used when speaking to superiors or to juniors.

The specific titles that describe one's duties, common in American companies, are virtually unknown in Japanese firms. For example, someone who would be called a "Senior Marketing Representative" in a U.S. firm might be a *kacho dairi* in Business Development Department Number Four. The lack of specificity in job titles and the associated absence of detailed job descriptions leaves each particular person's responsibilities ambiguous. The Japanese view is that this ambiguity provides flexibility for managers to tailor job activities to meet the abilities of the employees and to apportion tasks most efficiently among the members of a work group. It is also expected that employees will take the initiative to find useful things to do, thus expanding their activities. The lack of set job boundaries is thought to encourage such entrepreneurial behavior.

Rotation

As they move up in the company, employees are rotated from department to department, so that they move in a sort of spiral pattern toward the top. Whereas such rotational programs are limited to fast-trackers in American companies, they are the norm for most employees in Japanese companies. Sometimes it seems as though the company is grooming everyone to be able to become president of the firm, but this is not really the case. As time goes on those employees destined for the really top posts continue to be rotated widely, while others find themselves being rotated in one particular area of the company.

The rotation system means that employees of a Japanese company become generalists rather than specialists. The underlying concept is that raw talent (*noryoku*) is a generic quality; someone with ability should be able to carry out any job that is assigned. Transfers are accompanied by little or no formal training, even if the new post is in an unfamiliar area. Hapless employees often find themselves inadequately prepared for the tasks they are assigned and snap up the "how to do your

THE OBSESSION WITH TRAINEES

American affiliates of Japanese firms often have many expatriates who have been sent from Japan as "trainees"—sometimes as many as a dozen at a time. American employees often wonder why they are asked to give special presentations for these trainees or to coach them through their tasks. "What are those trainees doing here?" they ask.

Japanese companies' emphasis on trainees is not limited to their overseas affiliates. Within Japan, firms commonly trade trainees among themselves, and trainees are frequently sent to government offices and business-related nonprofit organizations.

The use of trainees has two roots. The first is the Japanese tendency to prefer actual experience over classroom study. Going somewhere, meeting people, and doing something is considered the best way to learn. The second cause of the trainee phenomenon is the lifetime employment system. Traineeships are considered part of a firm's investment in an individual. The traineeship is an experience that will enrich that person by expanding his knowledge or contacts. The company is willing to make large investments in individuals because they are expected to remain with the firm. Traineeships are a way to capture information within the company. The more know-how that a company's lifetime employees can soak up, the richer the organization as a whole.

job" books, such as *The Basics of Foreign Exchange Documentation* and *Step by Step Guide to Preparing Financial Statements,* that fill the shelves of Japanese bookstores.

There are both positive and negative aspects to this practice of rotating employees among diverse areas. On the positive side, employees are provided with variety and challenge and develop mental flexibility by constantly learning new tasks. The company has the flexibility to quickly transfer personnel from shrinking areas to growth areas. On the negative side, efficiency and competence are compromised by the fact that people often don't understand how to do their jobs. With so much internal movement, it is also difficult for the company to develop specialists who have in-depth knowledge of a particular area.

Unlike the situation in American companies, line managers do not have primary responsibility for personnel decisions. Although line managers affect the progress of their subordinates by submitting performance evaluations to the personnel department (which the subordinates usually do not get to see), they do not have a vested interest in obtaining raises or promotions for their subordinates or in preventing them from being moved to other departments, because they themselves are likely to soon be rotated to another position. For this reason, Japanese managers in the United States may not realize that American subordinates expect them to act as advisors and advocates on personnel matters.

Rotations as well as other personnel decisions such as promotions and compensation are determined unilaterally by the personnel department, with little or no input from the employees themselves. As a result, it is not necessary for Japanese employees to develop the well-defined career goals that are the hallmark of the fast-tracker in the U.S. corporate world. Forming elaborate goals is pointless if one is virtually powerless to make them come true. In the words of a young Japanese male employee at a major Japanese bank, "You could decide you want to work in X, but if the personnel department wants you to be in Y you have to do that. It's better to just go with the flow and try to do well with whatever you are given."

For this reason, Americans may focus more on the basic challenge and interest that a job provides than the average Japanese salaryman does. Americans choose their careers through the labor market. If they don't like what they are doing, they also have the freedom to do something about it and seek out something they like better. An American who is working in marketing, for example, has chosen that sort of work for a specific reason. His skills and personality are probably suited to it, and he probably derives intrinsic enjoyment from it. Meanwhile, a Japanese employee doing marketing in a Japanese company is doing it because that is the job to which he was assigned. He may find marketing uninteresting or even unpleasant. His personal characteristics may or may not be well suited to marketing work. In this take-it-or-leave-it situation, none of these factors matter because an individual Japanese employee has little control over where he is assigned in his company.

Refusing transfer orders from the personnel department would represent a huge black mark on one's record, so it generally isn't done. This is true even in cases where the transfer requires a move to another city or overseas. If a man is unwilling to uproot his family or disrupt his children's education, he will move to the new location alone rather than turn down the transfer. This practice is so common that it even has a name, *tanshin funin.*

There are two reasons why Japanese employees are willing to take whatever orders they are given. One is that they joined the company rather than a specific position, so there was an implicit requirement that they would loyally accept whatever work is given to them. Second, since there is virtually no external labor market, employees' only chance for career success (and even a stable livelihood) lies within their company. Thus it would be risky for them to be perceived as "difficult" and jeopardize their future prospects. This same mentality prevents employees from complaining about other aspects of their jobs or about personnel policies that they might find less than satisfactory.

Viewed in a positive light, this willingness of employees to do whatever is asked of them, and to accept company policies as given, is a manifestation of company loyalty and a mutually cooperative employer-employee relationship. Viewed in a negative light, employees are like vassals who have no choice but to obey the iron rule of the personnel department. Company policies and practices are shielded from the discipline of market forces that an external labor market would provide.

Compensation

Like the rotational and promotion systems, a Japanese company's compensation system is geared to an orderly internal pattern of career-long affiliation with the company. Separate salary ranges are not determined for individual positions, as they would be in an American company. The external labor market plays no role in shaping compensation. This is only rational since the company's employees are not looking outside the firm for other employment opportunities. Rather than different salaries for different jobs, there is one standard salary system that applies throughout the company. Pay is primarily based on internal personnel rank (which roughly but not exactly matches years of service, since better performers will receive promotions a bit more quickly than others who entered at the same time). This is considered more fair than individualized salaries because each person is employed by the organization at large and all employees are expected to share a common fate with the company.[6] Furthermore, individuals do not expect to be compensated for their specific skills, since they were developed at company time and expense. This contrasts with the American concepts of accumulating a resume of skills and accomplishments, investing in oneself by pursuing advanced education such as an M.B.A., and then leveraging these personal qualities to command a higher salary. Unaccustomed to the idea of linking an individual's pay to his skills, Japanese managers frequently view the salary and pay raise negotiation tactics of Americans as crass and unseemly.

This concept of fairness and an emphasis on teamwork also underlies the lack of performance-based compensation systems. It is thought that rewarding individual contribution undermines the harmony of a workgroup since everyone's contribution is important. Why should one person receive more pay when teamwork is considered the essential ingredient for success? Unfortunately, the de-emphasis on individual performance often creates a situation in which workers can continue to receive the same compensation even if they do not pull their weight. Shirkers who take advantage of this state of affairs are common, especially among those who have surmised that they have no chance of rising to the top. One Japanese woman who has had to work with several such people describes her company's system as "just like Communism."

The Personnel Department

The personnel department that designs the compensation system and plots the personnel transfers holds tremendous power within the organization. Everyone in the company treads lightly around the personnel department and there is always a great deal of speculation as to how its decisions are made. The department is headed up by a well-respected manager, usually a director of the company. However, although it is powerful, the personnel department is also lean in terms of numbers. The work involved in running the yearly college recruiting, planning personnel shuffles, and administering compensation and other routine matters usually keeps the personnel managers' hands full. There is no time, and no intention, to give significant individual attention to employees. Furthermore, unlike in the United States, there is no training or formalized qualification for a personnel manager. The department is staffed by up-and-comer line managers who have been assigned to personnel as part of their fast-track rotation, not by specialists in human resource management. The average Japanese personnel manager has little knowledge of subjects such as compensation system design, counseling techniques, or labor market theory. He may also have little interest in making major changes to personnel policy, since he is expecting to be rotated out of the department shortly.

NO SECOND CHANCE

How do Japanese companies deal with the inevitable fact that more people are needed at lower levels of the organization than are needed at the top? The upward spiral of employees is actually a cone-shaped spiral; fewer and fewer employees are in the running as one goes higher up. At each level there are those who are eliminated from the race. However, companies have traditionally been reluctant to fire superfluous employees, so they have developed several strategies for dealing with them. One is to simply stop moving some people around, allowing them to reach a plateau and perhaps build up a niche role in the organization. The second is to assign people to positions that simply have no work. The unfortunate managers who receive such posts are referred to as the *madogiwazoku* (the tribe that sits by the window) due to the placement of their desks in positions where they can enjoy the view. Often they have nothing to do but read the newspaper all day. A third strategy for dealing with surplus middle managers is to foist them off on subsidiaries. As a rule, major Japanese companies have a network of subsidiaries engaged in related businesses, whose managerial slots are filled by people assigned by the parent company. The Japanese recession of the early 1990s has forced Japanese companies to utilize these traditional tactics for dealing with superfluous managers even more aggressively, as well as to develop new tactics. (See Chapter 12.)

Given that a Japanese company's personnel management system is not geared to measuring individual performance, what determines who moves up and eventually makes it to the top? Of course, cream rises in any organization and the best performers will stand out on their own. But ability alone is not the only criterion. Two factors are important in an individual's perceived performance: his effort and his contribution to the performance of the group. Japanese managers tend to be concerned that everyone is giving their all and will often concentrate on measures of effort such as how long one stays in the office each night. Under this standard, even a stellar performer may be criticized if he leaves promptly at five o'clock; obviously he is not giving 100 percent, because giving his all would mean working longer. The second criterion, contribution to the group, has to do with cooperativeness. At its simplest level this means getting along with people. Thus, talented employees who have poor interpersonal skills are at an even greater disadvantage than they are in American companies. It also means that fast-trackers who are too arrogant and irritate their fellow employees will get their comeuppance eventually. Contributing to the group also implies a willingness to help coworkers with their jobs, even if it means staying late after one's own tasks are completed, and taking the initiative to seek out new and useful tasks that will ease the burden of coworkers or otherwise promote the interests of the group.

The difficulty in measuring whether one is "giving one's all" and "contributing to the group" means that there is a lot of room for subjectivity in personnel decision-making. Those who want to rise in the company must spend a great deal of time polishing their internal image and cultivating good relationships with superiors and coworkers. This is one of the reasons why Japanese businesspeople spend so much time going out together after work. It also explains why Yoshimichi Yamashita, president of Arthur D. Little Japan, has complained that "The typical Japanese executive has become far more adept at internal politics—'boozing and schmoozing'—than at external strategy."[7]

The need to maintain a good reputation within the firm is intensified by the fact that members of a *doki* cohort are a homogeneous group to begin with. They graduated from similar schools, and whatever unique skills they possess were likely to have been developed by the company. Everyone works hard, stays late, and makes sure that people like them. This creates stiff competition, especially when one gets below the top 10 percent or so of employees who truly stand out. In some sense the personnel department may be looking for reasons to disqualify people from the running, since in terms of performance (as evaluated by the system) they all appear similar. In this situation, continuing to move up often means just making sure you don't make any big mistakes. This is because the internal mechanism for noticing mistakes is much more developed than that for recognizing positive performance. The result is an extreme aversion to taking risks among Japanese middle managers. The downside is potentially devastating, while the upside may be overlooked. Both good work and mediocre work tend to fade into the background and can be quickly forgotten, while a major mistake will rivet people's attention. Many Japanese middle managers find it more expedient to avoid risks and downplay problems until they are transferred to their next position. Under the lifetime employment system, there may be no second chance.

THE JAPANESE MODEL OF A GOOD EMPLOYEE

A Japanese manager's idea of a model employee is determined by the lifetime employment system described above. The qualities that enable one to succeed in such a system are the ones that are valued. However, the free labor market system in the United States leads Americans to have different approaches to work. The following characteristics of a good employee in the Japanese system can clash with standard employee behavior in the United States.

Predictable

The Japanese employee is predictable and dependable. He will work with little complaint no matter how his company treats him, since the lack of an external labor market leaves him with few attractive options.

Thus, Japanese managers need not be concerned about whether or not their employees will become dissatisfied and leave. Ensuring employee satisfaction and preventing turnover are foreign concepts to a Japanese manager who is working under these traditional assumptions. When a Japanese employees quits, rather than being taken as a sign of a problem with the company, it is shrugged off as a problem with the individual employee—an inability to get along with coworkers, the personality of a perpetual malcontent, a lack of loyalty, or selfish job-hopping. Due to this way of thinking, Japanese managers often view Americans' job mobility quite negatively. Because their system does not encourage them to search for job satisfaction or to switch jobs in order to get ahead, Japanese will tend to assume that Americans are mercenaries who are only concerned with making more money.

Flexible

Because the Japanese employee has committed himself to staying with the same firm, the company views him as a flexible resource. He can be moved to different tasks in accordance with changing business needs. For example, if the firm decides to de-emphasize activity A and expand activity B, it will simply switch personnel from A to B, even if they are completely unrelated tasks. Similarly, employees who are asked to transfer abroad will virtually never refuse, even if it disrupts their personal lives. It is assumed that each employee will put corporate objectives above personal desires. To the Japanese company accustomed to managing the careers of its employees as it pleases, Americans, with their own well-developed goals and aspirations, may seem selfish, self-centered, and uncooperative.

Undemanding

The lifetime employment system is linked with the concept of long-term rewards. At the beginning of his career, even a high-level performer will not make much more than his contemporaries and may not move up noticeably faster. The system rewards good performance over the long run, in terms of decades, not years. In this context, it is pointless for the Japanese employee to be demanding in terms of salary or special treatment. It is also not necessary for the Japanese employee to call direct attention to his contributions as an individual. He is comfortable with shared responsibility and shared credit—his efforts and contributions will be recognized in the fullness of time. Thus, in the eyes of a Japanese manager, the American's desire for immediate recognition of individual accomplishments and willingness to openly ask for increased compensation seem self-aggrandizing and gauche.

10

Not All Employees Are Created Equal

I've stayed late, I've made more right recommendations than wrong ones, I've acquired some stature in their eyes, I've gotten some trust. You get the sense that they appreciate you, but that doesn't buy you anything extra. It doesn't change how they view me long term. I'm just a hired hand.

AN AMERICAN MANAGER
AT A JAPANESE BANK'S NEW YORK BRANCH

The preceding chapter described the personnel system for the core employees of a Japanese corporation—Japanese males who will stay with the company throughout their careers. While Japanese firms hire other employees as well, their status is not equivalent. Although Westerners generally consider anyone who works full-time to be an "employee," at Japanese firms employees are divided into various categories. These classifications go beyond the simple distinction between labor and management. The category into which a new e.nployee is placed is determined largely by his or her sex, age, educational level, and aspirations. While one category promises absolute job security and leads one on the path to management, the others are obviously dead ends with limited time frames. And once hired into a certain category, switching into another is usually not possible.

TWO-TIER EMPLOYMENT SYSTEM

The central group of white-collar employees is the *seishain*, who fall under the lifetime employment system described in the previous chapter. There is no term in English for *seishain* because there is no equivalent feature in western employment practices. Literally meaning "actual employee," it is often translated using awkward terms such as "regular staff member" or "permanent employee." The *seishain* is hired directly out of college, trained internally, and expected to stay with the same company until retirement. Male *seishain* are automatically put into the *sogo shoku*,[1] or "general work," category, which is a Japanese company's equivalent of the management track (although manufacturing firms often have a separate category for production workers). *Sogo shoku* are rotated around the company like interchangeable parts, receiving heavy doses of on-the-job training along the way. Throughout their careers *sogo shoku* slowly move up the corporate ladder, receiving gradually increasing responsibility and remuneration until retirement. In return for a lifetime of loyalty and service, the company gives *sogo shoku* a secure livelihood and an identity of which they can be proud.

In the past, only men could join the *sogo shoku* ranks and take their chances at trying to reach the executive suite. Only recently were female *sogo shoku* added to the corporate scene, a result of the Equal Employment Opportunity Law of 1986. Since this law was enacted, many major companies have begun admitting well-qualified women to the *sogo shoku* rolls. At this point it is too soon to tell whether these women will advance into management at the same rate as male *sogo shoku*. They face many hurdles, not the least being tradition-minded male colleagues and superiors and a lack of role models. Furthermore, the law itself does not specify any penalties for noncompliance, so firms are not as enthusiastic about affirmative action as American firms are in the United States.

The majority of women in Japanese companies, even if they have a college degree, are in the second *seishain* category, that of *jimu shoku*,[2] or clerical worker. These women are the so-called "office flowers" who brighten up the surroundings while operating the copy machines, typewriters, word processors, and teapots. *Jimu shoku* are seldom transferred

WORK AFTER MARRIAGE

Many Japanese women receive pressure from their companies to quit when they get married. While this reflects the traditional values held by some Japanese managers, it may also be a side effect of the seniority-based pay scale. By encouraging turnover among its female employees, a company keeps down their average age and average salary.

Women who marry coworkers often face particular pressure, since their spouses are more visible. One woman who married a man in her company was determined to continue working. Perturbed when she would not resign, a few months later the company transferred her husband to anoth-er part of the country. She was refused a transfer to the same location, effectively forcing her to quit.

Attitudes on working wives can vary even within the same company. One story making the rounds in Tokyo involves the wedding of two employees of the same bank. At the reception, the groom's boss used the toast to urge the bride to "devote herself to making a home and supporting her husband's career"—a thinly veiled suggestion that she quit. To the guests' amazement, the bride's boss then used his toast to deliver an impassioned plea for her to "chart her own course" and not leave the company!

---

between positions or locations and are unlikely to progress beyond the rank of senior clerk. Since *jimu shoku* are *seishain*, they are accorded lifetime employment, although few take advantage of it. Most quit when they marry or bear children.

Not all Japanese workers are lucky enough to obtain "elite" *seishain* positions. A company's implicit promise of lifetime employment extends only to a core group of employees that may make up as little as 20 percent of its workforce, depending on the particular industry and the state of the overall economy.[3] The other workers needed by the company are hired on a non-*seishain* basis.

These non-*seishain* are referred to by various terms, such as *shoku-taku* (contract employee), *paato* (full-time "part-timer"), *kogaisha no shain* (employee of a subsidiary), and *haken jugyoin* (employee sent from a temporary agency). These non-*seishain* employees, regardless of the content of their work, are viewed in a completely differently light by the company. Their position is inferior to that of the *seishain*. They are not members of the company family in the same way. The fact that they are not *seishain* makes their employment "temporary," even if they stay with the company for a number of years. They receive lower compensation

AMERICAN COMPANIES BEGIN TO GO TWO-TIER

The recent recession in the United States has prompted many American companies to downsize their workforces and rethink their approaches to staffing. The result is an emerging pattern that resembles the two-tier Japanese labor management model—reduced reliance on regular full-time employees, with increased use of part-time, temporary, and contract workers.º The ranks of these "contingent workers" are predicted to grow to make up half of the U.S. labor force by the year 2000.ᴾ

The difference is that in the United States this is a new phenomenon. In Japan it is entrenched—virtually every firm employs both *seishain* and non-*seishain* and has done so for decades. Furthermore, in Japan the distinction between core and noncore employees is sharper than in the United States. Even "permanent" employees of U.S. firms may be let go at any time, yet the stable long-term employment that Japanese companies offer *seishain* contrasts starkly with the non-*seishain's* lack of job security.

and benefits (with the exception of those *shokutaku* who have highly marketable technical skills) and have little job security or prospects for advancement. The personnel department doesn't give them training, evaluate their performance, or rotate them to other posts, and may not maintain even rudimentary records on them. They are hired to perform specific tasks, not to be groomed as generalists. They are not represented by the company union or, for that matter, any other union.[4] The repercussions of this distinction in employment status should not be underestimated, since the use of secondary employment categories is so deeply entrenched in Japanese personnel practices.

Since they can be hired and fired as needed, these non-*seishain* employees provide the flexibility that the company loses when it commits itself to lifetime employment for its *seishain*. For example, companies lay off temporary employees in economic downturns, using them as a cushion to protect the lifetime employment security of the *seishain*, and then hire new temporaries when things pick up again. Explains Victor Company of Japan personnel manager Mizuo Yoshida, "The point of having part-timers is so we can make adjustments according to production."[5] Using non-*seishain* as buffers in this way is an accepted practice because their relationship with the company is of a limited contractual nature—the company is purchasing well-defined services for a specific time period. The company owes its *shokutaku* and *paato* nothing more than the wages specified in their contracts. In the case of subsidiary and *haken jugyoin* employees, they are aware of their company's subordinate status and must accept the fact that *seishain* of the parent company control the circumstances of their employment.

FOREIGN HIRED HANDS

The two-tier system of core, all-purpose *seishain* employees and expendable, special-purpose non-*seishain* employees extends to Japanese companies' international operations. Most employees hired by Japanese firms overseas, despite whatever high-ranking titles they may hold, are in fact not *seishain* of the parent company in Japan. Usually they are officially categorized by the headquarters personnel staff either as *shokutaku* employees or as employees of a subsidiary. Either way, this means that locally hired employees are not "plugged into" the headquarters-controlled system that plans the careers of *seishain* and eventually moves them into management positions. Similarly, in Japan, non-Japanese employees (especially those who are not Asian) are most often hired on a *shokutaku* basis.

Being excluded from the core group of *seishain* can make non-Japanese employees essentially "foreigners" to the corporation as a whole, junior members of the company family. To the extent that senior management positions are reserved for the *seishain*, non-*seishain* status can significantly decrease the career prospects of non-Japanese employees, leading to a rice-paper ceiling.

To distinguish between their *shokutaku* in and out of Japan, Japanese companies often refer to their overseas employees as *genchi sutaffu*, which is rendered into English using terms such as "local employees" or "national staff." The *seishain* are in turn referred to as "rotating staff" or simply "Japanese staff." However, it is important to underscore that the *seishain*/non-*seishain* division is not made strictly on lines of race or nationality, but on where the employee was hired. Japanese nationals who are hired directly by the overseas office are also classified as local

LOCALLY HIRED JAPANESE

Many Japanese affiliates in the United States hire Japanese nationals on a local basis. These Japanese nationals may have attended an American college or graduate school, married Americans, or for some other reason decided to live in the United States. The situation of these locally hired Japanese employees often falls somewhere between that of Japanese expatriates and locally hired American employees. Fluent in the Japanese language and familiar with Japanese culture, they often possess the same workstyles as Japanese expatriates. On the other hand, they are often more fluent in English and more comfortable with American culture. Also,

their assimilation into the U.S. labor market and their non-*seishain* status may give them attitudes that are similar to the American employees. In fact, because they are more familiar with Japanese personnel practices, they may feel the exclusion from the *seishain* system more keenly.

Often, due to their understanding of both cultures, locally hired Japanese nationals become the interface between the expatriates and the American employees. Says one Japanese woman who works at the branch of a Japanese commercial bank, "I feel like I have to be a bridge between the two cultures."

staff and usually find that they have the same limitations on their career prospects as non-Japanese employees. The situation of these Japanese local staff members underscores the fact that the problems involved in integrating local employees go beyond the language and cultural issues often cited by Japanese executives.

From an American perspective, the realization that the company does not treat all employees equally can be disconcerting. What follows is one American's reaction to discovering how his company classified its non-Japanese employees.

A large Japanese bank had prepared a roster of all its employees. This roster was printed in Japanese and had been prepared by the head office's personnel department for use by Japanese employees. Jeff, a Japanese-speaking American working at the bank's headquarters, was given a copy. "When this thing landed on my desk, I thumbed through it to see how they had listed my department, and I didn't like what I saw. Then when I turned to the pages showing the overseas subsidiaries, I was flabbergasted."

The listing for Jeff's section contained the names of only half the section members—those who were Japanese. Jeff's name and those of the rest of the non-Japanese members of his section were at the end of the listing for the department, along with the names of the other half dozen non-Japanese employees from the department's various other sections. Their names were listed, under the heading "*Shokutaku*," in alphabetical order without any indication of their titles, responsibilities, or section affiliations. This was in sharp contrast to the way the Japanese staff were listed with their titles under the sections they were affiliated with. Jeff was outraged. "Looking at this listing, it didn't even look like I was a part of the team. It showed that I was regarded as completely peripheral!"

The listings for the bank's overseas offices weren't much different. Take, for example, the New York subsidiary. Its English-language annual report, prepared in New York, showed that the management team consisted of a Japanese president and four executive vice presidents, two Japanese and two American. However, the Japanese employee roster painted a different picture. Listed at the top of the page were all the head office Japanese staff who had been sent to work at the subsidiary—the president, the two executive vice presidents, and three first vice presidents. Under that, the names of the U.S.-hired staff appeared, listed in alphabetical order and without titles. The names of the two American executive vice presidents were interspersed with all the others. It seemed that, in the eyes of the head office personnel department, they were of no more note than the secretaries and clerks whose names were included on the same list. Jeff expressed amazement at what he saw—"from an American perspective, this was certainly hypocrisy."

DIFFERENT TREATMENT CAUSES FRICTION

The distinctions made between *seishain* and non-*seishain* are problematic because locally hired employees are not given the chance to become *seishain*, no matter how impressive their credentials, what valuable skills and experiences they possess, how long and loyally they have served the company, or how fluent their Japanese. Since only Japanese hired in Japan can become *seishain*, from an American standpoint there is discrimination in terms of opportunity. (A racial issue also arises here, since the expatriate *seishain* are of Japanese ethnicity, and the locally hired employees are usually not.)

The distinction between *seishain* and non-*seishain* would not be important if it were a mere formality used for administrative purposes. However, in practice the *seishain*/non-*seishain* distinction can be the source of differences in treatment. The following are some examples.

David had worked at a Japanese bank's New York branch for several years. He wished to move to Los Angeles for personal reasons, and since his bank had a branch there, he asked if it would be possible to be transferred. He was told that he was considered to be an employee of the New York branch only. If he wished to try to obtain a position at the bank's Los Angeles branch, David would have to quit and then reapply on the same basis as a complete stranger to the company. Not only does this sort of treatment suggest that non-*seishain* have second-class status, but it also represents a waste of the company's prior training of that individual. In many Japanese firms, the ability to transfer between offices is linked to one's formal status in the company, and *seishain* are the only ones who are eligible for transfers. This means that the experience-building and horizon-broadening aspects of transfers are reserved for *seishain*.

Gerald is a manager at a securities firm. Okabe, a younger Japanese expatriate, reports to him, according to the organizational chart. However, Gerald has no real power over Okabe because Okabe is managed under the Japan-based system. Decisions concerning Okabe's compensation and future advancement are made in Japan, with no consideration of Gerald's evaluation of his performance. As a result, Okabe often seems to ignore Gerald's directions and concentrates on pleasing the Japanese managers and polishing his image in the eyes of the head office. In effect, the fact that Okabe is covered by a different system allows him to flout the hierarchy of the local organization. This difference in status that results from the existence of two different systems is an important factor undermining the authority of American managers at many Japanese firms. In a study of a Japanese securities company in New York, sociologist Miwako Kidahashi observed that "The lack of significance of local officers as evaluators inevitably contributes to their lack of authority over the Tokyo staff, because rating power is a major tool by which authority is effectively exercised."[6]

In another example, many American employees of Japanese companies point out that while the head office personnel department may be lavish in its educational spending on Japanese employees, the local organization is unwilling to underwrite any type of educational program for the American employees. One American woman who worked for a Japanese commercial bank felt that "there is a two-class structure in terms of what Japanese and Americans get. The company is really tight with us. Outside seminars and training are nonexistent, unless it's free and then there's a chance you could go, but even then it is looked over seriously because it would take you away from work. I decided to study for a set of professional qualification examinations, and there was no support in terms of time off to study, or subsidies for test fees or seminars. But one of my Japanese colleagues had been sent to graduate school in the United States, all expenses paid!" Situations such as this signal that the company wants to invest in its "lifetime" *seishain,* while it views overseas employees as "temporary" or "peripheral."

As these examples suggest, many fundamental aspects of how personnel management is conducted at the overseas operation may be determined by whether one is a locally hired staff or a *seishain* sent from Japan. The main categories of difference are compensation, job security, opportunities for growth and advancement, and indirect effects.

Compensation and Fringe Benefits

Differing compensation levels for expatriates and locally hired employees result from the fact that Japanese expatriates' compensation is determined by the head office personnel department, while locally hired employees' compensation is determined by the subsidiary under the local payroll practices. To the extent that the philosophies and budgets of the head office personnel managers and the local personnel managers differ, gaps emerge between the compensation of the two different groups. For example, expatriates' compensation packages may be higher than those of the American employees due to various special allowances made for living outside Japan. While such a pattern is not unusual at multinationals in general, such differences serve to accentuate the fact that Japanese and American employees have different statuses.

Job Security

One of the most obvious contrasts in the personnel standards applied to Japanese and American employees can occur when there is a downsizing. In many cases, because a company has made a commitment of life-time employment to its Japanese *seishain*, it will transfer them back to Japan rather than lay them off when it downsizes its U.S. operations. However, because Japanese companies explicitly avoid making such commitments to their American employees, they feel free to lay them off American-style. While such layoffs are common practice at U.S. firms, at Japanese firms they serve as a reminder of the differences in employment status, since expatriates hold on to their jobs while Americans are let go. Such a difference in treatment can leave a company ripe for lawsuits. Several well-publicized recent court cases against Japanese companies have had this theme.[7]

Opportunities for Growth and Advancement

Limited opportunity for advancement is a frequent concern of Americans who work at Japanese companies.[8] Many middle- and upper-level managers find that they hit a rice-paper ceiling, above which only Japanese expatriates can rise. Employees at lower levels often see limited growth potential and feel that the company is unconcerned about grooming them for management positions. The following quote from a young American who left his job at a Japanese trading company dramatizes this outlook: "There was a high turnover of talented white-collar staff. There were few people I could look to as mentors and no clear path to show where I would be if I stayed on for ten years, since fewer than 5 percent of the general managers were American. The opportunities were limited. I knew I had better go elsewhere if I wanted to advance in the business world."

HUMANE OR INEFFICIENT?

To preserve their flexibility and to protect themselves legally, Japanese firms in the United States do not promise lifetime employment to their American employees. However, if there is no pressing need to downsize, Japanese managers may be reluctant to lay off U.S. employees. This approach is welcomed by some layoff-weary Americans as a more humane way to conduct business, while others see it less positively.

For example, Harold told the management of his bank that one of his subordinates was underperforming and should be dismissed. He was sternly told, "This is the clay that you have been given. As a manager, it is your job to mold it." Harold restructured the subordinate's activities to move him away from customer calling to financial analysis, his relative strength. The subordinate is now showing improved performance. Says Harold, "Management's attitude forced me to think harder about how I could develop his potential."

Some American managers are uncomfortable with this philosophy. Comments one manager at an electronics firm, "There is this obsession with keeping people around. People who have announced their intention to resign have been persuaded to stay with large salary increases. The Japanese seem to think that they lose face when someone leaves, and they would never consider firing someone. But I think we just end up with a lot of deadwood."

The lack of opportunities for growth and advancement appears to be a very common reason for Americans leaving or wanting to leave their positions at Japanese employers. In many cases, particularly if employees are young or ambitious, this factor seems to be significantly more important than compensation in affecting whether or not they decide to remain with the firm. Over time, the lack of growth and advancement opportunities may also outweigh factors such as compensation, work environment, and job content. A comment from an American banker gives insight into this line of thinking: "The Americans here don't see any future. They keep rotating Japanese in and out of the top spots. Consideration of Americans for those posts is out of the question. The people are nice, the work interesting, but I know I'm going nowhere. That's why I'm going to leave as soon as I get a chance."

Why do many Americans feel that the long-term opportunities for them are limited in Japanese-owned firms? The most obvious factor is that Japanese expatriates often dominate the upper-level positions. According to one headhunter who places executives in Japanese companies, "One of the frustrations that still remains for many Americans is that they feel they can never reach the top of an organization because the senior positions tend to be populated by Japanese who are sent every three to five years on rotation. That's a problem that's still remaining . . . I think it's very discouraging when you have a large percentage of the senior management—actually or almost 100 percent—being Japanese in the company. If you're a middle-level manager you feel 'What's the point?'" Such exclusion from upper-level posts is a frequent theme in discrimination lawsuits filed by American employees against Japanese companies.[9] The differences in future opportunities between local employees and Japanese expatriates is also a strong undercurrent in other types of internal friction at Japanese firms, because it is a significant determinant of the power relations in the organization.

The American concept of a career path is at odds with the *shokutaku* mentality that Japanese companies often use when hiring non-Japanese. At the recruitment stage, the *shokutaku* mentality and common American personnel practices are similar: Hire someone whose qualifications match the required job duties. However, usual American practice is that once hired, a person who performs well on the job will be given increasing responsibility, promotions, or rotation to another position within the organization. In contrast, a *shokutaku* is hired to do a specific job and only that job. Unlike the *seishain,* who are actively trained and groomed for increasingly important roles in the organization, *shokutaku* are there to utilize their existing skills. Because locally hired employees are thought of as *shokutaku* they aren't part of the company's overall human resource development strategy and the head office may not make any provision for their training or consider them for top management positions. Whatever training, development, and upward movement they receive is likely to come from within the local subsidiary, which may have limited resources or lack the authority or will to make personnel changes.

Japanese firms do not necessarily have written rules that prevent non-*seishain* from attaining certain positions. It is more a result of the fact that only *seishain* receive what the firm considers most important in filling such posts: training in the company's methods, exposure to many facets of the company's business, and the opportunity to develop a personal network and reputation within the company. An American banker contrasts his situation with that of his Japanese colleagues by saying "They come here for three to five years and they know they are going to get a new assignment at the end. It might be Tokyo, it might be London, it might be anywhere in the world. They are continuously challenged and they are trained to be good general bankers, because after their assignment here they might go into something which is completely different. And the Americans, we sort of sit here and never move. They may give us new titles, but it really doesn't mean much. It's just to make us happy. Our jobs never change, so we stagnate."

To the extent that the head office personnel department views locally hired employees as *shokutaku* under the jurisdiction of the overseas operation, it is unlikely to keep track of how many locally hired employees the company has in a given country and which of them has management potential. One hallmark of Japanese human resource management is that personnel decisions tend to be made on the basis of a generalized awareness within the company of the people available and the skills that they have demonstrated over an extended period of time. If the head office personnel managers (and other top managers with decision-making influence) are unaware of the skills and contributions of locally hired managers, they will not be considered when personnel decisions are made at the head office. Nor will they be looked upon as resources of the company as a whole that should be nurtured and valued.

A hypothetical example illustrates this phenomenon. Sam has been hired by the New York office of a major Japanese financial institution to help develop a new business area. He has a wealth of experience and connections in this area that he developed while working in a similar capacity at a blue-chip American bank. Tanaka, an up-and-coming Japanese expatriate, is assigned to work with Sam. Tanaka has little experience in this new business area, so his role consists primarily of monitoring Sam's work and learning about the business. Tanaka also keeps the head office informed about their progress and, when necessary, negotiates details with head office personnel.

A year and a half passes, and Sam's hard work has resulted in the development of a thriving new business area for the bank. The head office is pleased as punch: "We knew that Tanaka had a lot of talent!" But the head office has all but forgotten about Sam's existence. All communication with the head office has been written in Japanese with Tanaka's name on it, so he has come to be identified with the project. Perhaps the head office staff dimly remembers that there was some locally hired employee working with Tanaka, but they certainly aren't aware of the extent of his contribution. In fact, it is in Tanaka's interest to downplay Sam's role so that he himself may be perceived in the best possible light. Of course, Sam may receive some extra bonus or a salary increase through the locally managed compensation system in recognition of his efforts and accomplishments. However, it's Tanaka who is earning the "brownie points" at the head office that will enable him to climb the corporate ladder. As far as the head office is concerned, Sam isn't even on the ladder. He will not be considered for the posts that Tanaka will be considered for in the future.

The absence of attention from the head office to the tracking and training of American employees is often exacerbated by the fact that individual Japanese expatriates are unprepared to deal with American expectations about the role of direct supervisors in career planning and development. In Japan, an individual manager need not necessarily be concerned with the long-term development and career path of the people working below him. Those issues, along with compensation and promotion decisions, are handled completely by the personnel department. In contrast, U.S. central personnel departments do not enjoy as prominent a role, and personnel management decisions about individual employees are often largely in the hands of their immediate supervisors.

Thus, when a Japanese expatriate does not offer an American subordinate detailed information and advice about his or her career plans and prospects in the firm, he may in fact be acting no differently from how he would toward Japanese subordinates. From the American perspective, such a lack of career-related support and guidance becomes just another way in which Japanese managers are out of touch with their needs. In addition, with Japanese managers rotating back and forth from Japan every few years, American employees can slip through the cracks in the company's institutional memory. An employee may have been given certain expectations by one manager, only to see them forgotten or negated by the next manager. A further burden is placed on

American employees by the fact that they have to start from scratch and prove themselves to each new manager coming from Japan, rather than building on their prior accomplishments and reputation.

Indirect Effects

Because American employees are not *seishain,* they are not bound up in the complex web of ongoing human relationships that characterizes a Japanese firm. Over the course of their careers, Japanese build their credibility by trading favors and exchanging information with the contacts they have developed within the company.[10] As part of this process, an individual expatriate may invest extraordinary effort in fostering good relationships with the other Japanese in the office as well as colleagues back in Japan. Yet he may not be willing to extend the same information-sharing and relationship-building effort to an American employee. In his eyes, the American may be viewed as "here today, gone tomorrow"—in other words, the American is unlikely to represent a relationship that will prove valuable to the expatriate in the future. From a purely practical perspective, the busy expatriate may think, "Why should I expend valuable effort to communicate information to someone who may be gone soon? Because he is not a *seishain* he's of secondary importance, and even if I do him a favor he is unlikely to be able to do anything useful for me in return." Thus the individual incentives and actions of expatriates can reflect the *seishain*/non-*seishain* division and serve to enhance its importance.

THE "AMERICANIZATION" DILEMMA

"Americanization" implies the localization of managerial processes—putting greater decision-making power into the hands of American employees and reducing the number of expatriates in order to give Americans the majority of management positions. Such localization implies a movement away from the ethnocentric management model.

To the extent that a Japanese firm is able to "localize" or "Americanize" its management ranks and decision-making processes, it is a positive development. Some Japanese firms have made great strides in this direction by putting Americans in top positions, limiting the number of Japanese expatriates, giving the American operation more independent decision-making latitude, and conducting important communication in English. Americans at firms which have succeeded in localization will likely read this chapter and say to themselves, "So what?" Where localization is successful, distinctions between *seishain* and others have little importance. American employees are given high-ranking posts and commensurate responsibility despite the fact that they are not *seishain*.

Other Japanese firms find themselves unable to "Americanize" due to the powerful centripetal forces that characterize most Japanese organizations. They may localize personnel management for American employees by setting up an American-based system, and even place some Americans in highly visible positions, but their management processes remain focused on the head office in Japan. For Japanese companies that fit this pattern, true "Americanization" in the sense of polycentric style management is highly unlikely. The division between *seishain* and non-*seishain* prevents it.

In some cases, "Americanization" is espoused, but remains superficial. The Japanese managers make statements such as "We do things the American way" or "We are an American company that just happens to have a Japanese parent." They would like people to believe that they are no different from western multinationals in terms of their organizational structure and style. Yet large numbers of Japanese expatriates continue to be sent, and the company's way of doing things remains Japan-centered. Why do such firms claim to be "Americanized" or "Americanizing?" Sociologist Miwako Kidahashi suggests that, "Since Americanization is the normative expectation of the society, the company is more or less forced to present such an image, regardless of its intention or ability to do so, if it is to be favorably accepted."[11] To the extent that ethnocentrically managed firms attempt to create a facade of Americanization, they expose themselves to resentment and cynicism on the part of American employees, because the superior status of the *seishain* will eventually show through.

HOW THE SEISHAIN/NON-SEISHAIN
DISTINCTION AFFECTS YOU

The distinction between *seishain* and non-*seishain* may affect you greatly, or it may not affect you at all. It depends on your firm's size, structure, and policies. It also depends on your particular role within the company.

- *Firm size.* The *seishain*/non-*seishain* distinction is of less importance in large firms with extensive, localized U.S. presences. For example, in many large firms that have significant sales and manufacturing operations, there are ample career opportunities within the U.S. operation itself. These companies realize that they need Americans in key posts in order to operate effectively in the United States and have developed substantive career paths within the framework of their U.S. operations. On the other hand, at service-sector firms and manufacturers with smaller U.S. presences, the distinction between *seishain* and non-*seishain* may be a sharp one, with locally hired employees relegated to clearly subordinate roles.

- *Firm structure.* The more localized your firm's operations and the fewer the Japanese expatriates, the less important the *seishain*/non-*seishain* distinction. In firms that have large numbers of Japanese expatriates, and where the Japanese head office has significant day-to-day involvement in the U.S. affiliate's decision-making, the *seishain*/non-*seishain* division can loom quite large.

- *Policies.* The distinction between *seishain* and non-*seishain* can assume either great or little importance, depending on the policies of the individual firm. In some companies, employment categories are mere formalities and have minimal impact on how business is conducted. Other firms use the *seishain*/non-*seishain* distinction in nearly every aspect of their day-to-day operations, and it becomes a mechanism for excluding American employees from decision-making and career advancement.

- *Your role.* The *seishain*/non-*seishain* distinction may be less important to you if your job is a specialized one uniquely related to the

U.S. operation—for example, in legal affairs or personnel. If your post is one for which no Japanese are likely to be qualified, the fact that you are not a *seishain* may not affect your career prospects. Furthermore, if you are in a staff position that has the function of advising management, it may make little difference to your career potential whether the management you are advising is Japanese or American. The essence of the *shokutaku* concept is hiring someone with specific skills for a well-defined position. If you are comfortable with a specialist role, then your lack of *seishain* status may not be a significant issue. On the other hand, if you are in or aspire to a general management or line-management position, you may find that the posts above you are filled exclusively by Japanese expatriates.

• *Your location.* Your status as a *shokutaku* may be of particular importance if you are working in Japan. The next chapter will discuss this issue in further detail.

AMERICAN SEISHAIN?

Theoretically, one way for Japanese companies to solve the problems engendered by the non-*seishain* status of American employees would be to simply let them all become *seishain.* Or, employees who express interest or meet certain criteria (such as number of years worked for the company, rank attained, or a Japanese-language test) could be invited to become *seishain.* Yet, even if they were offered the opportunity to become *seishain,* most Americans would probably decline. This is because the personnel management methods for *seishain,* as described in Chapter 9, are highly rigid and do not place a high priority on meeting individual needs and recognizing individual performance. Most Americans would likely object to the loss of control over their careers that becoming a *seishain* would imply, as well as to the seniority-based pay system.

This issue is at the root of the problems that Japanese companies experience in managing American employees. Compared with U.S. practice, personnel management in Japan is extremely rigid. Japanese companies are accustomed to managing employees in a one-size-fits-all manner, with relatively little accommodation for differences in ability, skills, and performance among employees. They are also accustomed to managing employees who are locked into their jobs at one firm and are not looking to the external labor market. They can treat their Japanese employees in ways that would not be tolerated by analogous American employees, because they do not have to worry that they will leave in search of greener pastures or broader horizons. These Japanese-style personnel management methods would not satisfy American expectations.

Only by changing the personnel system for *seishain* to make it more similar to non-Japanese norms would Japanese employers be able to make it attractive for large numbers of their overseas employees to become *seishain*. The system would need to be made more flexible in order to accommodate employees who are not willing to accept sudden transfer orders from the company. It would also have to become more responsive to the needs and aspirations of employees than it is currently. It may be necessary for Japanese companies to make such changes anyhow due to the growing pressures on their domestic personnel systems (see Chapter 12), but they will not do so overnight.

ADDRESSING THE DISTINCTION BETWEEN JAPANESE AND LOCALLY HIRED EMPLOYEES

Some Japanese companies have begun to address the structural division between Japanese and American employees by blurring the lines between the two groups in terms of their functions and opportunities within the context of the U.S. operation. To the extent that your company is making or has made efforts in the following directions, it is a positive sign. On the other hand, if your company previously had some of these policies but has recently eliminated them, it is a step backward.

- *Conscious inclusion of Americans.* Some firms have adopted policies that make it easier for Americans to participate in decision-making, such as including Americans in all internal meetings, and limiting conversations and written communications to English. Another related effort is to increase English-language communication from Japan, and to involve American employees in contacts with head office.

- *Putting Americans in managerial posts.* Some firms have made conscious decisions to reduce the number of expatriates and put more Americans into managerial positions. Other firms have made the highly visible statement of putting an American in the top post.

- *Developing American employees.* Some Japanese companies have shown a willingness to invest in the development of their American employees by providing extensive training programs. These may take place in the United States or involve trips to Japan. The most progressive firms have instituted "reverse transfer" (*gyaku shukko*) programs that replicate for American employees the horizon-broadening rotations given to Japanese *seishain*. Under such programs, American employees are assigned to work in Japan for a period from six months to several years. During this time they are exposed to the company's overall business, deepen their understanding of Japanese

AN EXAMPLE OF MANAGEMENT TRANSITION

Several years ago, Nippon Credit Bank's New York branch decided, where possible, to groom locally hired employees to take over positions from expatriates. The American manager who now heads up the real estate area describes how the transition was made in his department from expatriate management to local management. "When I was hired, it was to come in as a comanager with a Japanese national. The understanding was that if my performance was satisfactory, then he would go on to another assignment and I would be the sole manager." He and the Japanese expatriate developed "a mutually comfortable working relationship," and discovered that they had "similar ideas about approaching business strategy, tackling problems, reading situations, and coming up with solutions." During that time "there was a slow, gradual transition of responsibility for the management of the loans." Also, the two comanagers went together to Tokyo for ten days, where the American manager learned more about headquarters and met Tokyo-based clients. Two years later, when the Japanese comanager was transferred to Paris and the American comanager took over responsibility for the real estate area, "It wasn't a sudden break . . . I had been working with my Japanese comanager on the management and decision-making, so it was a smooth transition."

BRINGING OVERSEAS EMPLOYEES TO JAPAN

Nissan Motor's program for bringing overseas employees to work in Japan is part of its long-term goal of localizing its overseas management. According to a Human Resources Development Department representative at Tokyo headquarters, "We rely on local staff members abroad. It's only reasonable that they should understand Japan to some extent, just as our Japanese employees need to understand about doing business overseas. Internationalization . . . depends on building up large numbers of people who have actual experience working outside their own country."

Nissan's Japan-based training program was begun in 1990, when twenty-eight engineers and their families were brought to Japan for eighteen months from the company's manufacturing subsidiaries in Australia, Spain, Mexico, the United Kingdom, and the United States. An analogous program for middle managers was begun in 1992. The six individuals who took part were assigned to the Legal, Information Systems, Overseas Purchasing, Overseas Service, and Production Control departments at headquarters.

So that they can work side by side with Japanese staff, all trainees are required to have completed 100 hours of Japanese-language training before arriving in Japan. They then receive 200 hours of additional instruction before beginning work.

culture and the company's business methods, and develop networks of relationships within the company. Some Japanese firms in the United States have also begun to experiment with developmental transfers within the U.S. operation.

In addition to the types of activities described above, many Japanese companies have attempted to finesse the process of "internationalization" by hiring young foreigners to work at the head office in Japan. The idea is to treat them like young Japanese employees, training them in the company's business and corporate culture. These employees will then ripen into ideal managers for the firm's overseas operations—combining the best aspects of Japanese and American employees. However, this approach can have a variety of pitfalls, not only for the company but especially for the individual non-Japanese employee. In fact, the basic structural issue of the *seishain*/non-*seishain* division is often at the root of the problems that Japanese companies have in retaining and effectively utilizing the non-Japanese employees whom they hire to work in Japan.

11

Working in Japan for a Japanese Company

Sometimes I meet people from our overseas offices. One thing they always complain about is the conversations in Japanese that go on all the time. Sometimes I will be put in a difficult position. We'll be in a meeting with someone from the overseas office and one of the Japanese will turn to me and speak in Japanese, with the person who doesn't speak Japanese sitting right there wondering what we are saying. Also, sometimes I feel guilty because I send letters in Japanese to our overseas sales people, even though I know that there are non-Japanese who work with them. It says my name at the top and then all the rest is in Japanese. They must wonder what I'm saying. And when people from our overseas offices come to Japan, I wonder how honestly they talk with me. Because I speak Japanese and work in the Japanese office, I am one of them.

AMERICAN WORKING AT A JAPANESE ELECTRONICS FIRM IN TOKYO

Recently, it has been something of a fad among large Japanese companies to hire non-Japanese as white-collar workers for their head offices. Having foreign faces around is tangible evidence that a company is active in the international arena. The Japanese press's glamorization of this trend, combined with spurs from the Ministry of International Trade and Industry (MITI) to "internationalize" in response to the trade and investment frictions of the 1980s, has created a sort of social pressure for companies to jump on the foreigner-hiring bandwagon. At companies that don't currently hire many non-Japanese, personnel managers tend to feel that they are behind the times. One trading company is reportedly so self-conscious about this issue that it deliberately exaggerates the number of foreign employees at its head office to inquiring journalists.

Of course, Japanese companies have many reasons for hiring foreigners that are more substantial than just social pressure. A company may have any one or more of the following motivations for hiring a particular individual: to use their special skills or knowledge, to fill areas where Japanese applicants are scarce, or to create an "international" atmosphere at the head office.

Special skills or knowledge. For certain posts, a non-Japanese may be more qualified than a Japanese due to the very fact that he or she is not Japanese. For example, translators, language instructors, writers, international advertising and public relations coordinators, and liaisons with overseas offices and customers are naturally able to perform more efficiently and effectively in their native languages and cultures than Japanese employees using a second language. Marketing specialists, international purchasing officers, credit analysts, and lawyers draw on specific knowledge of conditions in their home countries that few Japanese are likely to possess. By using non-Japanese in such posts at the head office, Japanese companies can strengthen their ability to do international business.

Substitute for Japanese personnel. Japanese companies may also recruit non-Japanese in areas where there is a shortage of qualified Japanese personnel. For example, this is the motivation behind many manufacturers' recent efforts to recruit research and development staff from overseas. Yet the current recession and evaporation of the overall labor shortage may be reducing this motivation for hiring non-Japanese.

Creating an "international" atmosphere at the head office. "Internationalization" is one of the most commonly cited motivations for hiring non-Japanese to work in the head office. Undoubtedly, sprinkling a few foreigners among the head office departments helps staff members to

Julie studied Japanese at the University of Washington. After graduating, she worked in retail until a job offer from a small Japanese computer firm enabled her to fulfill her dream of working in Japan.

"Originally, I was hired to be a liaison for product maintenance. But eventually that became a minor role. Everyone asked me to do other things, since I was the only native English speaker in the company. Finally one day I asked if I could change the title on my card to something more descriptive of what I'm actually doing."

Julie's activities range from interacting with suppliers and existing distributors, to negotiating new distribution agreements. "Small high-tech companies like this one don't have the resources to do international work. I provide that resource for them." She feels that her greatest job difficulty is technical rather than cultural. "I don't have a high-tech background, so often I have difficulty understanding the technical details. I get frustrated with my own ignorance." Other than that, however, Julie's job satisfaction is high. "I really enjoy what I'm doing. Sure there are frustrations to working in the Japanese environment, but you just have to accept the way things are done here."

---

become more at ease working with non-Japanese. The different approaches to day-to-day business and interpersonal relations that non-Japanese bring to the table can also bring a breath of fresh air to stagnant policies and practices.[1] These goals are admirable—but only when combined with more concrete job responsibilities. "Internationalizing" alone is a pretty vague job description, and herein lies the danger of this motivation for recruiting non-Japanese. Just hiring foreigners for the sake of internationalization risks making them into mere decorations. Commented one woman working in Tokyo, "My company really wasn't sure why it needed me when it hired me. It just wanted me as a brand name accessory, like a luxury leather handbag. It's as if my Ivy League degree were a status symbol, like Gucci or Chanel." While some are able to carve out interesting and satisfying niches for themselves as "internationalizers," unfortunately many foreigners end up becoming "pet *gaijin* (foreigners)" who are displayed to customers and reporters, but don't have any real responsibilities.

HOW YOU CAN FIT IN

The most immediate challenge for you as a non-Japanese working in Japan is adapting to everyday life in the Japanese workplace. The cultural issues discussed in earlier chapters weigh even more heavily when in Japan. Japanese expatriates in the United States are expected to make a significant effort to learn English and adapt to American work habits. Conversely, when you are in Japan, the burden is on you to adjust. The major issues you are likely to encounter include:

Language.   Learning Japanese, or improving your existing skills, is essential. Try to convince your company to subsidize lessons (many do). If you are at an intermediate level, start reading Japanese newspapers and learn how to write memos and reports in Japanese. (As you progress, keep in mind that as your Japanese improves, you'll be expected to become more subtle, more polite.)

Salaries.   Japanese pay scales, particularly for younger employees, tend to be significantly lower than those in America, and raises are gradual. This is the reference point that a Japanese firm is working from when it considers your initial salary as well as the amount of your annual salary increase. This may make it difficult for you to obtain the compensation that you might otherwise command in the United States, or at a foreign firm in Japan. This is particularly true now that Japanese firms are tightening their belts—foreign employees may be viewed as expensive, expendable luxuries.

Vacations.   Foreign employees are likely to experience the same pressure that is placed on Japanese employees not to take their vacation days, or at least not to take too many of them at once. You may find little sympathy for your desire to take all your days off at one time so that you can visit your home in the United States. Also be aware that in Japan, sick-day allowances are virtually nonexistent—you may have to use your vacation time if you come down with the flu.

Long hours.   Copious overtime and obligatory after-work business gatherings almost always come with the territory. If you don't go along, you'll be left out.

Special opportunities. Your situation as a non-Japanese may give you special opportunities that are not open to your Japanese colleagues. Your native English abilities may be called upon for high-profile or glamorous projects that involve international topics. You may receive more personal attention from superiors and top executives than a comparable Japanese employee. These opportunities should of course be pursued, but be aware of the potential for jealousy from Japanese colleagues.

Lack of interesting work. Many foreigners at Japanese companies find themselves with little worthwhile to do. This may be a result of one or more of the following factors. First, it is common for young Japanese employees to do routine work for years, so managers may not understand why a non-Japanese employee expects challenging assignments immediately. One American who joined a major electronics firm found himself sorting the department's incoming faxes for weeks on end. When he complained to his superior, the response was "When I first joined the company, I spent the first three years transcribing telexes. You

SPECIAL ISSUES FOR WOMEN WORKING IN JAPAN

Western women working in Japan often must confront expectations that are shaped by the role of Japanese women in their company. The expected behaviors may include wearing a schoolgirlish uniform, serving tea, and tidying up around the office. Many western women feel compelled to refuse, and this can antagonize not only the men in the office, but particularly the Japanese women. Ultimately, each person has to strike a balance between her principles and avoiding open warfare in the office.

One American woman working at a Japanese computer company decided not to protest taking a turn vacuuming the office, reasoning, "All the other women are doing it, so fighting it would just create a big stink. I'd rather spend my energies on my work." Meanwhile, an American woman at another firm caused an uproar in her company by wearing suits instead of the women's uniform. Finally the company relented: it made the uniform optional for all female employees throughout the company.

The difficulty of these symbolic issues for women working in Japan is balanced by advantages that western men may not enjoy. Japanese businessmen are very curious about western businesswomen. This can get you increased attention and greater access to upper-level executives.

can learn a lot that way, so stop complaining." Second, a manager may feel that he needs time to become comfortable with, and learn to trust, the new foreign employee. Third, your manager may not know how to use a foreign employee effectively. This is particularly true when, as is apt to happen, personnel departments plunk foreigners down in sections that have not necessarily requested them and are unprepared to receive them. Unable to understand your talents and motivations, your manager may not know what to do with you. He may give you menial tasks to keep you suitably busy, or nothing to do at all.

If you find yourself in the situation of having insufficient or unstimulating activities, you should take it upon yourself to find something substantive to do. Saying to yourself, "they hired me, they should figure out how to use me" is the wrong approach. Look around, talk to people, learn about the company's activities, and find out where you can add value. Try to make yourself useful in any way you can. Your boss will usually be willing to jump on any reasonable suggestion you might have for a new activity (as long as it doesn't require spending any money!), since it's embarrassing to have you sitting around doing nothing. Look at the situation as an opportunity rather than a problem. The company has given you the chance to shape your job and to explore what you would like to do and how you can best contribute.

SEPARATE PATH TO NOWHERE

Perhaps the most frustrating aspect of working in Japan is that you will be expected to fit in and act like a Japanese, but you can never be accepted in the same way as a Japanese. Being a foreigner working in a Japanese company is a sword that cuts both ways. You can use your foreign status to demand better pay and perks and to disregard some petty rules and protocol, but to the extent you do so, you call attention to yourself and set yourself further apart.

The fact that one cannot be fully accepted in the same way as a Japanese employee is partially due to racial, linguistic, and cultural factors.

SPECIAL ISSUES FOR MEN WORKING IN JAPAN

Just because Japan is a male-dominated society doesn't mean that as a man you will immediately be accepted as "one of the guys." Many Japanese men feel uncomfortable around western men, a result of pervasive negative stereotypes and competitive feelings. Typical western male aggressiveness may also be out of place in the Japanese workplace environment. Furthermore, since most Japanese language teachers are women, many western men speak overly feminine Japanese (find a male Japanese tutor if possible).

This discomfort on the part of the men in the office may be balanced by a great deal of interest from the "office ladies." However, one of the worst things you can do is to be labeled as someone who is only interested in the women in the office. Platonic friendships with members of the opposite sex are less common in Japan than in the West, so you may be misunderstood if you are perceived as spending too much time with female employees. Office romances should be avoided and handled extremely discreetly if they do develop.

Making the effort to attend office drinking parties and joining a company sports team or club are good ways to develop friendships with both male and female colleagues. Also, if you live in the company dormitory, be sure to participate in the various dorm activities.

However, an even more important factor is the unequal employment category to which non-Japanese are usually relegated. Although many companies hire non-Japanese from Asia (especially Asians who have attended Japanese universities) on the same basis as Japanese employees (*seishain*), non-Japanese are usually hired on a contractual basis (*shokutaku*). This classification leads to a rice-paper ceiling for many foreigners working at Japanese companies in Japan.

Non-Japanese who did not attend Japanese universities are usually able to accept the fact that they won't have the same status as Japanese employees when they first join the company. At this point, not only is the company checking them out, but they are checking the company out as well. Also, for those who see working at a Japanese company as a temporary position rather than a career, the *shokutaku* status is ideal. The problem with keeping non-Japanese as straight *shokutaku* comes over time when those who work hard, produce solid business results, and demonstrate a commitment to the company find that they do not have the same opportunities to progress as *seishain*. They are not on the same career ladder and are not given the same developmental opportunities. As non-Japanese *shokutaku* realize that their ability to advance in Japanese firms is hindered, many Japanese companies see high turnover of their foreign employees.

Unfortunately, this high turnover has only served to strengthen the stereotype of non-Japanese employees as job-hoppers with little loyalty. The Japanese company is likely to perceive itself as having bent over backward to accommodate foreign employees and make them happy. Unable to understand the motivations of non-Japanese employees who are accustomed to thinking of themselves as participants in a wider labor market, a Japanese company may not realize how its policies (or lack thereof) contribute to the turnover of non-Japanese employees. In order to encourage non-Japanese employees to stay with the firm for more than a few years, guarantees are needed, in the form of policies and precedents, that their efforts and loyalty will indeed be rewarded.

In formulating appropriate policies for foreign employees, Japanese companies will need to consider four issues:

- How can the company best utilize the skills and energy of non-Japanese employees?

- How can the company recognize the contributions of non-Japanese employees hired in Japan and confer on them appropriate status within the organization?

- How can the company make it possible for non-Japanese employees hired in Japan to remain with the firm if they want to return to their home country?

- How can the company provide career opportunities to non-Japanese employees who wish to remain in Japan and make their careers there?

Unfortunately, few Japanese companies have given serious thought to these questions. As a non-Japanese considering joining or remaining with a Japanese company in Japan, you should evaluate your future career potential in light of your company's response to these questions. In the long term, they are even more important than short-term considerations such as salary and working environment.

POLICIES FOR FOREIGN EMPLOYEES

If a Japanese company were to consider how it could reward foreigners hired in Japan for their contributions and confer upon them the status that would make a career with the firm attractive to them, what possibilities might there be? One option is to create a separate career path for *shokutaku*. The second option is to institute a mechanism by which *shokutaku* can become *seishain*. The following paragraphs will describe the policies of two companies: Fuji Bank, which has created a separate career path for *shokutaku*, and Sony, which invites non-Japanese to become *seishain* after a trial period as *shokutaku*.

Fuji Bank

Fuji Bank started hiring non-Japanese for line positions eight years ago but had a poor track record of keeping them on board. In an attempt to reduce this turnover, the company instituted a formal career path for the non-Japanese *shokutaku* at the head office. After putting in time and producing results, a *shokutaku* becomes eligible for the ranks of assistant manager and manager. This is the same scale in effect for the bank's locally hired staff at its overseas offices. This equivalency means that it is possible for a non-Japanese who works at the head office and achieves a certain rank there to return to his home country and join the local Fuji organization at the same level.

Recently, two head office non-Japanese employees, both in their sixth year at the bank, were the first to be promoted to the rank of assistant manager. In a touch that showed sensitivity to the subtle nuances of rank in a Japanese organization, the personnel department sent "assistant manager chairs"—they have arms—to replace their old armless chairs. These two employees are considered to be prime candidates to be sent to work in their home countries in the future. The exact logistics of such a move have yet to be formulated, but at least a system is in place that assures non-Japanese employees that it is possible and would be encouraged by the bank. In fact, the bank explicitly considers its non-Japanese employees at headquarters to be future top management material for its overseas offices.

When the career ladder for non-Japanese at the head office was established, the bank decided to keep them under the auspices of the International Division, which oversees the roughly two thousand locally hired staff around the world. The internal memo that established the promotion program for non-Japanese *shokutaku* did, however, leave open the possibility for a conversion to *seishain* status. This is an area that eventually will need to be addressed since some non-Japanese may prefer to stay in Japan rather than return to their home country. Also in need of long-term consideration will be the fact that two employment systems still exist—one for Japanese, another for non-Japanese.

Sony

Sony is widely known as one of the companies that has most aggressively recruited non-Japanese staff for its offices in Japan and has a progressive approach to human resource management in general. There are currently about a hundred non-Japanese *shokutaku* at Sony, primarily in the engineering and research areas but also distributed throughout other functions such as corporate planning and corporate communications.

Until four years ago, all non-Japanese who were not graduates of Japanese universities were classified at *shokutaku*. At that time, the company conducted a survey of its non-Japanese employees and found that many of those planning to make a career with the company were uncomfortable with their year-to-year contract status. They disliked being treated as special and felt that they ought to be part of the regular work force or at least be given that opportunity. As a result of that survey and the ensuing discussions, the decision was made to give employees the option of becoming *seishain*, and a number of employees did in fact request that their status be changed. Those who chose to become *seishain* had their personnel matters transferred from the auspices of the International Human Resources Group to the Head Office Human Resources Group. As a result they are employed under the same policies and procedures as the other *seishain*.

A Sony spokesman describes *seishain* status as offering a "more stable, secure position" within the company. Currently, most non-Japanese employees are hired on a *shokutaku* basis, and after two or three years are given the option of remaining *shokutaku* or switching to *seishain* status. The spokesman notes that "the company is now encouraging more non-Japanese people to seek *seishain* status . . . We see non-Japanese and Japanese employees very much on the same level, not just serving the company for a limited time year to year. We would like to see them dedicate themselves for a longer term and try to establish themselves on a long-range career plan. *Seishain* status would certainly help . . . for longer range plans." However, he acknowledges that some employees have other goals, and the company understands and respects that. The choice is left to the individual, and no one is forced to become a *seishain*.

Non-Japanese employees have become well assimilated into Sony's day-to-day business functions and are making valued contributions. For example, one American employee with a master's degree in chemical engineering, an M.B.A., and work experience with major American oil and high-tech companies joined Sony four years ago. He was looking for a position based in Japan, and was attracted by the progressiveness of Sony's personnel policies and its strong emphasis on international business. After participating in the six-week stints at a manufacturing facility and a retail sales outlet that are standard for new Sony employees, he was assigned to a planning area. His assignments have included worldwide production allocation, product strategy, and site selection for an overseas production facility. After only two years (and a switch to *seishain* status) he was promoted to manager. The promotion was primarily a result of his performance, while the fact that he had been a manager in his previous job was also taken into consideration. Overall, this employee feels that his experience has been "very positive" and is "looking forward to the future opportunities" at Sony. With a Japanese spouse, he envisions himself based in Japan long-term, but says he is prepared to go "wherever the company needs me to go."

For those non-Japanese employees who wish to return to their home country, as a general principle Sony encourages them to consider working in the local Sony subsidiary. As the Sony spokesman put it, for non-Japanese employees who have worked at the headquarters or manufacturing facilities in Japan, "Having learned how we do our business should certainly be a plus if they move to our subsidiaries overseas." However, whether a position can be found for every person who desires one "depends on what type of career he or she is looking for and what kind of opening we may have outside of Japan . . . [as well as] the individual's skills and experience levels." As a general rule, he states, "we do try to keep our employees in our subsidiaries . . . but it all depends on the situation. If there are no openings that fit this person, then we may have to part with each other."

If a non-Japanese with *seishain* status wished to return to their home country, their status and experience would be accounted for when they moved to the new position in their home country. To some extent this is still a theoretical issue, as there are only a few cases where non-Japanese *seishain* have been transferred. However, the company is careful to point out that it has an established policy of "moving people around for experience's sake." Japanese employees are sent to the United States or the United Kingdom for two-to-three-year stints. The company is moving locally hired staff around within the European Community, as well as between the United States and the United Kingdom. Thus, transferring non-Japanese *seishain* employees can be seen as part of this wider effort.

Of course, Sony didn't develop this ability to integrate non-Japanese into its operations overnight. To some extent it has been a process of trial, error, and further refinements, as demonstrated by the survey it conducted of non-Japanese employees. Through this process of continuous improvement, Sony has been able to develop policies and procedures that enable it to utilize the potential of non-Japanese employees. As the company spokesman put it, "Sony's been fairly globalized for a long time and having come through all these obstacles we've become fairly well adaptable to various situations, and flexibility is certainly one key point that we cherish here."

FROM HEAD OFFICE EMPLOYEE
TO OVERSEAS MANAGER

As the above example shows, hiring non-Japanese to work in the head office can be seen as a strategy for enriching the firm's domestic human resources. With the rise of marriages between Japanese and foreigners, the number of non-Japanese who want to reside in Japan permanently will surely grow. There are also those who want to remain in Japan because it offers a better standard of living than their home country, because they want to make use of the Japanese-language skills they so painstakingly acquired, or simply because they enjoy the country. A company's personnel policies should be flexible enough to offer those non-Japanese who plan to stay in Japan long-term the same career opportunities that are available to Japanese.

However, most non-Japanese working for Japanese firms in Japan probably want to return to their home countries eventually. This is also the usual expectation of the Japanese firm, and Japanese companies often say their goal in hiring non-Japanese to work in Japan is to develop future managers for their overseas operations. The new graduates from foreign universities will be blank slates on which the company can write its own values and ways of doing things. After being properly trained in Japan they will be able to return to their home countries to work in the company's subsidiaries. These Japan-trained non-Japanese will thus become "Janus-headed" managers with an understanding of and loyalty to the parent company while possessing the language and cultural background that will make them more effective overseas than a Japanese expatriate.[2]

This is a nice plan in theory, but it is too soon to tell whether it will work in practice. Unfortunately, few Japanese companies have developed concrete strategies for how to make such a plan workable, and many non-Japanese employees find other alternatives in the meantime. If it truly desires to train a future cadre of overseas managers from scratch, a Japanese company needs to be able to offer a mechanism for overseas transfer, without a loss of status, for employees who start their careers in Japan. It also needs to integrate them smoothly into the local operations once they arrive.

IF YOU'RE TRANSFERRING
TO YOUR FIRM'S U.S. OPERATION

As someone who has worked at the head office in Japan, you will have several potential advantages if you join your company's subsidiary in your home country. You will be able to interface more easily with the head office as well as the Japanese expatriates. Being familiar with Japanese culture, you will be accustomed to Japanese management and decision-making processes. You will also have developed a sensitivity to the internal politics of the head office and forged a network of relationships with the head office staff that will enable you to "work the system" effectively.

However, you may discover that your transfer to the overseas operation results in a decrease in your status. The Fuji Bank and Sony examples cited above demonstrate two mechanisms for maintaining the status of non-Japanese employees when they return to their home countries. However, most companies have not yet established such mechanisms. For example, Stan worked for a trading company in Tokyo and enjoyed being treated in exactly the same way as the Japanese employees. When the company transferred him to the United States, he became a local employee and immediately felt a rapid decline in his standing. As one of the local employees, Stan was ranked far below the Japanese expatriates, and was treated accordingly. In a similar case, John, a man who had worked for an automobile company in Japan, returned to the United States and was given a job in the local operation. When he encountered some personnel-related difficulties John contacted the head office, but was told, "You're a local employee now, you don't have anything to do with us."

Furthermore, your company may find it challenging to integrate you into the local organization. It may be difficult to find a position that suits your skills and experiences. Locally hired employees may look upon you with curiosity, and even suspicion or distrust. Your closer ties with the Japanese expatriates and your ability to elicit faster responses from the head office may invite their jealousy.

Your biggest potential hurdle as a person who has worked at the head office is gaining respect from the locally hired staff for your job skills. The common profile of Americans who are hired by the head offices of Japanese companies—liberal arts graduates who have studied Japanese—is very different from the engineers, business majors, and accountants who most likely populate the firm's U.S. operation. This difference alone is liable to cause friction, as you are likely to be perceived as having Japanese language skills but lacking professional credentials. This is exacerbated by the fact that non-Japanese working at the head offices of Japanese companies often fill headquarters-oriented staff positions in areas such as international public relations, international advertising, international human resource management, or international planning that have no direct counterparts in the U.S. operation. Of course, such positions are usually interesting and challenging, and may offer the non-Japanese employee in Japan the best opportunity to make a significant contribution to the company. However, such positions are not necessarily good preparation for line management in the company's overseas operations. Unless you can bring skills that are relevant to and valued by the U.S. operation, you will have difficulty gaining the trust of your locally hired colleagues and finding a productive niche in the local organization. In the words of one young American who works at the head office of a large Japanese manufacturer and is scheduled to be transferred to the United States, "I have to be able to show that I'm not just a Japanese whiz, but that I'm also an expert in production."

IF YOU DECIDE TO LEAVE THE COMPANY

You may decide to return to the United States, but quit rather than transfer to your firm's local subsidiary. You may not feel that there is a future for you in your firm, you may want to pursue something different, or your firm may have little or no presence in the U.S. market. Nevertheless, the primary issue is the same as for those who decide to join their current firm's local operation—transferable skills are of the utmost importance. Contrary to what you may have thought when you started studying Japanese and decided to work in Japan, and what people tell you at cocktail parties, employers will not necessarily fall all over themselves to hire you when you get back to the United States just because you speak Japanese and have lived in Japan.

Despite all the lip service in the American press about the need for more people with foreign-language skills, American companies generally aren't interested in Japanese-language ability in and of itself. Everyone will tell you, "Oh, with your Japanese ability and experience, you'll be really marketable!" Unfortunately, this is just a platitude. Many American firms would rather stick with what's comfortable—someone with a standard background, not a Japanese adventure. Interviewers may ask, "So, why did you decide to go work in Japan?" in the same tone of voice they might query, "So, why did you decide to go to Mars?" There are few set positions for foreign-language speakers in American firms, and the larger ones will often say, "We handle the Japanese market out of our Tokyo office." For those specialist positions that are available, the competition can be intense, and truly superior language skills are often necessary. Since more and more Americans are studying Japanese and spending time in Japan, your language and cultural skills alone are unlikely to make you a highly sought after commodity.

Unless you plan to become a translator or interpreter, your cultural awareness and language ability are only valuable in conjunction with more concrete, marketable skills. Thus, those with technical specialties such as engineering or computer science are in the best position, and those with liberal arts degrees in the most precarious. Going to graduate school is one way to pair a specific qualification with a Japanese background, but once you are there you may encounter the same issues. For example, in the increasingly competitive M.B.A. job market, someone with an exotic Japanese tinge to their resume may be at a disadvantage in comparison with classmates who have cultivated more mainstream business skills. John Campbell, professor of political science at the University of Michigan and a founder of the school's Center for Japanese Studies, cautions, "If you know Japanese and have an M.B.A., it will cost you an extra $5,000 in starting salary and take you a few extra months to find a job . . . You're viewed as peculiar."[3]

KEEP YOUR GOALS FIRMLY IN MIND

Working for a Japanese company in Japan can be an intense and exciting learning experience. It is the best way to improve your Japanese-language ability and understand the inner workings of a Japanese corporation. Your unique status as a non-Japanese may entitle you to juicier work assignments and broader exposure than you might obtain in an American firm. If you plan to make a career with the same company in its overseas operations, starting out in Tokyo is a terrific way to learn the corporate culture, make contacts, and earn a reputation within the organization.

On the other hand, if you're not careful (or are extremely unlucky), a stint with a Japanese company in Tokyo can be a career negative. Adapting to daily life in a Japanese workplace can be enormously frustrating. Also, your company may not have a framework in place to offer long-term career opportunities to non-Japanese. And the work you do may not leave you with skills that are readily transferable to the U.S. labor market. In order to overcome these negatives, you should remain clearly focused on your personal goals—the reasons why you are working for a Japanese company in Japan and the benefits you expect to derive. If you play your cards right, the result could be an excellent experience.

12

How the Japanese Approach to Personnel Management Is Changing

In the long run we are going to have to have a fluid labor market. To some extent, there is something we can learn from the U.S. experience.

KEIO UNIVERSITY ECONOMIST ATSUSHI SEIKE[1]

Change, or at least the talk of it, is on everyone's mind. . . .The next few years will see a paradigmatic shift in the way large Japanese companies nurture company loyalty and compete within a modified employment system.

DOUGLAS SHINSATO, MANAGEMENT CONSULTING PARTNER,
DELOITTE TOUCHE TOMATSU'S TOKYO OFFICE[2]

Due to economic, social, and demographic changes in Japan, the lifetime employment system and the associated personnel management practices are facing new threats to their continued existence. Japanese companies are being forced to reevaluate their approach to personnel management as well as corporate management in general. They are discovering that the changing environment is rendering the hallowed practices of Japanese management less effective.

Japanese corporate leaders and pundits are using strong words. A Nomura Securities executive exclaims that "Basically everything about the way we are doing business has to change,"[3] and a MITI bureaucrat talks of the need for a "cultural revolution."[4] Even American newspapers are heralding the end of the Japanese lifetime employment system. What has prompted this rapid change in tenor? What is making this recession different from others? Are the resulting changes really so profound? Will the lifetime employment system really crumble? If so, what will take its place? And how will these changes impact Americans who work for Japanese firms?

FRAYING AROUND THE EDGES

Even during the go-go "bubble" years of the late 1980s, the challenges to traditional Japanese personnel management were beginning to mount. At the time, the biggest concern of corporate personnel managers was a worsening labor shortage. This labor shortage prompted many Japanese firms to experiment by hiring women, non-Japanese, and midcareer employees from other companies to do work formerly done by male *sogo shoku*. However, these experiments usually did not grow beyond a limited scale and did not change the essence of how companies' personnel systems worked. The most prominent response of large firms was to step up their traditional efforts to recruit new male college graduates, setting off a mad scramble to sign up as many college seniors as possible.

Otherwise, the flush of rising sales and healthy profits enabled Japanese companies to largely ignore the growing threats to their traditional personnel management style. When the stock and real estate markets crashed, the yen rose to new heights, and Japan plunged into a recession, the labor shortage quickly evaporated. This has brought Japanese companies face-to-face with the real personnel problems that were brewing below the surface:

Buildup of managers over forty. Aggressive hiring during the high-growth years and Japan's version of the baby-boom generation, the *dankai sedai,* has led to a cluster of managers who are now in their forties. As it ages, this bulge of workers is wreaking havoc with Japanese companies' carefully balanced seniority promotion and compensation systems, which depend on having more people at the lower levels than at upper levels. The situation has resulted in more managerial-age employees than there are managerial posts. Given that Japanese companies cannot expect to duplicate their explosive growth rates of the past, they will not be able to grow themselves out of this predicament.

Bloated white-collar ranks. Although rapid improvements in blue-collar productivity enabled Japanese firms to expand production while only modestly increasing manufacturing employees during the 1980s, these same firms have experienced significant increases in their white-collar staff.[5] The result is a large overhead burden for Japanese firms.

Inefficiency of white-collar workers. In contrast to Japan's state-of-the-art factories, its offices seem like a throwback to the past. Few employees use personal computers, and scores of clerks do nothing but shuffle paper. As companies have grown, many have allowed bureaucracy to proliferate. The consensus decision-making process, with its endless meetings and review of *ringisho*, has bogged down white-collar productivity. Also, the lifetime employment system is highly tolerant of shirkers who don't do their fair share of work, since such "free riders" can count on sticking around and advancing regardless of their actual performance. (For this reason, in Japan the "corporate ladder" is often referred to as an "escalator"—upward movement is not necessarily dependent on one's exertions.) The factors combine to make Japan's white-collar workers surprisingly inefficient by American standards.

Insufficient number of specialists. Although they have been building up large white-collar staffs, Japanese companies lack the right mix of employees. The traditional white-collar training and rotation pattern has focused on developing generalists who have broad exposure to a wide variety of areas. As technologies become more complex and businesses expand globally, companies are finding that they do not have enough employees who have the necessary highly developed specific skills.

Lack of creativity. As Japanese business is forced to shift its focus from cost leadership to innovation and high value-added products, it is realizing that it needs more creative risk-takers among its employees. However, the traditional personnel management system has encouraged just the opposite—passivity, conformity, and conservatism. Japanese executives are now wondering how to shake their companies out of a dull, bureaucratic lethargy.

Strain on Japanese family life. The corporate culture of long hours, heavy entertaining, drop-of-the-hat transfers, and posting of husbands away from their families (*tanshin funin*) have taken their toll on Japanese family life. Many Japanese men only see their children on weekends and have little time to spend with their wives.

Changing values of younger Japanese. Japan is experiencing a growing generation gap between the older generation that struggled to build Japan from the ashes of war into an economic power and the younger generation that has grown up in affluence. Younger Japanese are less likely to derive their entire identity from their jobs and place a higher value on free time, leisure pursuits, and family life.

These problems have been exposed in a glaring way by the bursting of Japan's economic bubble and the plunge in corporate profits. Companies have suddenly awoken to the fact that many aspects of their time-honored personnel management methods—lifetime employment, seniority-based promotion and compensation, and avoidance of lay-offs—have become handicaps rather than assets. Many of the sources of strength now look like sources of rigidity and inefficiency. Comments Toru Katsurada, a director and head of personnel for Fujitsu, "These unique Japanese systems were a plus during the era of high economic growth. But now we are going into an era where we can't expect growth anymore."[6]

This change in the environment has left Japanese companies confused about what to do. Faced with heavy overstaffing and inefficiency, they know they need to change, but are unsure how. On the one hand, it is difficult for them to abandon the cherished traditional personnel management methods, the only system they and their employees know. On the other hand, many Japanese executives are beginning to envy the flexibility of American companies to reduce employment as needed. The challenge for Japanese managers is how to make the necessary changes in their personnel management without destroying the employee loyalty that has been one of Japan's greatest strengths.

HOPING FOR ATTRITION

What are Japanese companies doing in the face of their personnel management challenges? The answer varies from firm to firm. Some companies have understood the magnitude of the problems described above and have undertaken measures that are earnest and innovative. Other firms are sticking to their traditional methods as much as possible, in the hopes that they can ride out the storm until things improve.

Downsizing and Costcutting

Major Japanese companies are facing an overwhelming need to downsize in the face of stagnating sales and plunging profits, particularly in their overstaffed white-collar ranks. Fuji Research Institute Economist Masaru Takagi estimates that there are 1.5 million "in-house unemployed" in Japan who remain on corporate payrolls although they have little or no work to do;[7] 67 percent of companies surveyed by Japan's Economic Planning Agency predicted that they would soon have too many managers,[8] and 46 percent of companies polled by the Labor Ministry feel that they have too many employees overall.[9]

This overstaffing collides with the historic corporate taboo against discharges. As in the past, Japanese companies are highly reluctant to lay off workers. They are making every effort to streamline personnel costs in other ways before taking that step of last resort.

Hiring cutbacks. Many Japanese companies have drastically reduced or frozen new hiring of college graduates. This has resulted in an astonishingly bleak employment situation for college seniors. Women in particular have suffered from this trend, since clerical "female only" jobs are often the first to see reduced hiring, and firms are losing the urge to experiment with placing women in management track (*sogo shoku*) positions. Many companies are hoping that scaled-back hiring in combination with natural attrition will lead to the desired shrinkage in the number of employees.

Slashing overtime.   Companies have begun to restrict the overtime put in by their employees in a movement referred to as *jitan*. Such actions have the dual purpose of cutting costs (since most salaried workers are paid overtime) and of meeting government pressure to cut working hours.

Shrinking bonuses.   Japanese workers have come to expect that the customary twice-yearly bonuses will make up a significant proportion of their total compensation, although unlike salaries, bonus amounts are not guaranteed. Firms have taken advantage of this gray area by sharply reducing the size of their bonuses.

Shedding of part-time and contract workers.   Designed to be an expendable workforce that can be easily let go in times of recession, these temporary workers are seeing their contracts canceled in droves.

Accelerated transfers to subsidiaries.   Expanding on a tactic used to deal with superfluous employees even in good times, major companies are attempting to foist off ever larger numbers of employees on subsidiaries. There are signs, however, that these subsidiaries are becoming stuffed to the gills as well.

Aggressive early-retirement programs.   Japanese companies are starting to offer early-retirement inducements similar to those offered by downsizing American firms. These programs reportedly have an element of coercion and are not much different from actual layoffs, both in their impact on the individuals affected and overall employee morale.[10]

Uncomfortable window seats.   Some companies are so desperate to get rid of employees without the public appearance of conducting layoffs that they resort to harassing and embarrassing them into quitting of their own volition. Traditionally, being one of the window sitters (*madogiwazoku*) has been a comfortable sinecure for unneeded employees. Recently, however, many Japanese firms have purposefully made these positions less attractive, hoping that employees will resign. This new breed of window seat posts includes assignments to dimly lit basement offices or remote branches in the boondocks and demeaning make-work activities such as chopping wood and writing essays on current events.[11]

However, for a growing number of companies, even these measures are not sufficient, and they have had to announce actual layoffs as well. This abandonment of the lifetime employment promise has shocked and demoralized Japanese workers. Although the layoffs, early retirement offers, and downsizing through attrition announced by Japanese firms cannot compare in scale to corporate America's bloodletting of the last decade, they have had an extremely negative impact on Japanese consumer confidence and the morale of individual workers.

For the middle-aged and older Japanese who toiled to produce Japan's economic miracle, corporate Japan's unilateral retraction of the lifetime employment promise is tantamount to a betrayal. Having traded loyalty and devotion in return for assurances of stability, they are distraught to see those promises revoked. As for younger Japanese, recent events are deterring them from developing the deep company loyalty that characterized their elders. Polls indicate that Japanese in their twenties are less likely to express feelings of company loyalty and more willing than those in their thirties or forties to switch jobs.[12]

It is possible that Japanese companies have opened a Pandora's box by breaching the social contract of lifetime employment and damaging the traditional bond of trust with employees. In the future, it may prove difficult for them to manage employees who see themselves as participants in a wider labor market. As Japanese social commentator Taichi Sakaiya remarks, "Japanese companies don't have the 'humanware' to manage employees who don't possess loyalty to the company. In America you have professional ethics and team spirit [as ways to motivate workers], but Japanese companies don't have these. So when [their] employees stop being loyal, Japanese companies will have trouble."[13]

Yet, Japan's labor market will not come to resemble the fluid U.S.

employment picture overnight. For one, most Japanese firms will, for the time being, continue to preserve lifetime employment (or at least the appearance of it) to the extent possible. Second, although larger Japanese companies have broached the lifetime employment tradition with layoffs and early retirement offers, their hiring and promotion practices continue to conform to the traditional pattern. No mechanisms have been adopted for American-style hiring for specific positions, and the labor market is still undeveloped. Third, Japanese workers generally are not welcoming the demise of lifetime employment. They are unprepared for the prospect of job-hunting and continue to cling to the ethos of loyalty to and identification with the company that has been promulgated by Japanese business for decades.

Performance-based Compensation

Performance evaluation has recently become a hot topic in the Japanese business press as high-profile companies such as Fujitsu and Honda have adopted performance-based compensation programs for managerial employees. These programs are generating interest because they are seen as a way to stimulate higher levels of performance. The new interest in these programs is also of note because it represents such a tremendous departure from the way Japanese employers have managed personnel in the past. The very idea of explicit individual performance evaluations tied to salary levels flies in the face of traditional Japanese personnel management's emphasis on team efforts and seniority-based compensation.

The move toward performance-based compensation programs has not been a stampede. Only 14.6 percent of companies surveyed by the Japan Federation of Employers' Associations had such systems in 1992, a small increase over the 10.4 percent in 1991.[14] Such programs typically face resistance from the very managers who are their target, because the prospect of such evaluations is so unfamiliar and nerve-wracking.

Another barrier to the successful adoption of such programs is the upper-level managers who are entrusted with performing the evaluations. Japanese firms that have instituted such programs, such as Tokyo

Gas and Hankyu Electric Railway, report that their managers are reluctant to make large distinctions between employees.[15] This mirrors the reaction of Japanese expatriates in the United States when faced with the task of executing performance evaluations. Masatake Fujii, a director and in charge of personnel at Sunstar, says of his company's performance evaluation system, "Having to face a subordinate and give him an evaluation makes managers uncomfortable. And all managers feel fondly toward their subordinates. So, even if you have a dynamic system, the evaluations still end up being mild anyway. This tendency is even more pronounced when the evaluation will have a direct impact on the subordinates' salaries."[16]

Internal Job Posting

Several companies have instituted programs of internally posting available positions, allowing employees to apply for job openings within the company. In a country where employees passively accept the assignments doled out by the personnel department as a matter of course, such programs are a novelty. These programs are also opportunities for both employees and employers to dabble in labor-market type activities such as interviewing and matching qualifications to job requirements. Additionally, companies are beginning to learn that employees who choose their own posts are happier and more productive.

New Types of Management Positions

Creation of specialized posts for middle-aged employees other than the typical line management positions is another trend. NEC and Nissan Motor are among the firms that have recently established such positions.[17]

New Value on Strong Leadership

President Takashi Kitaoka of Mitsubishi Electric has made headlines in Japan with the organizational overhaul he has conducted since taking office in June 1992. His innovations include replacing the typical "bottom-up" consensus-building style with a strong leadership "top-down" approach, and giving division heads the final authority to decide on capital expenditure decisions of less than $4.5 million without sending *ringisho* up to the president's office.[18] It remains to be seen, however, whether other companies will follow suit.

Overall, there is a feeling of questioning and experimentation in the air as Japanese companies struggle to dismantle the practices of the high-growth years and adopt more flexible ones while maintaining the loyalty and motivation of their employees.

This atmosphere of questioning is mirrored by Japanese individuals, who have been shocked by the willingness of companies to abandon the lifetime employment promise. They are questioning the values that form the linchpin of Japanese personnel management, and wondering whether the sacrifices expected of them by their companies are worth it. As columnist Masahiko Ishizuka wrote recently in the *Nihon Keizai Shinbun* newspaper, "Japanese workers are now revolting against 'corporatism,' their enslavement to the corporation and its mores. Bluntly speaking, Japanese people are starting to see themselves as underpaid and exploited."[19] Keep in mind, however, that this "revolt" is a quiet one, taking place in the minds of workers but not necessarily surfacing in their words and actions. Still stability-minded, and lacking a fully functioning labor market to turn to, most corporate employees are staying put if they can.

In summary, although the changes taking place in Japanese personnel management are interesting, the Japanese labor market will not come to resemble that of the United States anytime soon. What is likely is for both individual Japanese and their companies to begin thinking more deeply about the nature of the employer-employee relationship, and to consider issues of productivity and motivation more carefully. Over the longer term, it's likely that many of the Japanese personnel practices and corporate norms that Americans find to be the most puzzling will be reexamined and changes begun.

IMPACT ON AMERICAN EMPLOYEES
OF JAPANESE FIRMS

What impact will the Japanese recession, the personnel management woes of Japanese companies, and the debate on the nature of the lifetime employment system have on the American employees of Japanese firms?

In the Short Term

•   *Even less risk taking.* Now that Japanese employees are beginning to lose trust in the promise of lifetime employment, they are likely to become even more conservative and risk-averse. This should hold for both managers stationed in the United States and those at company headquarters in Japan. It's still true that Japanese organizations don't give second chances. The difference is that now the penalty for a mistake is perceived to be harsher—instead of a comfortable seat by the window, it may be a dreaded *kata tataki* (tap on the shoulder), the Japanese version of a "pink slip."

•   *Further belt-tightening.* The pressure on profits will cause many Japanese companies to pinch pennies and cut costs wherever possible. This may result in even tighter scrutiny of spending requests from overseas operations.

•   *Increased layoffs outside of manufacturing.* If a Japanese firm is desperate enough to trim staff at home, it certainly will not be averse to laying off U.S. workers. The potential for downsizing is particularly great in industries that have been hit hard by Japan's banking crisis, stock market crash, and real estate slump.

•   *More manufacturing positions.* Many manufacturers are adding capacity and increasing output in the United States to cope with the strength of the yen against the dollar. This should mean a further increase in the availability of manufacturing positions for Americans at Japanese firms.

In the Long Term

The huge gap in personnel management practices between Japan and the United States underlies many of the difficulties that Japanese firms have in managing their American employees. As a labor market begins to develop in Japan and Japanese companies change their personnel management practices to be more focused on the individual, there is bound to be a favorable impact on their ability to understand and manage Americans. Also, the increased flexibility in Japanese personnel management may begin to soften the rigid distinction between *seishain* and non-*seishain*, or even make it attractive for Americans to become *seishain*.

Moreover, given the current spirit of experimentation and openness to new ideas, the U.S. operations of Japanese firms could be at the forefront in helping to develop a blend of the best of both countries' personnel management styles.

Conclusion

When Americans work together with Japanese, the contrasts between the two countries' management styles and business culture are emphasized. Japanese and Americans approach the employment relationship, manager-subordinate interaction, and even basic communication with different expectations and motivations. Each group finds aspects of the other's behavior to be puzzling and frustrating because it persists in measuring with its own cultural yardsticks. Many Japanese firms and managers never learn to appreciate the skills and strengths of their American employees, while many Americans overlook the potential benefits of the Japanese management style.

The differences occur at two main levels. The first level involves language and interaction style, the short-term issues discussed in Part 2. Not only do few Japanese and Americans speak each other's languages well, but the proper approaches to business communication and decision-making in the two cultures are diametrically opposed. Many Japanese and Americans stumble over this first level of difficulty and never establish effective cooperative relationships. Japanese managers often overlook the need to adapt their communication style when working with Americans, while those Americans who do not learn how to interact effectively with Japanese hurt their own chances of becoming trusted. This lack of smooth interaction helps give rise to the rice-paper ceiling, as Japanese firms are reluctant to entrust Americans with managerial positions if they do not feel comfortable working closely with them.

Yet these issues of language and interaction style are relatively superficial and easily solved in comparison with the second level of differences, those involving personnel management practices and career patterns. Japan lacks a fluid American-style labor market, and Japanese companies and managers are unaccustomed to American personnel practices such as interviewing, salary negotiations, and performance-based compensation and promotion. Because the Japanese system rewards those who stay with the same company and devote themselves to group goals, Japanese companies are uncomfortable with Americans' labor mobility and emphasis on individual efforts and rewards. This causes them to view American employees in a different light from Japanese employees and to keep them in a separate category. Meanwhile, whereas American employees often become frustrated with the effects of being treated differently from Japanese employees, few would be willing to be managed under traditional Japanese personnel practices such as seniority-based compensation and promotion and unilateral job assignments made by personnel managers. Although in the long run this gap may narrow as Japanese companies are forced to reevaluate their personnel management practices, the sharp contrast in labor market structure between the two countries will continue to be a source of difficulty for Japanese firms and their American employees. As long as Japanese firms feel that they cannot use the same personnel management system for all their employees worldwide, the rice-paper ceiling will remain in place.

YOUR DECISIONS

As an employee of a Japanese firm, you will need to decide how to handle both the short-term issues of communication and the long-term issues of career opportunity.

In the short term, your thoughts should be focused inward on what you can do to improve your ability to work effectively in a Japanese company environment. What adjustments may be necessary in your work style and communication methods? How can you form better relationships with Japanese colleagues and superiors? How can you cultivate a better understanding of Japanese business methods, culture, and language?

The long-term issues are more difficult, because they are less in your control as an individual. Each American employee of a Japanese firm should ask him- or herself: How does the firm's management and personnel structure affect me and my career opportunities?

There is no simple answer. In assessing your long-term potential with a given Japanese firm, you will need to consider whether becoming part of the company's in-group is really possible. Does the fact that you are not Japanese mean that you will always be excluded from certain information and decision-making? Or does your company offer substantive career opportunities to American employees?

The answer to these questions depends on your company's attitudes and policies. Unfortunately, in some Japanese firms you will end up beating your head against the wall—they will probably never learn to integrate any Americans into their management processes. This is, of course, a sign of their poor management, and in the long run it will adversely affect their ability to do business internationally.

In some firms, if you have special talents that you can bring to bear, or are able to work skillfully within the organization, you can develop a unique and satisfying niche despite the company's overall reluctance to put Americans in positions of authority. This is particularly true if your performance and interpersonal skills have inspired the trust of your Japanese superiors and colleagues. Also, if you possess Japanese-language skills or cross-cultural communications skills, you can develop a special role as an interface between the Japanese and American organizations.

A Japanese company's U.S. subsidiary may offer excellent opportunities to American employees—ones that may be even better than those provided by American firms in terms of job content, pay, benefits, or job security. This is particularly likely to be the case in firms that have large

U.S. operations with well-developed local human resource management systems that provide a variety of career paths to American employees. In addition, many Japanese companies across the spectrum have made conscious decisions to put Americans in upper-level managerial positions and have instituted wise policies that minimize distinctions between American and Japanese employees.

In other words, the penetrability of the rice-paper ceiling depends on many factors. It depends on you, your abilities, your efforts, your personality, and your luck. It depends on the openness, flexibility, and vision of the individual Japanese expatriates you work with. And it depends on the willingness of your company, both at the U.S. subsidiary level and at the head office level, to make the necessary efforts to identify and develop promising non-Japanese employees.

Japanese firms tend to have longer time frames for training, recognizing, and promoting employees. As a result, Japanese managers will frequently tell restive American employees to "be patient." However, in some Japanese companies it's worth being patient; in others it's not. The discussion in this book can be summarized by recommending that you consider three types of factors in evaluating the long-term career prospects in your firm: yourself, the Japanese managers, and the company as a whole.

Yourself

- At what point in your career are you? What are your goals?

- What do you value most about a job and an employer: Opportunities to learn and develop? Growth and advancement potential? The chance to do a particular type of work? Stability? Salary and perks?

- What kind of work do you do: Blue-collar? White-collar? Managerial or professional? Specialist? Generalist? Line? Staff?

- What are your personal skills? Do you have special skills that appeal to a Japanese firm, such as Japanese-language ability or experience living in Japan?

- How effectively are you able to work with Japanese superiors and colleagues? Do they trust you? What kind of reputation have you developed?

- How well do you enjoy the work that you are doing? Is it challenging and interesting? Does it match your long-term goals?

- What other job opportunities are currently available to you, and how do they compare to your current position?

Your Managers

- What is the attitude of the Japanese managers at your firm toward American employees: Are Americans routinely excluded, or are specific efforts made to include Americans in managerial processes? Are the Japanese managers willing to trust and delegate authority to Americans?

- How much of an effort do the Japanese managers make to understand American society and to face difficult cross-cultural issues?

- Do the Japanese managers try to sweep conflicts under the rug, ignoring the concerns of the American staff? Or have they recognized problems and taken action to address them?

Your Company

- What is the importance of international operations and U.S. markets to your company as a whole?

- To what extent has your company put Americans in key decision-making positions?

- How many Japanese expatriates are there, and what is their power and importance? Do they occupy all the upper-level positions or act as a shadow network subtly controlling decision-making? Are there few expatriates, and only in those positions where coordination with Japan or technology transfer are necessary? Specifically, are the positions you aspire to consistently filled with Japanese expatriates?

- How large is the office/operation you are working in? If it is small, is it likely to grow and be profitable, providing future opportunities to American employees? Or is it large and diversified, with ample career paths?

- How strong and active is the company's U.S. human resource function?

- How much independence does the U.S. operation have from the Japanese parent company in its day-to-day operations?

- How does the company regard the role of Americans in the firm? How sharp are the distinctions between *seishain* and non-*seishain*?

- Does your company's head office in Japan make an effort to reach out to overseas employees and incorporate them in the firm as a whole, for example, by providing opportunities for training or long-term assignments in Japan?

IN CLOSING

Depending on the answers to the questions above, you can draw various conclusions. If you are uncomfortable with your work or with the Japanese company environment, if your Japanese manager has a bad attitude toward American employees, and if the company's policies consistently treat overseas employees as peripheral and temporary, these are all signs that you should consider other opportunities. If you enjoy your work, anticipate further challenges and growth, get along well with your Japanese colleagues, and feel that your company has an open (or steadily improving) stance toward non-Japanese employees, it may be worth it to stick around. The most difficult situation is faced by those who like their jobs and are comfortable working with Japanese managers, but see little chance for advancement and complete indifference on the part of the parent company.

Americans in white-collar and professional positions tend to look at their careers in two- to three-year increments. Anyone should be willing to give a Japanese employer a chance for this time period (after carefully checking them out beforehand, as described in Chapter 3). Japanese firms will remain significant sources of employment opportunities in the United States, particularly in certain regions and industries. It would be foolish for Americans to avoid them on a blanket basis simply because some have dismal records in their management of American employees. Furthermore, working in a cross-cultural environment can be an opportunity for personal growth.

After you have been with your firm for a few years you will be able to evaluate the answers to the questions above and make choices that are appropriate for you and your personal career goals. Japanese *seishain* have no labor market to turn to for alternatives, but as an American, you do. Ultimately, Japanese companies' ability to provide employment opportunities that are attractive to Americans for periods of longer than just a few years is the real test of their ability to create strong organizations in the United States.

It is my hope that the information presented in this book will be useful for potential and current American employees of Japanese firms. Not every issue discussed here will be applicable to each Japanese company's U.S. operations. Each employment situation must be evaluated on its own merits, whether the company has its headquarters in Japan, the United States, or any other country. If the company is Japanese, it means that there are potential cultural and structural issues you should be aware of. However, this does not mean that a Japanese employer will necessarily provide a poor working experience. If you and your company both work to address these issues, a job at a Japanese firm can be a terrific opportunity.

Appendixes

---

1. DISCRIMINATION LAWSUITS AGAINST JAPANESE FIRMS IN THE UNITED STATES

Many lawyers and consultants agree that discrimination suits against Japanese companies have grown widespread. This is presumably due, at least in part, to the cultural and structural issues described in this book. At the same time, some employees may see Japanese companies as deep-pocketed and vulnerable and bring suits that probably wouldn't stand up in court. Some defense attorneys for Japanese companies claim that "many of their courtroom opponents are extortionists who threaten to whip the jury into a Japan-bashing frenzy if they aren't offered a handsome settlement."[1] It has also been suggested that Japanese companies may not necessarily be facing a disproportionate number of discrimination charges, given that they employ so many people in the United States. In the litigious American environment, any firm, regardless of its nationality, is exposed to the risk of lawsuits.

Discrimination cases against Japanese employers generally fall into two categories (although certain suits span both categories): cases charging discrimination on the basis of age, race, or gender, and cases in which Americans were fired, prompting charges of wrongful discharge or national origin discrimination. In cases where discrimination against women and minorities is charged, attention is paid either to a hiring process that systematically favors certain groups, a lack of promotional opportunities for certain groups, or the fact that employees in one group were systematically paid less than those in other groups. In cases where the plaintiff was discharged, attention often focuses on the fact that Japanese nationals were not fired or that the plaintiff was replaced by a less-qualified Japanese national.

A significant element in many of these cases is the dual employment system that Japanese companies tend to use in the United States: one system and set of standards for American employees, and another for Japanese expatriates. The argument is made that the dual nature of a Japanese company's personnel system is inherently discriminatory against Americans or certain subsets of Americans. Plaintiffs in cases where this is an issue tend to focus on evidence suggesting that management positions and promotional opportunities are reserved for Japanese, on the generous salaries and benefits paid to expatriates but not available to American employees, and on the fact that Japanese employees appear to have lifetime employment while no such system applies to Americans. Additional incidents such as the occurrence of meetings that only Japanese were allowed to attend and Japanese expatriates' derogatory comments about Americans are also frequently cited in these cases.

Nevertheless, due to a unique legal doctrine, discrimination cases against Japanese companies turn on more than just the question of whether the alleged discrimination actually took place. When the first batch of discrimination cases against Japanese companies began to crop up in the late 1970s and early 1980s, a debate began about what rights a cold-war era trade treaty gave Japanese companies in the area of personnel policy. After World War II, the U.S. government signed bilateral Treaties of Friendship, Commerce, and Navigation (FCN treaties) with a variety of friendly countries. Generally, these treaties sought to foster international commerce by giving each signatory's companies the ability to conduct business in the other signatory's country without being subject to laws that would unduly limit their ability to do business. Doing business without undue restriction was defined as encompassing the right to choose specialist personnel. The relevant portion of the U.S.-Japan FCN treaty[2] states that "Nationals and companies of either Party shall be permitted to engage, within the territories of the other Party, accountants and other technical experts, executive personnel, attorneys, agents and other specialists of their choice." Ironically, it was the United States that insisted on inclusion of this provision; Japan was opposed.[3]

On the basis of the clause "of their choice," some Japanese firms (as well as foreign multinationals from other countries that have similar treaties with the United States) have argued that the treaty gives them the right to hire employees as they please regardless of the strictures of U.S. civil rights laws that prohibit discrimination on the basis of race, color, religion, sex, or national origin.

The landmark case in this area, *Sumitomo Shoji v. Avagliano*,[4] prompted a 1982 U.S. Supreme Court decision. Female employees of the Japanese trading company's U.S. subsidiary contended that they were discriminated against in favor of male Japanese employees, effectively being denied opportunities for advancement within the company. The court ruled that because Sumitomo Shoji America was incorporated as a U.S. company, it was subject to U.S. laws, including civil rights laws. This was an important clarification, particularly since the majority of Japanese companies' American operations are incorporated as U.S. subsidiaries. However, a 1991 ruling on a later case[5] modified this all-or-nothing precedent by ruling that the FCN treaty allows discrimination in favor of the citizens of the foreign nation. This interpretation is possible because Title VII explicitly forbids discrimination on the basis of race, color, sex, religion, and national origin, but is silent on the subject of citizenship.

Future cases will undoubtedly explore arcane legal issues raised by the conflict between this international treaty and domestic civil rights laws. For example, does permitted discrimination on the basis of citizenship result in forbidden discrimination on the basis of national origin, race, or sex because Japanese expatriates are all of Japanese race and national origin and are almost always male? The point is that neither the FCN treaties nor the U.S. civil rights laws were written with these sorts of situations in mind. The FCN treaty was written before Title VII was a glimmer in anyone's eye. And Title VII itself was written in response to problems of discrimination against minorities in the U.S. domestic context. Clearly American (and international) law hasn't caught up with the challenges posed by international personnel policies that extend across borders and affect employees of more than one nationality.

Individuals who believe that they have cause to sue a Japanese employer should seek qualified legal counsel. Your Rights in the Workplace by Dan Lacey (Berkeley: Nolo Press, 1991) is also a useful reference to help evaluate the potential legal merits of your situation.

2. SURVEY METHODOLOGY

This section describes the methodology used to conduct the survey reported in Chapter 2. A database of major multinationals from the United States, Japan, and Europe was compiled as the union of two sets: the *Business Week* Global 1000 (15 July 1991) and the Fortune 500 lists (The *Fortune* 500, 29 April 1991 and The *Fortune* 500 Largest Foreign Companies, 22 July 1991). The *Business Week* list ranked companies on the basis of stock market value, while the *Fortune* lists ranked companies on the basis of sales volume. In order to remove from the database those companies that were unlikely to have multinational operations, all companies described as being utilities were eliminated, and for American companies all those that were not also listed in the *Directory of*

American Firms Operating in Foreign Countries (11th edition, New York: World Trade Academy Press, 1987) were removed. The resulting list contained 918 firms: 272 headquartered in the United States, 309 headquartered in Japan, and 337 headquartered in Europe.

In order to facilitate a greater response rate, translations of the survey into Japanese, German, and French were prepared by native speakers familiar with business vocabulary. The Japanese version was sent to the firms headquartered in Japan; the German version to firms headquartered in Germany, Switzerland, and Austria; and the French version to firms headquartered in France and Belgium. Firms headquartered in other countries all received English versions of the questionnaire.

The survey was designed to be filled out by one individual at each firm. One response per firm was deemed adequate because the majority of the questions in the survey are factual in nature and presumably would not vary widely from respondent to respondent. It was decided that the most logical choice to receive the questionnaires would be an individual responsible for the international human resources function, who would be familiar with the relevant statistics, policies, and problem areas. One questionnaire was mailed to each firm, addressed "Manager—Int'l Human Resources." The first mailing yielded an inadequate response, so a second mailing was sent approximately three months later to the same list of firms.

The 81 responses received were as follows: 23 from Europe (3 from France, 3 from Germany, 1 from Switzerland, 13 from the United Kingdom, and 2 from the Netherlands), 34 from Japan, and 24 from the United States. The majority of the individuals completing the survey were managers in the human resources or international departments of their firms.

Further details of this study are presented in Rochelle Kopp, "International Human Resource Policies and Practices in Japanese, European, and U.S. Multinationals," *Human Resource Management Journal* 33, no. 4 (Winter 1994).

3. JAPANESE-LANGUAGE
STUDY MATERIALS FOR BUSINESS

As the number of non-Japanese studying the Japanese language increases, the selection of Japanese-language textbooks is growing. However, much of what is available is not geared to a businessperson's needs. The following materials are recommended for use by employees of Japanese companies as supplements to more standard grammar and writing-based texts. It is not meant to be an exhaustive list—new business-oriented Japanese texts are being published all the time. Many of the books listed here can be found in American bookstores that also carry Japanese-language books. Full addresses of publishers are given for books published in Japan or not readily available in North Amercan bookstores; write to the respective publishers for ordering information.

Beginning

Executive Japanese. By Hajime Takamizawa. All conversations are business related. Includes interesting articles in English on Japanese business culture. (ASMIK Corporation, 4 Ageba-cho, Shinjuku-ku, Tokyo, Japan 162)

Japanese for International Businessmen. By Ken Butler. Two cassette tapes also available. Practical conversations. (ALC Press, 2-54-12 Eifuku, Suginami-ku, Tokyo, Japan 168)

Intermediate and Advanced

Japanese for All Occasions. By Anne Kaneko. Useful basics for every imaginable occasion, both in business and everyday life. A must for anyone working in Japan. Includes section on letter writing. (Charles E. Tuttle)

Office Japanese. By Hajime Takizawa. Practical topics include meetings, telephone conversations, office equipment, and *nemawashi*. (ALC Press, 2-54-12 Eifuku, Suginami-ku, Tokyo, Japan 168)

Advanced Japanese—Social and Economic Issues in Japan and the U.S. By Yoshiko Higurashi. Stresses intercultural communication skills. About half the lessons are specifically on business topics: negotiations, the Japanese concept of service, and basic business manners. (Harcourt Brace Jovanovich Japan, Ichibancho Central Bldg., 22-1 Ichibancho, Chiyoda-ku, Tokyo, Japan 102)

Nihon de Bijinesu—Nihongo Hyogen to Bijinesu Manaa (Business in Japan: Japanese expressions and business etiquette). By Mineko Horiuchi and Chieko Ashidaka. Entirely in Japanese, this book is for advanced students. Although somewhat condescending in tone, it is useful because it shows just what is *really* expected in the Japanese context. (Senmon Kyoiku Shuppan, 7-7-7 Nishi Shinjuku, Shinjuku-ku, Tokyo, Japan 160)

Rules for Conversational Rituals in Japanese. By Haruo Aoki and Shigeko Okamoto. Not strictly a business book, this is a useful guide to confoundingly fuzzy Japanese expressions. For example, the authors dutifully translate a sentence as "I am not involved in this matter, but I promise you that I will order an immediate and thorough investigation and solve the problem in a forward-looking posture," then note that it really means "I won't do a damned thing." (Taishukan Publishing Company, 3-24 Kanda Nishiki-cho, Chiyoda-ku, Tokyo, Japan 101)

Writing Letters and Reports

Jissen Nihongo no Sakubun (Japanese expository writing practice). By M. Sato, C. Kano, K. Tanabe, Y. Nishimura. Helpful if you want to improve your ability to write reports in Japanese. (Bonjinsha, c/o Japan Book Center, The Water Garden, Suite 650 East, 2425 West Olympic Boulevard, Santa Monica, CA 90404)

The Business Letter. Edited by Bussan Kenshu Center. Although this book is designed to help Japanese write English letters, the Japanese translations it provides are quite helpful to students of Japanese. (Yuhikaku, 2-17 Kanda Jinbo-cho, Chiyoda-ku, Tokyo, Japan 101)

Business Bunsho Surasura Jiten (Dictionary for easy business-letter writing). By Kazuo Oka. Japanese business-letter style is so difficult that there are many books on the market to help Japanese write them better. This is one of them; any store carrying Japanese books will likely have others. (Paru Shuppan, 8 Honshiomachi, Shinjuku-ku, Tokyo, Japan 160)

Tegami no Kakikata—Kisetsubetsu Bunreishu (Letter writing: Example sentences organized by season). By Toshiko Atoda. This is also a book intended for native speakers and is for general rather than business-only use. It includes set phrases for the opening and closing paragraphs of letters that are appropriate for each month of the year, and also provides many sample greetings for New Year and summer cards. (Ikeda Shoten Witch Books, 43 Bentenmachi, Shinjuku-ku, Tokyo, Japan 162)

Dictionaries

Talking Business in Japanese. By Nobuo and Carol Akiyama. This compact guide is surprisingly complete for its size. (Barron's Educational Series)

The Shogakukan Japanese-English Dictionary of Current Terms (*Saishin Nichi-Bei Hyogen Jiten*). By Keisuke Iwatsu and Michihiro Matsumoto. Contains a complete set of financial statements, a list of major Japanese companies, and sample tax returns, as well as many current business terms that other dictionaries often leave out. (Shogakukan, 2-3-1 Hitotsubashi, Chiyoda-ku, Tokyo, Japan 101)

The Dictionary of Loanwords (Katakanago no Jiten). Many Japanese business terms are borrowings from English. This dictionary can help you to decipher them when they are rendered in the *katakana* syllabary. (Shogakukan, 2-3-1 Hitotsubashi, Chiyoda-ku, Tokyo, Japan 101)

Japanese-English Dictionary—Fundamental 1,200 Business and Banking Terms (Fundamental 1,200 Waei Kinyu Yogo Jiten). Edited by the Yasuda Trust and Banking Company. Contains many words not found in other dictionaries. Packed with detailed explanations. (Keizai Horei Kenkyukai, 3-21 Ichidani Honmuramachi, Shinjuku-ku, Tokyo, Japan 162)

Current English Financial Terms (Waei Kinyu Yogo Jiten). Edited by Minoru Hanada. Chock full of example sentences to help you render Japanese financial terms into English. (The Japan Times, 4-5-4 Shibaura, Minato-ku, Tokyo, Japan 108)

Kenkyusha's English-Japanese Dictionary for the General Reader (Riidaazu Eiwa Jiten). Edited by T. Matsuda. If you are a serious user of Japanese, your library should include a good English-to-Japanese dictionary. This one is particularly complete and accurate. (Kenkyusha, 2-11-3 Fujimi, Chiyoda-ku, Tokyo, Japan 102)

Kenkyusha's New Japanese-English Dictionary (Shin Waei Daijiten). Edited by Koh Masuda. For serious Japanese-based work you will also need a comprehensive Japanese-to-English dictionary. This one is a favorite of translators, who have dubbed it the "Green Goddess." (Kenkyusha, 2-11-3 Fujimi, Chiyoda-ku, Tokyo, Japan 102)

Imidas. This annual publication looks like a telephone book and is the best source for current terms and their proper usage. Japanese experts in virtually every field, from biotechnology to finance to advertising, are asked to write essays on current developments. The new terms that appear are then indexed in the back. (Shueisha, 2-5-10 Hitotsubashi, Chiyoda-ku, Tokyo, Japan 101)

4. SUGGESTED FURTHER READING ON JAPANESE CULTURE, SOCIETY, AND BUSINESS

Abegglen, James C., and George Stalk, Jr. *Kaisha: The Japanese Corporation.* New York: Basic Books, 1985.

Brannen, Christalyn, and Tracey Wilen. *Doing Business With Japanese Men: A Woman's Handbook.* Berkeley: Stone Bridge Press, 1993.

Emmot, Bill. *Japanophobia: The Myth of the Invincible Japanese.* New York: Times Books, 1993.

Fields, George. *From Bonsai to Levi's—When West Meets East: An Insider's Surprising Account of How the Japanese Live.* New York: Macmillan, 1983.

Kato, Hiroki, and Joan Kato. *Understanding and Working with the Japanese Business World.* Englewood Cliffs, N.J.: Prentice Hall, 1992.

Rauch, Jonathan. *The Outnation: A Search for the Soul of Japan.* Boston: Harvard Business School Press, 1992.

Reischauer, Edwin O. *The Japanese Today.* Cambridge, Mass.: Harvard University Press, 1988.

Rohlen, Thomas P. *For Harmony and Strength: Japanese White-Collar Organization in Anthropological Perspective.* Berkeley: University of California Press, 1974.

Rowland, Diana. *Japanese Business Etiquette.* New York: Warner Books, 1985.

Sakaiya, Taichi. *What is Japan? Contradictions and Transformations.* New York: Kodansha International, 1993.

Sullivan, Jeremiah J. *Invasion of the Salarymen: The Japanese Business Presence in America.* Westport, Conn.: Praeger, 1992.

van Wolferen, Karel. *The Enigma of Japanese Power.* New York: Alfred A. Knopf, 1989.

White, Merry, *The Japanese Overseas: Can They Go Home Again?* New York: Free Press, 1988.

Zimmerman, Mark. *How to Do Business with the Japanese: A Strategy for Success.* New York: Random House, 1985.

Notes

Chapter 1: What Happens When Japanese Companies Hire Americans?

1 U.S. House Committee on Government Operations, *Employment Discrimination by Japanese-Owned Companies in the United States: Hearings before the Employment and Housing Subcommittee of the Committee on Government Operations,* 102nd Cong., 1st sess., 1991, 211.

2 Ibid., 359–60.

3 Ibid., 359.

4 Ibid., 37.

5 Ibid., 1.

6 Yoshihiro Tsurumi, "The Ghost of McCarthyism Haunts Japanese Firms," *Pacific Basin Quarterly* (Summer/Fall 1991): 15.

7 Bureau of Economic Analysis, Economics and Statistics Administration, U.S. Department of Commerce, *Foreign Direct Investment in the United States: Operations of U.S. Affiliates of Foreign Companies—Preliminary 1991 Estimates,* U.S. Department of Commerce, 1993, Table F-4.

8 U.S. House Committee on Government Operations, *Employment Discrimination,* 178.

9 Daniel Bob and SRI International, *Japanese Companies in American Communities* (New York: Japan Society, 1990), 41.

[10] "Labor Letter," *Wall Street Journal*, 29 August 1989, A1.

[11] Yoshihiro Tsurumi, quoted in "Differences Between U.S. Workers and Japanese Managers Wind Up in Court, *New York Times*, 9 September 1990, and John Gillespie, Intercultural Specialist at Clarke Consulting Group, quoted in "Japanese Firm Settles Suit by U.S. Employees," *Newsday*, 9 November 1990, 47.

[12] See the Bibliography for a selection of academic works concerning the international human resource management of Japanese firms.

[13] "Suits Boom Against the Japanese," *National Law Journal*, 22 June 1987, 1.

Chapter 2: Personnel Management
Problems in Japanese Multinationals

[1] Robert B. Reich, "Who Is Them?" *Harvard Business Review*, March–April 1991, 81.

[2] Appendix 2 provides more information on the survey methodology. The full results of this study are discussed in Rochelle Kopp, "International Human Resource Policies and Practices in Japanese, European, and U.S. Multinationals," *Human Resource Management Journal* 33, no. 4 (Winter 1994).

[3] The following definitions are based on Peter Dowling and Randall Schuler, *International Dimensions of Human Resource Management* (Boston: PWS-Kent Publishing, 1990), 36–37, 48–51, and David Heenan and Howard Perlmutter, *Multinational Organization Development* (Reading, Mass.: Addison-Wesley, 1979), 17–21.

[4] Yoram Zeira, "Management Development in Ethnocentric Multinational Corporations," *California Management Review* 18, no. 4 (Summer 1976): 34–42.

[5] See, for example, Rosalie Tung, *The New Expatriates: Managing Human Resources Abroad* (Cambridge, Mass.: Ballinger, 1988). This argument has also been made to me informally by several Japanese executives.

[6] Dowling and Schuler, *International Dimensions*, 30.

[7] "Japanese Wary on U.S. Operations," *Wall Street Journal*, 9 June 1992.

[8] Shigeru Komago, "Subsidiaries in U.S. Post Record Losses," *Nikkei Weekly*, 5 April 1993, 7.

[9] Speech at University of Chicago Graduate School of Business, 8 April 1992.

[10] Henry DeNero, "Creating the 'Hyphenated' Corporation," *McKinsey Quarterly*, no. 4 (1990): 165.

[11] This topic is discussed in depth in Merry White, *The Japanese Overseas: Can They Go Home Again?* (New York: Free Press, 1988).

[12] See Appendix 1 for a discussion of some of the legal details of this issue.

[13] Christopher Bartlett and Sumantra Ghoshal, *Managing Across Borders: The Transnational Solution* (Boston: Harvard Business School Press, 1989), 92.

[14] Ibid., Chapter 2.

[15] Ibid., 92.

Chapter 3: Checklist—Evaluating a Potential Japanese Employer

[1] Alfredo Lanier, "Alex Warren: Bridging the Gap Between Cultures and Technologies," *GSB Chicago*, Winter 1991, 13.

[2] See Appendix 1 for further discussion of the legal issues involving Japanese firms in the United States.

[3] This phenomenon has been noted by several observers: Hideki Yoshihara, "The Bright and Dark Sides of Japanese Management Overseas," and Malcolm Trevor, "Japanese Managers and British Staffs: A Comparison of Relations and Expectations in Blue-Collar and White-Collar Firms," both in Shibagaki, et. al., ed., *Japanese and European Management* (Tokyo: University of Tokyo Press, 1989); Thomas Lifson, "The Managerial Integration of Japanese Business in America," *The Political Economy of Japan*, vol. 3 (Palo Alto: Stanford University Press: 1992); and Hideo Ishida, "Nihon Kigyo no Jinteki Shigen Kanri no Kokusaiteki Tekiosei" (The international adaptability of Japanese companies' human resource management), in *Ho to Keizai no Kihon Mondai* (Fundamental issues in law and economics) (Tokyo: Keio University Industrial Research Institute, 1990).

[4] Vladimir Pucik, Mitsuyo Hanada, and George Fifield, *Management Culture and the Effectiveness of Local Executives in Japanese-Owned U.S. Corporations* (Ann Arbor: University of Michigan, 1989), 69–71.

[5] Joann Lublin, "The American Advantage: It Often Doesn't Pay to Work for a Foreign Company's U.S. Unit," *Wall Street Journal*, 17 April 1991, R4.

[6] Ibid.

[7] Wyatt Company, *A Report on the Survey of Human Resource Management in Japanese-Owned Companies in the United States* (Washington, D.C.: Wyatt Company, 1990), 9–10.

Chapter 4: How You Can Succeed at a Japanese Company

[1] See Appendix 4 for a list of recommended reading.

[2] See Appendix 3 for a list of recommended study materials for business Japanese.

[3] John E. Rehfeld, "What Working for a Japanese Company Taught Me," *Harvard Business Review*, November–December 1990: 167–76.

Chapter 5: Understanding the Japanese Expatriate

[1] Nihon Zaigai Kigyo Kyokai (Japan Overseas Enterprises Organization), *Kokusaika Yoin Ikusei Kenkyu Iinkai Hokokusho* (Report of the Committee on Development of Human Resources for Internationalization) (Tokyo: Nihon Zaigai Kigyo Kyokai, 1989), 31.

[2] Rosalie Tung, *Key to Japan's Economic Strength: Human Power* (Lexington, Mass.: Lexington Books, 1984).

[3] Nihon Zaigai Kigyo Kyokai, *Kokusaika Yoin Ikusei*, 37–40; Hiroko Nishida, "Beikoku Funin Shain ni Hitsuyo na Kyoiku to wa, Jo" (Necessary education for employees sent to the U.S., part 1), *Jinzai Kyoiku* (Human resource development), August 1992, 10–13; Yosei Sugawara, *Silence and Avoidance: Japanese Expatriate Adjustment—Summary of the Results of a Thesis Project*, California State University San Bernadino, 1993 (mimeograph).

[4] Kunio Odaka, *Japanese Management: A Forward-Looking Analysis* (Tokyo: Asian Productivity Organization, 1986), i–ii.

[5] Robert Neff, "Japan's Hardening View of America," *Business Week*, 18 December 1989, 63.

[6] Bob and SRI, *Japanese Companies*, 63.

[7] Karel van Wolferen, *The Enigma of Japanese Power* (New York: Alfred A. Knopf, 1989), 267–68.

[8] James Risen, "Firms Deny Bias; Japan Car Plants in U.S. Hire Few Blacks, Study Says," *Los Angeles Times*, 13 September 1988, sec. 4, p. 1.

[9] James Risen, "Accusations of Racism; Japanese Businesses Unfair, Blacks Say," *Los Angeles Times*, 9 August 1988, sec. 4, p. 1.

[10] Anne Tergesen, "Heightening Corporate Awareness of U.S. Minority Issues Is Group's Aim," *Japan Times*, 28 November 1989.

[11] Bruce Stokes, "Questioning Japanese Hiring Policies," *National Journal* 21, no. 18 (6 May 1989): 1125.

12 Suzanne Alexander, "Japanese Firms Embark on a Program of Lavish Giving to American Charities," *Wall Street Journal*, 23 May 1991, p. B1.

13 "Hispanic Institute Aims to Forge Ties with Japan," *Wall Street Journal*, 5 July 1991, p. B1.

Chapter 6: Strategies for Coping with the Karate-Teacher Manager

1 Shigeki Koga, "Budding Film Director Wants to Rove a Borderless Celluloid World," *Nikkei Weekly*, 19 July 1993, 11.

2 Michael Shapiro, "In the Master's Shadow," *Winds*, March 1989, 40.

3 Ibid., 42–44.

4 Lanier, "Alex Warren," 13.

5 Jennifer Crockart, "International Management Skills," *Wafu*, October 1991, p. 5.

6 Rehfeld, "What Working for a Japanese Company Taught Me," 170.

Chapter 7: Participating in Japanese-Style Decision-Making

1 Edwin O. Reischauer, *The Japanese* (Cambridge: Harvard University Press, 1982), 165.

2 James Abegglen and George Stalk, Jr., *Kaisha, The Japanese Corporation* (New York: Basic Books, 1985), 178–79.

3 Ibid., 8–9, 52.

4 John Kageyama, "Commentary: Japanese Managers and American Employees," *Pacific Northwest Executive*, July 1989.

Chapter 8: Out of the Loop

1 Doron Levin, "Adjusting to Japan's Car Culture," *New York Times*, 4 March 1992, p. C1.

2 Miwako Kidahashi, "Dual Organization: A Study of a Japanese-Owned Firm in the United States" (Ph.D. diss., Columbia University, 1987) is an extended investigation of why a dual organization exists at one Japanese firm in the United States. This term was also used in Ishida, "Nihon Kigyo no Jinteki Shigen Kanri," 56. Malcolm Trevor uses a similar term, "dual

employment system," in *Japan's Reluctant Multinationals: Japanese Management at Home and Abroad* (New York: St. Martin's Press, 1983), 125, 187.

Chapter 9: The Japanese Lifetime Employment System

[1] Jacob Schlesinger and Masayoshi Kanabayashi, "Many Japanese Find Their 'Lifetime' Jobs Can Be Short-Lived," *Wall Street Journal*, 8 October 1992, p. A1.

[2] Readers who wish to explore this topic in greater depth should refer to the general descriptions in Hideo Inohara, *Human Resource Development in Japanese Companies* (Tokyo: Asian Productivity Organization, 1990); Masahiko Aoki, *Information, Incentives, and Bargaining in the Japanese Economy* (Cambridge: Cambridge University Press, 1988); and Trevor, *Japan's Reluctant Multinationals*, Chapter 3. Also, Thomas Rohlen, *For Harmony and Strength* (Berkeley: University of California Press, 1974), is an in-depth case study of one Japanese bank's personnel management.

[3] Yumiko Ono and Christopher Chipello, "Japan's No. 1 Ad Agency Confronts New Playing Field," *Wall Street Journal*, 11 August 1992.

[4] Aoki, *Information, Incentives, and Bargaining*, 72.

[5] Ibid., 96.

[6] Inohara, *Human Resource Development*, 111.

[7] Yoshimichi Yamashita, "Japanese Executives Face Life Out of the Nest," *Wall Street Journal*, 16 December 1991, p. A14.

Chapter 10: Not All Employees Are Created Equal

[1] The exact term used may vary from company to company.

[2] The exact term used may vary from company to company.

[3] Ann R. Klee, "Worker Participation in Japan: The Temporary Employee and Enterprise Unionism," *Comparative Labor Law* 7 (1986): 366.

[4] Ibid.

[5] Quoted in Schlesinger and Kanabayashi, "Many Japanese Find Their 'Lifetime' Jobs Can Be Short-Lived."

[6] Kidahashi, "Dual Organization," 73.

[7] Mackentire v. Ricoh Corp. (c90-20077), Aflague v. Kyocera Int'l Inc. (4th

Dist Ct App, No. D-006594), Porto v. Canon USA (28 FEP 1679 [N.D. IL 1981]), Ristow v. Toshiba America Inc. (CD Cal, No. CV-86-0164), and Fortino v. Quasar (751 F.Supp. 1306 [N.D. IL 1990]).

8   Pucik, Hanada, and Fifield in *Management Culture* made the same observation.

9   For example, Sumitomo Shoji v. Avagliano (457 US 176, 72 L.Ed.2d 765, 102 S.Ct. 2374 [1982]), Speiss v. C. Itoh (643 F.2d. 353 [5th Cir. 1981]), Adames v. Mitsubishi Bank (751 FSupp. 1548 [E.D. NY 1990]), and Yap v. Sumitomo Corporation of America (WL 29112 [S.D. NY 1991])

10 Lifson, "Managerial Integration," 246–52.

11 Kidahashi, "Dual Organization," 85.

Chapter 11: Working in Japan for a Japanese Company

1   Hideki Yoshihara, *Genchijin Shacho to Uchi Naru Kokusaika* (Using local nationals as top managers of overseas operations, and the internalization of internationalization) (Tokyo: Toyo Keizai Shinpo Sha, 1989), discusses in detail the benefits of head office internationalization and the role of non-Japanese employees in helping to bring it about.

2   Allan Bird and May Mukuda, "Expatriates in Their Own Home: A New Twist in the Human Resource Management Strategies of Japanese MNCs," *Human Resource Management* 28, no. 4 (Winter 1989): 437–53.

3   Martin Justin, "Why Johnny Can't Compete," *Journal of the American Chamber of Commerce in Japan*, Summer 1991, 5.

Chapter 12: How the Japanese Approach to Personnel Management Is Changing

1   Jacob Schlesinger, "Japan Begins to Confront Job Insecurity," *Wall Street Journal*, 16 September 1993, p. A20.

2   Douglas Shinsato, "Japan Tries to Get the Size Right," *Wall Street Journal*, 28 June 1993, p. A16.

3   Emily Thornton, "Japan's Struggle to Restructure," *Fortune*, 28 June 1993, p. 85.

4   Jacob Schlesinger, Michael Williams, and Craig Forman, "Japan Inc., Wracked by Recession, Takes Stock of Its Methods," *Wall Street Journal*, 29 September 1993, p. A4.

5 Shintaro Hori, "Fixing Japan's White-Collar Economy: A Personal View," *Harvard Business Review*, November–December 1993: 160–63.

6 Andrew Pollack, "Japanese Starting to Link Pay to Performance, Not Tenure," *New York Times*, 2 October 1993, p. 1.

7 Schlesinger, "Job Insecurity."

8 "'Free Titling' Lets Employees Invent Own Jobs," *Nikkei Weekly*, 5 July 1993, p. 11.

9 Michael Williams, "Japanese Economy Seems Headed For Its Worst Post-war Recession," *Wall Street Journal*, 1 November 1993, p. A14.

10 Thornton, "Japan's Struggle," 86–88.

11 David Sanger, "Layoffs and Factory Closings Shaking the Japanese Psyche," *New York Times*, 3 March 1993, p. 1; Yumiko Ono, "Unneeded Workers in Japan Are Bored, and Very Well Paid," *Wall Street Journal*, 20 April 1993, p. A1.

12 Hori, "Fixing Japan's White-Collar Economy," 164–65.

13 Speech to the Japan America Society of Chicago, 13 July 1993.

14 Pollack, "Japanese Starting to Link Pay to Performance," p. 6.

15 Koichiro Sakai, Yutaka Matsuda, Yumiko Matsuhira, and Kosaburo Hira, "Nattoku Dekiru Chingin" (Wages that everyone can agree on), *Nikkei Business*, 8 March 1993, 16–17.

16 Ibid., 16.

17 "'Free Titling' Lets Employees Invent Own Jobs."

18 Tetsuya Iguchi, "'Top-down' Leader Holds Mitsubishi Reins," *Nikkei Weekly*, 20 September 1993, p. 12.

19 "Japan Changes Its Work Habits," *Wall Street Journal*, 7 April 1992, p. A12.

Notes to Sidebars

a U.S. House Committee on Government Operations, *Employment Discrimination by Japanese-Owned Companies in the United States: Hearings before the Employment and Housing Subcommittee of the Committee on Government Operations*, 102nd Cong., 1st sess., 1991, 19.

b Ibid., 24.

c Ibid., 38–39.

d Ibid., 191.

e Ibid., 190.

f   U.S. House Committee on Government Operations, *Employment Discrimination*, 106.

g   Ibid., 491.

h   DeNero, "Creating the 'Hyphenated' Corporation," 159.

i   Pucik, Hanada, and Fifield, *Management Culture*, 22.

j   Hideki Yoshihara, *Anketo Chosa no Shukeihyo* (Report of survey results) (Kobe: Kobe University, 1993), 5.

k   Momoo Yamaguchi and Setsuko Kojima, *A Cultural Dictionary of Japan* (Tokyo: Japan Times, 1986), 341.

l   Taichi Sakaiya, *What is Japan? Contradictions and Transformations* (New York: Kodansha International, 1993), 223.

m   Edwin O. Reischauer, *The Japanese* (Cambridge, Mass.: Harvard University Press, 1982), 213–14.

n   An example of a company that uses this terminology is described in Kyoko Shibuya, "How Do the Japanese Companies Grow in the American Soil?" (Ph.D. diss., Columbia University, 1990), 77. Professor Hideo Ishida of Keio University Business School first called my attention to the fact that this expression is frequently used by Japanese companies (personal conversation, July 1992).

o   Peter Kilborn, "New Jobs Lack the Old Security in Time of 'Disposable Workers,'" *New York Times*, 15 March 1993, p. 1; Steve Lohr, "More Workers in the U.S. Are Becoming Hired Guns," *New York Times*, 14 August 1992, p. 1; Janice Castro, "Disposable Workers," *Time*, 29 March 1993, 43–47.

p   Lance Morrow, "The Temping of America," *Time*, 29 March 1993, 41.

Notes to Appendix 1

1   Mark Thompson, "Japan Inc. on Trial," *California Lawyer*, May 1989, 44.

2   Treaty of Friendship, Commerce, and Navigation between the United States and Japan, 4 U.S. T. 2063, Article VIII(1).

3   Fortino v Quasar 950 F.2d 389 (7th Cir. 1991), at [6].

4   Sumitomo Shoji v. Avagliano (457 US 176, 72 L.Ed.2d 765, 102 S.Ct. 2374 [1982]).

5   Fortino v Quasar.

Glossary
of Japanese Terms

Aisha seishin: Company loyalty, devotion to one's company.

Bucho: Department manager. Often translated in English as "general manager."

Burakumin: Descendants of feudal period lower castes who continue to suffer discrimination.

Chutosaiyo: Midcareer hiring; a person who has switched companies mid-career.

Dankai sedai: Japan's baby-boomers.

Doki: The group of employees who entered a company in the same year.

Fude mame na hito: A good correspondent.

Fuku shacho: Vice president. This term is used in a more restricted sense than the English term "vice president," referring only to the rank directly below president of the company.

Gaijin: Foreigner, non-Japanese.

Genchi sutaffu: Locally-hired employees of an overseas subsidiary or office.

Gyaku shukko: Reverse transfer program in which locally-hired overseas employees are assigned to work in Japan, usually for a period ranging from six months to two years.

Habatsu: Competing factions within an organization.

Haken jugyoin: Employee sent from a temporary agency.

Hanko: Signature seals, used in place of a signature on formal company documents.

Ikebana: Japanese flower arrangement.

Jicho: Second in command. Often connoted in English titles by the words "deputy" or "assistant."

Jikan ga kakaru: Phrase meaning "It will take time."

Jimu shoku: Clerical workers, usually female.

Jitan: Recent efforts by Japanese companies to cut employees' overtime hours in response to falling profits and government pressure.

Jomu: Managing director. Signifies a more senior board member than *torishimariyaku*.

Kacho: Section chief, team leader.

Kacho dairi: Assistant section chief.

Kaicho: Chairman.

Kaizen: Continuous improvement.

Karoshi: Death from overwork.

Katakana: Japanese syllabary used to write words of non-Japanese origin.

Kata tataki: A "tap on the shoulder" that informs a worker he or she is being laid off.

Keidanren: Federation of Economic Organizations, the leading Japanese business association.

Koan: Answerless riddles used in Zen Buddhism.

Kogaisha no shain: Employee of a subsidiary. Lower in status than a *seishain* of the parent company.

Kohai: One's juniors; colleagues who are younger than oneself. Also used to refer to younger graduates of one's university.

Kuroko: Stagehands in the Japanese traditional theatre who dress in black to remain unobtrusive.

Madogiwazoku: Surplus middle managers who are given make-work jobs. This term, which literally means "the tribe that sits by the window," is derived from the practice of giving these workers seats "by the window," away from the center of activity.

Nemawashi: Discussing ideas with key decision-makers prior to formal submission of a proposal.

Nihonjinron: Anthropological "theories of Japanese uniqueness" that have recently enjoyed popularity in Japan.

Nihonteki keiei: Japanese management.

Noryoku: Raw talent, management potential.

Osaki ni shitsurei shimasu: Apologetic phrase used when one leaves the office before others. May be shortened to *Osaki ni* when used with close colleagues.

Paato: Temporary worker. Considered to be "part time" even if full-time hours are worked.

Ringisho: Proposal document that is circulated widely through management as part of the formal approval process.

Seishain: Permanent employees of a company, for whom there is an assumption of lifetime employment.

Senmu: Senior managing director. Signifies a more senior board member than *torishimariyaku*.

Senpai: One's seniors; colleagues who are older than oneself. Also used to refer to older graduates of one's university.

Sensei: A term of highest respect, used to refer to one's teacher. The term is also used in addressing professors, doctors, and lawyers.

Shacho: Company president.

Shitencho: Branch Manager.

Shokutaku: Contract employee.

Sogo shoku: White-collar, management-track positions.

Sore wa chotto muzukashii desu: Phrase meaning, literally, "It's a bit difficult." A polite way of saying "no."

Tanshin funin: The state of living apart from one's family as a result of corporate transfer.

Torishimariyaku: Director. In Japanese firms, the majority of board members have risen through the ranks of the company. There are few outside directors.

Tsukiai nokori: Custom of not leaving the office until others have also completed their work.

Uchi/soto: Inside and outside; insiders and outsiders.

Wan man kodo: Autocratic management style which ignores the necessity for *nemawashi* and consensus-building.

Bibliography

A body of academic literature has emerged that examines how Japanese firms manage their international human resources. This literature provides evidence for a consistent pattern in Japanese companies' international human resource management: use of Japanese expatriates in a large proportion of overseas managerial positions, a reluctance to consider locally hired employees for many managerial positions, friction between Japanese expatriates and local employees, and difficulty recruiting and retaining high-caliber local employees (particularly managers and other white-collar employees). These similar observations have emerged despite the fact that the researchers have used a variety of methodologies and examined different industries and geographical areas. The following are some of the significant works that have explored these issues:

Bartlett, Christopher, and Hideki Yoshihara. "New Challenges for Japanese Multinationals: Is Organization Adaptation Their Achilles Heel?" *Human Resource Management* 27, no. 1 (1988): 19–43.

Beechler, Schon Laureen. *International Management Control in Multinational Corporations: The Case of Japanese Consumer Electronics Subsidiaries in Southeast Asia.* Ph.D. diss., University of Michigan, 1990.

Bird, Allan, and May Mukuda. "Expatriates in Their Own Home: A New Twist in the Human Resource Management Strategies of Japanese MNCs." *Human Resource Management* 28, no. 4 (Winter 1989): 437–53.

Bob, Daniel, and SRI International. *Japanese Companies in American Communities.* New York: Japan Society, 1990.

Cole, Robert, and Donald Deskins. "Racial Factors in Site Location and Employment Patterns of Japanese Auto Firms in America." *California Management Review* 31, no. 1 (Fall 1988): 9–22.

Dalbello, Ron, Richard Madigan, Jim Noble, Prema Venkat, and Allan Bird. *Rough Times at Nomura.* New York: New York University Stern School of Business, 1991. Mimeographed case study.

Fucini, Joseph, and Suzy Fucini. *Working for the Japanese: Inside Mazda's American Auto Plant.* New York: Free Press, 1990.

Heise, H. J. "How Japanese Work Out As Bosses in Germany." In *Japanese and European Management,* edited by Kazuo Shibagaki, Malcolm Trevor, and Tetsuo Abo. Tokyo: University of Tokyo Press, 1989.

Inohara, Hideo. *Human Resource Development in Japanese Companies.* Tokyo: Asian Productivity Organization, 1990.

Ishida, Hideo. "Transferability of Japanese Human Resource Management Abroad." *Human Resource Management* 25, no. 1 (1986): 103–20.

―――. "Nihon Kigyo no Jinteki Shigen Kanri no Kokusaiteki Tekiosei" (The international adaptability of Japanese companies' human resource management), in *Ho to Keizai no Kihon Mondai* (Fundamental issues in law and economics). Tokyo: Keio University Industrial Research Institute, 1990.

Johnson, Richard T. "Success and Failure of Japanese Subsidiaries in America." *Columbia Journal of World Business,* Spring 1977, 30–37.

Kidahashi, Miwako. *Dual Organization: A Study of a Japanese-Owned Firm in the United States.* Ph.D. diss., Columbia University, 1987.

Kobayashi, Noritake. "The Patterns of Management Style Developing in Japanese Multinationals in the 1980s." In *Japan's Emerging Multinationals: An International Comparison of Policies and Practices,* edited by Susumu Takamiya and Keith Thurley. Tokyo: University of Tokyo Press, 1985.

Lifson, Thomas. "The Managerial Integration of Japanese Business in America." In *The Political Economy of Japan,* vol. 3. Palo Alto: Stanford University Press, 1992: 231–66.

Matsusaki, Hiro. "Japanese Managers and Management in the Western World: A Canadian Experience." In *The Functioning of the Multinational Corporation,* edited by Anant Negandhi. New York: Pergamon Press, 1980.

Negandhi, Anant. *Quest for Survival and Growth: A Comparative Study of American, European, and Japanese Multinationals.* New York: Praeger, 1979.

————, Golpira Eshghi, and Edith Yuen. "The Management Practices of Japanese Subsidiaries Overseas." *California Management Review* 27, no. 4 (1985).

Nishida, Hiroko. "Beikoku Shinshutsu Nikkei Kigyo de Hataraku Nichibei Jugyoin no Aida no Communication Gap" (The communication gap between Japanese and American employees at Japanese companies operating in the U.S.). In *Borderless Jidai no Kokusai Kankei* (International relations in the borderless era). Tokyo: Hokuki Shuppan, 1991.

Park, S. J. "Personnel Management of Japanese Subsidiaries in West Germany." In *Japanese and European Management*, edited by Kazuo Shibagaki, Malcolm Trevor, and Tetsuo Abo. Tokyo: University of Tokyo Press, 1989.

Pucik, Vladimir, Mitsuyo Hanada, and George Fifield. *Management Culture and the Effectiveness of Local Executives in Japanese-Owned U.S. Corporations.* Ann Arbor: University of Michigan,1989.

Sethi, S. Prakash, Nobuaki Namiki, and Carl Swanson. *The False Promise of the Japanese Miracle.* Marshfield, Mass.: Pitman Publishing, 1984.

Shibuya, Kyoko. *How Do the Japanese Companies Grow in the American Soil?* Ph.D. diss., Columbia University, 1990.

Trevor, Malcolm. *Japan's Reluctant Multinationals: Japanese Management at Home and Abroad.* New York: St. Martin's Press, 1983.

————. "Japanese Managers and British Staffs: A Comparison of Relations and Expectations in Blue-Collar and White-Collar Firms." In *Japanese and European Management*, edited by Kazuo Shibagaki, Malcolm Trevor, and Tetsuo Abo. Tokyo: University of Tokyo Press, 1989.

Tsurumi, Yoshihiro. "The Best of Times and the Worst of Times: Japanese Management in America." *Columbia Journal of World Business*, Summer 1978, 56–61.

White, Michael, and Malcolm Trevor. *Under Japanese Management: The Experience of British Workers.* London: Heinemann, 1983.

Yoshihara, Hideki. *Genchijin Shacho to Uchi Naru Kokusaika* (Using local nationals as top managers of overseas operations, and the internalization of internationalization). Tokyo: Toyo Keizai Shinpo Sha, 1989.

————. "The Bright and Dark Sides of Japanese Management Overseas." In *Japanese and European Management*, edited by Kazuo Shibagaki, Malcolm Trevor, and Tetsuo Abo. Tokyo: University of Tokyo Press, 1989.

Yoshino, Michael Y. *Japan's Multinational Enterprises.* Cambridge, Mass.: Harvard University Press, 1976.

Index